PHILOSOPHY
AN INTRODUCTION

Antony Flew has been Professor of Philosophy in the University of Reading since May 1973, and previously since 1954 held the same position at Keele. He has taught as a visiting Professor in ten or more other universities in the United States, Canada, Australia and Malawi, as well as doing lecture tours for the British Council in Thailand, Argentina and Brazil. From his earliest days as a Lecturer first in Oxford and then in Aberdeen he has always been enthusiastic about teaching philosophy to people who have no wish to devote their whole lives to the subject, and his own writings have concentrated on those philosophical problems which relate most closely to practical life. His books have included *A New Approach to Psychical Research* (1953), *Hume's Philosophy of Belief* (1961), *God and Philosophy* (1966), *An Introduction to Western Philosophy* (1971), *Crime or Disease?* (1973), *Thinking about Thinking* (1975), *The Presumption of Atheism* (1976) and *Sociology, Equality and Education* (1976). He had also edited philosophical anthologies, including *Body, Mind and Death* (1964), and the Pelican Classic edition of *Malthus: An Essay on Population* (1971).

TEACH YOURSELF BOOKS

PHILOSOPHY
an introduction

Antony Flew

*M.A. (Oxon.), D. Litt. (Keele), Professor of Philosophy,
University of Reading*

TEACH YOURSELF BOOKS
Hodder and Stoughton

First Impression 1979

Copyright © 1979
Antony Flew

British Library C.I.P.

Flew, Antony
 An introduction to philosophy. — (Teach
 yourself books).
 1. Philosophy
 I. Title   II. Series
 100   B72

 ISBN 0-340-24501-8

Phototypeset in V.I.P. Garamond by Western Printing Services Ltd, Bristol Printed and bound in Great Britain for Hodder and Stoughton Paperbacks, a division of Hodder and Stoughton Limited, Mill Road, Dunton Green, Sevenoaks, Kent (Editorial Office: 47 Bedford Square, London WC1 3DP), by Hazell Watson & Viney Ltd, Aylesbury, Bucks

Contents

It must be of itself that the divine thought thinks (since that is the most excellent of things), and its thinking is a thinking about thinking.

Aristotle: Metaphysics

How charming is divine philosophy
Not harsh and crabbed, as dull fools suppose

John Milton: Comus

What is the use of studying philosophy if all that it does for you is to enable you to talk with some plausibility about some abstruse questions of logic, etc., and if it does not improve your thinking about the important questions of everyday life . . . ?

Ludwig Wittgenstein

ACKNOWLEDGMENTS

The publishers wish to thank Hutchinson Publishing Group Ltd. for permission to use extracts from H. J. Paton's translation of Kant's *Groundwork of the Metaphysic of Morals*, and *The Moral Law*.

Preface

This book, like all the others in the Teach Yourself Series, is written for those who want to learn, and who are ready to make an effort. It therefore has two indices, an Index of Notions as well as the more usual Index of Names. The idea is that both of these may be used, particularly the first, not only for purposes of occasional reference but also as instruments of systematic revision. This concluding list of notions is itself significantly longer than it might have been. For I have often parenthetically and in passing explained terms which, though not essential to the immediate task in hand, keen readers will certainly want to become acquainted with.

The Bibliography, on the other hand, is austere. It is intended to cover all but only the works in which reference happens to be made in the text. The object was to produce an adequately full and precise, yet economical and unobtrusive, system of referring. For the same reason wherever, as so often, quotations are made from texts which have appeared in various editions and paginations, I have employed any available edition-neutral method of reference. The different job of recommending further reading is mainly done not in the Bibliography but in the paragraphs headed 'Now read on', after the end of the final Chapter VII. I must also warn that in quoting authors from earlier centuries, especially those who wrote in languages other than English, I have not always reproduced the exact text given in the particular edition described in the Bibliography. Though never, I trust, distorting meanings I have sometimes changed punctuation or provided my own translation: the aim was always to make this book read more smoothly.

It is unfortunate that our standard typefounts provide for only two kinds of inverted commas, single and double. I use the single to indicate: first, the titles of articles or chapters; second, direct speech not attributed to anyone in particular; and, third, that some word or expression is being either philosophically mentioned or questionably used. I use double inverted commas exclusively in order to make verbatim quotations from named sources. Two other less than universal typographical practices will be explained and justified when they first appear (pp. 32, 37, and 115).

Finally, there are four helpful people to thank. Lydia Greeves and her to me unknown publisher's reader both made many suggestions. Most of these, to the considerable improvement of the resulting book, I have followed. Even where in issues of substance I could not agree I always tried, especially in the suggestions for further reading, to take account of these differences of view. Kate Pippett and Elizabeth Arthur transformed my largely legible yet unlovely manuscript into a typescript in which what I had written looked vastly better than it did before; or, perhaps, than it is.

Antony Flew

Reading, May 1978

CHAPTER I

On what philosophy is

'My own philosophy is, the more sex the better.' It was in these or perhaps rather coarser terms that a certain already very successful American psychoanalyst, the future author of a runaway best-selling popular manual, once expressed to me the central feature of his personal world-outlook and value-system. When we speak of someone taking something philosophically, when — say — a leading accountant is invited to improve some ceremonial occasion by expressing his philosophy of accountancy, or when people in the eye of the media are signed up to contribute to a series on 'My Philosophy of Life', it is in the same in its place perfectly reputable sense that the word is used. In that most common understanding philosophy is a matter of a comprehensive view, usually embracing both value commitments and beliefs about the general nature of things; and a view in which, typically, particular and ephemeral urgencies are seen in a somewhat withdrawn perspective and with a certain detachment.

However, whether for better or for worse, the sense in which the word refers to the subject of a Teach Yourself Book, and to the discipline practiced in Departments of Philosophy within institutions of tertiary education, is, although not wholly unrelated, quite different. A good first answer to the immediate question, 'What is this subject, this discipline?' finds its inspiration in a distinguished Cambridge professor. The story is told that the preferred response of G. E. Moore (1873–1958) was to gesture towards his bookshelves: "It is what all those are about." So let it be said first that philosophy is the main subject of most of the writings of Plato; of Aristotle's *Metaphysics* and *Nicomachean Ethics*; of large parts of the works of St Thomas Aquinas, Duns Scotus, and William of Ockham; of the *Meditations* of Descartes; of the *Ethics* of Spinoza and the *Monadology* of Leibniz; of Locke's *Essay concerning Human Understanding*; of Berkeley's *Three Dialogues* and *Principle of Human Knowledge*; of Hume's *Inquiry concerning Human Understand-*

ing and Kant's *Critique of Pure Reason*; and, finally, in the present century, of Moore's own *Principia Ethica*, of Russell's *Our Knowledge of the External World* and *Mysticism and Logic*, and of Wittgenstein's *Tractatus Logico-Philosophicus*.

1. *Is it a definition that we want?*　This first answer will not satisfy; nor is it, without supplementation, satisfactory. An importunate inquirer demands a definition, as did the Socrates of Plato's earlier dialogues: 'How can anyone', such a person asks, 'sensibly believe anything about philosophy, much less begin seriously to study the subject, if they cannot even say what philosophy is? Answer me that, you who are paid to know and to teach.'

In meeting this challenge we can both say a little more about the nature of philosophy and do some. A. N. Whitehead (1861–1947) once remarked, with no more than the amount of exaggeration and distortion inevitable in any such epigram, that later philosophy consists in a series of footnotes to Plato (About 427-347 BC). All Plato's publications, with the exception of a handful of letters, are in the form of dialogues. In most of these the leading role is that of a character called Socrates. It is, of course, an issue of scholarly dispute how far this dramatic representation is faithful to the realities of the historical Socrates, whom Plato certainly knew and revered. It is even suggested sometimes that, where an unsound argument is in the dialogues either left unchallenged, or even accepted as valid, Plato himself was fully aware of this but deliberately presented error as material for philosophical training. Such intimate and speculative biographical questions are of no concern to us here.

It is, however, certain that Socrates, who left no writings, was put to death in 399 BC, when Plato was in his late twenties. Socrates is mentioned in various other extant sources, and also represented – very differently – by both the dull but worthy historian Xenophon and by Aristophanes, the superlative master of Old Comedy. I shall here simply take for granted what seems in fact to be the dominant view: that in the earlier dialogues the Platonic Socrates is not too far removed from the old man known to the young Plato; but that later, and in particular from the beginning of Book II of *The Republic*, the Platonic Socrates is more and more a mere mouthpiece of the writer.

In his earlier dialogues Plato typically represents a Socrates pressing questions about some virtue or other value. In *Laches*, for instance, the master question is, 'What is courage?'; in *Charmides* 'What is temperance?'; and in Book I of *The Republic* – indeed, officially, throughout – 'What is justice?'. Such questions are pressed with double force upon recognised paragons of these particular virtues: the gallant old soldier Laches in the first; the famously temperate Charmides in the second; and in the third the respected senior citizen Cephalus. Through the dialectic, through the refutation by question and answer which is the Socratic elenchus, it emerges always that no one – not even, or especially not, the paragons themselves – is able to give an account which is both self-consistent and compatible with established verbal usage. The dialogues end with all the particpants having to accept, with varying degrees of good or ill grace, that we do not know. The superior wisdom of Socrates lies in the fact that he alone began by knowing that he did not know. Thus Book I of *The Republic* ends: "For when I do not know what justice is I am hardly likely to know whether it is an excellence or not, or whether he that possesses it is unhappy or happy" (354C).

The conclusion seems irresistible. Yet it can and must be resisted. For whyever should we allow, what Socrates is assuming, that to know what justice is, or to know what anything else is, either is, or must be manifested in, a capacity to provide a satisfactory definition of the word 'justice', or of whatever other word it may be? The assumption becomes still harder to justify when it is so extended that to pass as satisfactory the definition is required to provide: not just a rough and ready summary of the present usage of what may be in some ways a vague term; but a clearcut and correct determination of how it should be applied in all possible cases – including all marginal cases and cases involving unforeseen and perhaps unforeseeable novelties. Whatever the possibilities and the merits of such an exercise, the result must be, not a defintion of the word in its present meaning, but a redefinition. For us the immediate necessity is to distinguish, as neither the Platonic Socrates nor Plato himself ever did, between two quite different interpretations of the key form of expression, 'know what something is'.

In the present context this has to be construed in what ought to strike us as a curious and artificial way. To know here what, for instance, courage or temperance or justice are is to be able to produce definitions satisfactory to Socrates. Yet this is not at all the ordinary, the everyday interpretation; although it is precisely and only when given that ordinary, everyday interpretation that the concluding sentence of the previous paragraph expresses an obvious truth.

For, consider, when his fellow Athenians allowed that the hero Laches knew what courage is they surely meant only that he was abundantly acquainted with examples of courage, and no doubt of cowardice too; and that he could be relied on to recognise courage for what it is. These fellow

5

Athenians would not have been inclined to withdraw their claim, to accept that what they had said had been shown to be false, simply because poor Laches had been by the cross-examining of a notorious philosophical gadfly reduced to embarrassment and silence. Nor should we accept this. The paradoxical and seemingly irresistible conclusion drawn by Socrates depends upon a subtle and significant equivocation.

The first moral for us is that definition is at best not so universally important as Plato's Socrates believed. A definition (the *definiens*) is normally, as it were, longhand for the shorthand word or expression to be defined (the *definiendum*). We should not, therefore, expect it to be either illuminating or even possible thus to explicate the meaning of every word and expression in other more numerous but perhaps simpler or more familiar words. Some words have to be, and are, explained and understood directly; by reference not to other words but to what it is that is to be talked about. This necessarily applies to the most elementary and basic terms of any language. But it also happens to be true of other terms too; and, in particular, a first understanding of what philosophy is cannot be conveyed by producing a definition of the world 'philosophy'.

Suppose we had to explain what giant pandas are, to someone unfamiliar with the appearance of those extraordinarily engaging creatures. We should not attempt to think up a definition of the expression 'giant panda'. Instead we should try to point to specimens or, failing that, models or pictures; maybe adding a few words on recognition points and on any other species with which this one might be confused. Or suppose, coming much closer to our actual concern, that we had to explain what mathematics is to people who had done little or no mathematics. A definition might perhaps be constructed here. Yet even if it could be this would not help our inquirers. Their need is, first to be reminded of any specimens with which they happen already to be acquainted, and then to be given some more. Time enough after that to make the revealing general remarks, and to indicate possible confusions. So it is with philosophy. To acquire an understanding of what philosophy is, it is essential to become acquainted with a range of specimens. The remarks and the warnings can be appreciated properly only as or after that acquaintanceship is achieved.

Nor is it sufficient in either case, in order to get that acquaintanceship, uncomprehendingly to confront what happen to be examples of the activity under consideration. We should not be becoming acquainted with a piece of mathematical activity as such if, although we were in fact watching a pure mathematician at work, we either had no idea at all of what was going on or else mistakenly believed that he was just doodling. Furthermore, in both cases, it is a condition of even this minimal observer's understanding of what is in process that the observer should be at least to an equally minimal extent a participant. He does not of course need to be able to follow a bit of what may be very advanced mathematical work. But he must himself be doing or have done some sums, or some geometry, or some algebra. So similarly with philosophy. To recognise doing philosophy as doing philosophy we have ourselves to follow or to have followed some philsophical argument, and thus ourselves to be doing or to have done some philosophy.

It is an encouraging thought that this necessary albeit not sufficient condition has already been met by every reader who has managed to keep in touch so far. For the apparently irresistible paradox presented by Socrates at the end of Book I of *The Republic* constitutes a paradigm case, a possible — indeed now, if not before, an actual! — textbook example of a philosophical thesis. The consequent criticism of this thesis, by developing a fundamental distinction between two different interpretations of the key form of expression 'know what something is', and by uncovering something about what are and are not conditions of communication and understanding, constitutes in consequence a paradigm case, a textbook example, of doing philosophy. The danger with this first illustration is, not that it will be too difficult, but that it will seem too easy. That risk, however, has to be accepted as a pedagogic cost; just as anyone who deploys live and exciting illustrations has to be aware of, and to adjust to, the fact that these may sometimes maintain interest only at the cost of distracting attention from whatever they were intended to illustrate. Any damage done will have to be undone later.

2. *A logical inquiry about concepts*. Even with that single Socratic example as so far our only paradigm some useful remarks can be made about the nature of philosophy. These remarks are in place here at the beginning because they are needed to remove popular misconceptions. First, philosophy is a logical inquiry about concepts. Precisely what and how much is involved in having a concept has been itself a matter of philosophical dispute, in particular whether there is some essential connection with an ability to form mental images. But for the moment it is enough to say that, if you possess a certain concept — the concept, for instance, of causality — then you must be adequately seized of the meaning of the word 'cause', and be competent to use it, or some synonym, or some equivalent in some other language.

Not every enquiry about concepts, nor even every logical enquiry about concepts, is philosophy. Nevertheless, philosophy is concerned with concepts, and with concepts in their logical aspects, rather than with discovering or explaining what goes on in the non-linguistic world. If you are thinking of what are listed as subjects in a university calendar, then the affinity is again with mathematics; rather than with physics or biology, or a host of other disciplines concerned to discover what in fact happens, and why. (Here, by the way, we should notice a long obsolete third sense of the word 'philosophy'. It was in the 1600's and 1700's often equivalent to our 'science'. This third sense survives – fossilised – only in the official titles of some old established chairs: the Professors of Natural Philosophy in Aberdeen and of Experimental Philosophy in Oxford are physicists both; and not, in our sense, philosophers.)

The fact that it is concerned in its own way with concepts makes it possible to confound philosophy with psychology, while the fact that having and using concepts is always and necessarily a matter of being able to use and of using words or word-substitutes means that all philosophy – not just some one exclusive and temporarily dominant group of 'Linguistic Philosophers' – is committed to its own kind of concern with language. Many of the greatest philosophers of the past failed fully to distinguish philosophy from psychology. This confusion was for a long time in many countries institutionalised in a departmental structure which brigaded practioners of the two disciplines together. In Britain several Departments of Philosophy, or of Philosophy and Psychology, gave birth to independent Departments of Psychology only after the end of the Second World War. But that is not today's besetting confusion. In so far as we deal with that at all, the treatment will be at the end of Chapter III, by disentangling the philosophy from the psychology and physiology of perception.

What we have to begin to grasp right away is that, and why, and how, all philosophy is essentially concerned with language. This statement will strike most readers as scandalous. To say this, surely, is to say that all the problems of philosophy are merely verbal; and, therefore, trivial?

It is not. In the first place, and quite generally, to say that this is that never is by itself to say that this is *merely* that, that this is that *and nothing else*. Yet anyone who has ever uttered public statements about anything must have been made aware that it is one of the commonest reporting errors to put down someone who said, only, that this is that for having said, recklessly, that this is *merely* that. (Let us christen it 'The It-is-merely Fallacy'.)

In the second place, and particularly, it is wrong to think that everything which is in any way verbal, and concerned with language, must be by the same token trivial. The trouble here is that all the usual models of disputes about words do in fact happen to be trivial disputes. We think perhaps of amateur philologists arguing the merits of those Old World monosyllables 'lift' and 'car' against their polysyllabic New World alternatives 'elevator' and 'automobile'. Or we may be reminded of the evasiveness of official spokesmen: of the (British) Minister who insisted that no one had been 'dismissed', while conceding that 'some labour had been released'; of the (American) Air Force Officer who protested, 'It's not *bombing*, its air support.'

But these are the wrong models. For philosophical problems, and the issues which they put at stake, may be deep not trivial. The philosopher's peculiar interest in language is not in the grammatical form but in the semantic content. It is, in one word, logical. When Socrates concludes that, if he does not know what justice is or what virtue is, then he cannot know anything whatever about either justice or virtue, he throws the whole possibility of knowledge into question. Misguided his conclusion may be; and, as we have argued, is. But trifling it is not.

When Socrates talks about knowledge, and hence about the meaning of the word 'knowledge', he is not concerned with how many letters or syllables are possessed by a particular English (or Greek!) vocable; nor with whether that vocable is or is not euphonious. (My dictionary explains 'vocable' as a near equivalent to 'word'; but adds, "especially with reference to form rather than meaning".) Socrates is thus concerned with what is logically implied, and what is logically presupposed, when something is said to be known. These logical involvements are inseparably connected with questions of meaning. For what is logically implied by the statement that something is known is whatever can be validly deduced therefrom. (By definition: this is validly deduced from that, if, and only if, you could not simultaneously deny this and assert that without thereby contradicting yourself. The shorthand for 'if, and only if' is 'iff'.)

That Socrates, like his philosophical successors, was discussing content not form, concepts not vocables, comes out most clearly when we think of the principles of translation. Had he indeed been discoursing on the shape of a particular Greek vocable, the faithful translator would have been in professional duty bound to leave that vocable untranslated. In reality Socrates was talking about the concept of knowledge; which is the meaning of the word 'know', the use to which that word is put. Since that use, that meaning, cannot but be the same for every genuinely equivalent term in any language, a correct translation has to replace every occurrence of the Greek vocable by an appropriate English equivalent.

A second example will serve both to make the conceptual and logical character of philosophy still more manifest and to reinforce the point that what is in this way verbal is not for that reason trifling. Later we shall be devoting a whole chapter to the philosophical problems of free will. At this stage it suffices to notice how they arise, and what they are. Typically the perplexities begin, as so many other philosophical perplexities begin, with a consideration of what seem to be the presuppositions and implications of something which is not itself philosophical at all. The usual difficulty is that these apparent consequences of what we either know or believe that we know conflict, either with one another, or else with what seem to be the presuppositions and implications of something else which we know or think we know. It is the truth of the first of the last two statements which leads people to ask about the philosophical implications of this or that — especially, in our time, of new branches of scientific inquiry and of new developments of scientific theory. The modestly serviceable saw is: 'Science tells us what happens, and why. Philosophy asks, "So what?"' It is the truth of the second observation which enables philosophers to claim that one of their professional functions is to toil as diplomats, striving to resolve clashes between rival intellectual sovereignties.

More particularly and more concretely, philosophical perplexities about human responsibility and the freedom of the will arise against both a secular and a religious background. In the one case it goes like this. It seems to be an inescapable assumption of much of our ordinary life that all of us on many occasions are agents, able to do or to abstain from doing this or that at will. Equally it seems to be both a presupposition and an implication of the achievements of the scientists — and most importantly here of the aspiring human scientists — that in truth there are no such open alternatives; and that everything which happens — human conduct not excluded — really, ultimately, and in the last analysis, happens necessarily and unavoidably. In the other case the ostensible antinomy, the ostensible contradiction, is between: on the one hand, the first assumptions of the secular case, sharpened by a religious drive to emphasise the ineffable wickedness of sinners freely choosing wrong alternatives; and, on the other hand, the essential conviction that everything in the creation is absolutely dependent upon the will of God, who is nonetheless not the author of sin in any sense which would make it unjust for Him to punish sinners enormously and eternally.

In both these two cases the philosophical problem is to show that the actual (which may well not be the ostensible) assumptions and implications either are or are not logically compatible. Do they or do they not contradict each other? Accordingly the practice is growing of calling those who pitch for the one position Compatibilists, those defending the other Incompatibilists. Both rival theses are obviously about the logical relations, and the lack of logical relations, between different concepts and different propositions. Yet the issues at stake could scarcely be more important, or less trivial. In the religious case the question is whether a once orthodox kind of world-system is fundamentally incoherent, in the secular it is whether the sciences of man can leave room for individual choice and responsibility. (By the way: in the usage of philosophers, as opposed to those of businessmen or playboys, a proposition is in the first instance whatever can be assumed, believed, asserted or denied; so that whatever can come after 'believe that' or 'assume that' in a grammatical sentence is presumed to express a proposition. When we want to speak of a proposition, but not of any proposition in particular, we introduce the anonymous proposition p.)

It is especially worthwhile thus to insist upon the true nature of the philosophical problems of freewill, because they are so often, even by people paid to know better, misrepresented. It will not do, not but what it is nevertheless done, to prejudice every relevant philosophical issue by taking it for granted that everything has already been settled in the Incompatibilist sense.

Such a presentation is obnoxious on three main counts. First, it is prejudicial. Second, it ignorantly conceals that most of those classical philosophers and philosopher-theologians who published treatments of any of these questions concluded for some kind of Compatibilism: although we cannot as philosophers allow the weight of authority to be decisive, any sincere inquirer before becoming an Incompatibilist has to take the measure of this Compatibilist opposition. Third, it misrepresents as the philosophical problems issues of a quite different category. These other issues arise only if and when we have found ourselves forced to accept Incompatibilist answers. The truth is that, although the philosophical questions spring from clashes between the apparent implications and presuppositions of commitments which all parties are almost irresistibly inclined to accept, and although anyone who concludes that these clashes cannot be resolved has to decide which of the incompatibles ought to be abandoned; the philosophical questions themselves are about what does or does not follow, what is or is not logically presupposed, and what is or is not compatible. Such questions are, therefore, in senses at least for the moment sufficiently explained, essentially logical and conceptual in character.

3. *Philosophy and linguistic philosophy*.   I have already suggested in passing that the 'Linguistic Philosophy' so frequently hailed and farewelled in the decades since the Second World War is neither a particular branch of philosophy nor a distinctive school of philosophers. In showing this, something more can be brought out about the nature and grounds of the philosopher's concern with language.

(i)   The traditional divisions of his field are produced by trying to mark off different areas of discourse within which and from which his problems arise. Since many of the philosophically most interesting notions find application almost everywhere, this attempt results in a lot of awkwardness and cross-classification. At first things seem quite straightforward. The problems about the presuppositions and implications both of moral discourse generally and of particular moral terms belong to philosophical ethics. The corresponding problems for aesthetic appraisal belong to philosophical aesthetics. Those for the various disciplines rated as – in the broadest sense – sciences belong to the philosophy of biology, the philosophy of psychology, the philosophy of history, and so on.

But then the trouble starts. We find that much material is claimed by more than one pigeonhole. Take the freewill problems, for instance. Both philosophical ethics (also called moral philosophy) and the philosophy of religion bid for the religious collection. On the secular collection the philosophy of religion can have no hold. But its sole importunity is replaced by a hubbub of claims from the philosophy of every human science, and some others too. Again, the Socratic questions entertained above were actually put with reference to aesthetic and moral notions. But his conclusions must apply with equal force to all knowledge. They belong therefore just as much to every other branch of philosophy. They are also the prerogative of epistemology; which is, by definition, the study of philosophical questions about knowledge.

Unsatisfactory though this unsystematic system of area divisions therefore is, it does decisively preclude the possibility of introducing 'philosophy of language' as another exclusive yet at the same time all-inclusive area title. So anyone wishing to provide useful employment for the expression 'linguistic philosopher' is best advised to apply it simply to those who choose to make much of what is in fact a necessary and unavoidable preoccupation of all philosophy: who regularly prefer, for instance, what Rudolf Carnap (Born 1891) christened the Formal Mode of Speech – speaking of the word 'cause' or the expression 'causal connection' – rather than any Material Mode of Speech – such as speaking of the concepts of knowledge or of causal connection, or of the essential natures of knowledge and causality.

In this understanding the great disadvantage of a linguistic philosophy, the main reason against practising as a linguistic philosopher, is that so many, including even professional teachers of the subject, will insist upon making the invalid inference that whatever is in any way linguistic must be on that account trivial. Some go on to protest that such was not the philosophy known to and done by Plato, Aristotle, and the other great men of old. They insinuate that an alien intruder is today supplanting the rightful heirs to that perennial tradition. Some wretched cuckoo is 'selling our truth right for a mess of verbiage'.

The more than compensating advantage of doing philosophy sometimes – not always – in the linguistic mode is that this practice underlines the basic truth that access to the concepts and conceptual relations which are the subject matter of philosophical inquiries is and can only be through the use, and hence the correct usage, of the appropriate words and word-substitutes. It is not good enough to grope with closed eyes for some introspective revelation. Even if illumination comes it can still be tested only by reference to a knowledge of correct usage. (That mention of word-substitutes was to cover the finicking fact that something else may be made to do the job of a word. For example: King George VI had a favourite campfire song in which gestures replaced the words 'chest', 'nut' and 'tree'. The use of a word, as of a chisel or of anything else, is the job it does. The usage is the way in which it is employed.)

In the case of words use depends absolutely upon usage. Take, for instance, the English 'table'. This has the meaning which it does have, expresses the concept which it does express, only and precisely because, and for so long as, it is by convention correct to utter it or to refrain from uttering it, to apply it or to refuse to apply it, on those occasions when, and to those objects to which, it is and is not now applicable.

There is of course no physical reason – no reason, that is, other than those of past history, present convention, and human choice – why any particular conceptual job should be allocated to any particular vocable. Certainly too the resources of different languages differ, with many words in some possessing no strict equivalents in others. But there are far more cases in which it is, for as near as makes no matter all practical and theoretical purposes, the same job which is done, under the different conventions which constitute different languages, by different vocables. The concept of table, for instance, which is not the exclusive property of any language, is expressed equally adequately by all the various vocables which happen to have been chosen by Italian, German, Latin, and Greek — respectively 'tavola', 'Tisch', 'mensa' and 'trapeza'.

(ii)   Once the subject of various linguistic conventions has been raised it becomes important to see exactly what is and is not a matter of convention. So consider a deservedly famous exchange in Lewis Carroll's *Through the Looking Glass*. Humpty Dumpty has just explained that by 'glory' he meant "there's a nice knock-down argument for you:"

> 'But "glory" doesn't mean "a nice knock-down argument",' Alice objected.
> 'When *I* use a word,' Humpty Dumpty said in a rather scornful tone, 'it means just what I choose it to mean — neither more nor less.'
> 'The question is,' said Alice, 'whether you *can* make words mean so many different things.'
> 'The question is', said Humpty Dumpty, 'which is to be master — that's all' (Chapter VI).

(a)   It is indeed. But if we are to be masters, not entrapped by our own and other people's words, then we have to recognise: not only, as Humpty Dumpty does, that the meaning of a vocable is determined by its usage, which is in its turn a matter of collective human decision rather than of the order of nature; but also, as Humpty Dumpty conspicuously does not, that it is enormously difficult and costly for an individual to adopt and observe a fresh usage if this conflicts with whatever is established by the conventions of his language group.

Certainly there is no physical obstacle in the way of our adopting the new usage proposed by Humpty Dumpty, the usage in which 'glory' is employed on all and only those occasions where previously the right thing to say would have been 'a nice knock-down argument'. There is no question but that mankind rather than nature is the master here. Nevertheless the very attempt to do such a thing constitutes an obstacle to the free flow of communication between any innovating Humpty Dumpty and the rest of us. For the most part we are — like Alice — either so out of touch as not to know what is going on, or so conservative as to wish to continue in familiar verbal ways. Furthermore, since verbal habits are just as much habits as any others, they can be very difficult to change; even when there are good reasons so to do, and even when the proposed change has been properly proclaimed in advance to all concerned. Nor will all the old associations fall into their new places smoothly and automatically. Humpty Dumpty may remember to say 'glory' now wherever he used to say 'a nice knock-down argument'. But that is no guarantee that, even for him, the replacement word will at once acquire the appropriate associations of logical appraisal, or lose the now inept overtones of chivalry.

It is remarkable that psychologists and sociologists, who of all men should be most aware of how much we are the creatures of conditioning, seem to be no less inclined than lesser breeds to replace familiar public forms of speech by esoteric professional jargon, and to propose new usages going dead against the grain of old habits. It will not resist mentioning one precious find, an article where the plain word 'people' is systematically replaced by the jargon expression 'societal members'. So the new *Genesis* reads: 'And God (or perhaps the sociologist) created societal members in his own image, male and female societal members created he them'.

But a more subtle and more influential example is provided by the American sociologist Thorstein Veblen (1857–1929). In his classic *The Theory of the Leisure Class* he first insists on introducing the strongly offensive 'conspicuous waste' (Veblen, pp. 97ff.). He then immediately protests that, since what and all he is doing is pure and neutral social science, this phrase is throughout to be read as a detached and evaluatively non-committal description. No one should be surprised, however, to find that his own actual usage is not consistent with these stated intentions; while readers regularly construe his key phrase in its traditional sense as an expression of strong, maybe well-warranted, disapproval. As so often with such perverse verbal prescriptions it is hard not to suspect some strain of calculating disingenuousness. Compare, for instance, the protests of some professing socialists that what they themselves mean by the word 'socialism' does not include – perhaps even precludes – state or other public ownership and control of the means of production, distribution, and exchange. Such protests, it seems, never shake the day to day allegiance of the protesters to parties urging and implementing always more and never less nationalisation; nor diminish their inclination to judge by peculiarly privileged and undemanding standards those countries which are in the disclaimed sense as near as makes no matter fully socialist.

(b)   A second comment on the Humpty Dumpty exchange is that it is ruinously wrong to infer, as is nowadays too often done; from the premise that it must ultimately be a matter of social decision both what vocables are employed for what jobs and what concepts are available in the language; to the conclusion that it is similarly a matter of collective determination whether this does or does not follow from that, and whether this or that proposition is true. There is much more to be said about this, as about almost everything else. But the crucial points to seize are: that what follows from a proposition depends, not upon what vocables happen to be recruited to express that proposition, but upon what it means; and that the truth-value of a proposition – whether it is true or false – depends both upon what it means and upon what are the actual facts about which it may be making some assertion.

The invalid inference becomes especially tempting here, if we think of such tautological truths as 'All husbands are male' or 'There's ne'er a villain living in all Denmark but he's an arrant knave'. For our knowledge of these vacuous verities would remain unthreatened whatever facts were turned up by sociological and criminological investigations. Their truth, therefore, is grounded in the very meanings of the words. So, it might seem that it must be possible, by doing an individual or collective Humpty Dumpty, to make these truths false and others true.

If it does seem so, then what seems is haywire. For, if we were to change the usage and hence the use of any or all the words involved, we should not thereby alter the truth-values of either or both of the original propositions. We should instead simply be bringing it about that the original vocables now expressed other propositions, or perhaps become mere incoherent strings of words.

The same invalid inference is also applied to substantial scientific propositions, usually as one element in a constellation of confusions about the nature and implications of the sociology of knowledge. Thus one contributor to a very widely used textbook – the same, incidentally as prefers 'societal members' to 'people' – lays it on the line: "Scholars also have traditionally sought to discover 'objective' knowledge and have had to contend with the fact that the search for and discovery of such knowledge is socially organised. . . . The implication is this: if objective knowledge is taken to mean knowledge of a reality independent of language . . . then there is no such thing as objective knowledge" (Young, p. 128: and compare Flew 1976a, Ch. 2 and 3).

Pause for a moment to puzzle out what is going on – and wrong. The clue lies in a crucially significant and typically sloppy shift in word-order. The conlusion drawn is that there is no such thing as "knowledge of a reality independent of language". The premises justify no more than a statement that there is no such thing as knowledge independent of language. The truth is that the truism that knowledge must be articulated in concepts, and that these have all to be expressed in a language of some sort, has no tendency to show that knowledge cannot be – as it often is – of realities independent of language. There is astronomical knowledge; which, like all knowledge, is thus articulated. Yet the stars will continue in their courses long after the last earthly astronomer is dead, just as they did before. The concepts of astronomers, like all concepts, have to be expressed in words or word-substitutes. So, if the vocabulary of astronomers is penurious, their knowledge cannot but be correspondingly restricted. But no manoeuvres with words, no givings of meaning to nor taking of it from particular vocables, ever do, or ever could, create or change the realities of the universe around us.

The quoted statement just discussed is a centrepiece of a loose system of demoralising and obscurantist ideas. This has for some time now been powerfully preached both from the radio pulpits of the Open University and in the lecture-rooms of the University of London Institute of Education. Since these ideas are all supposed to be implications of the sociology of knowledge the treatment of them here has served, both as part of a brief discussion of what is and is not conventional in language, and as an illustration of the nature and possible importance of the philosophy of sociology.

(iii) But to show that the linguistic philosopher, who sees merit in sometimes doing philosophy in the linguistic mode, can nonetheless be truly a philosopher, it is best to go back yet again to our very first example. It was, after all, drawn from the writings of one of the first of the great men of old. Socrates concludes that if I do not know what something is I cannot know anything else about it. How does he support this philosophical conclusion?

He supports it by describing homely instances and by getting his hearers to agree that these make his point. 'How can I sensibly say anything about Meno', he asks in the dialogue *Meno*, 'if I do not know who Meno is?' Although, not being a linguistic philosopher, he never makes this explicit, Socrates is in effect appealing to every word-trained person's knowledge of what it would be correct to say; whether in Greek or in any other language possessing equivalent terms. My own criticism rested on the same kind of appeal, perhaps made slightly more explicit. The tactic was to contrast: on the one hand, the new-fangled criteria which Socrates had introduced for the application of the key form of expression 'know what something is'; with, on the other hand, the established criteria of ordinary, everyday standard usage. I then pointed the moral. Only when that expression is read in the pedestrian sense determined by established usage can the Socratic conclusion qualify as proved. But Socrates, for no sufficient reason given, insists that this conclusion still remains incontestably true even when the key phrase is construed in his own made-to-measure interpretation. The beginning of this discussion was perhaps not obviously linguistic, whereas its development ostentatiously is. Yet the whole thing is uniformly a paradigm of philosophy.

4. *Parochialism and obviousness.*   The previous three sections have given a preliminary account of what philosophy is. Two objections will be put, that the account is parochial, and that the philosophical truths instanced are truisms. Meeting these objections can bring out more about the nature of the discipline.

(i) The charge of parochialism may refer to either geographical or ideological blinkers: the short list of great examplars in the second paragraph of the present chapter consisted entirely of European names; and it did not include those of Marx or Lenin. 'Surely', someone will say, 'both India and China have had famous philosophical traditions; and is not Marxism-Leninism the official philosophy of an ever-rising proportion of the peoples of the world?'

(a) Famous though these traditions are, a large part of what they offer is philosophy only in the quite different sense explained right at the beginning; and, for present purposes, dismissed. The best introductions known to me are both published by the Princeton University Press: *A Source Book in Indian Philosophy* edited by S. Radhakrishnan and C. A. Moore; and *A Source Book in Chinese Philosophy* edited by Wing-tsit Chan. Where these do present conceptual inquiries of the sort with which we are here concerned, and this is far more often the case in the former volume than the latter, one feels an urgent need for a new class of interpreters. What is wanted, and what so far scarcely exist, are people with a formidable combination of qualifications. These new interpreters need to be — at least — not only fluent translators between two languages, but also at home in two traditions which have until comparatively recent times developed in almost total isolation one from the other. Such super-cultural bridgebuilders may emerge, perhaps in places like Hong Kong and Singapore, or among the large and growing Asian community in Britain. But, until they do, the author of a book such as this had better be parochial rather than risk spreading misunderstandings.

In the Chinese case the remarkable thing is how little we find which is recognisable as philosophy in the present sense; although there may be some change in this picture after the original literature has been thoroughly searched by scholars equipped with all the necessary skills, both sinological and philosophical. Certainly the reader of the Wing-tsit Chan anthology has to go a long way before he meets what looks like a philosophical thesis, and the few such he does find are neither presented as the conclusions of argument nor subjected to critical examination. It is this lack of argument which decisively disqualifies. For philosophy, as we understand the term, is essentially argumentative. It is this, incidentally, which makes it so excellent a mental training. There can be few of the many careers undertaken by philosophy graduates which they do not pursue the more effectively for having thus acquired a greater capacity and inclination to examine an argued case as an argued case, determining what does and does not support what, what does and does not follow.

Approaching the Chinese source book with these interests we have, however reluctantly, to pass by Confucius and Mencius. They are both of their kind splendid. But that is not the kind we are presently seeking. 'The Natural Way of Lao Tzu' and 'The Mystical Way of Chuang Tzu' are, again, not for us now. Of Mo Tzu and his followers the Editor remarks in oddly inept self-commentary: "All speculation aside, the fact remains that they may have represented the working class." He continues: "One thing is certain, and that is, philosophically Moism is shallow and unimportant. It does not have the profound metaphysical presuppositions of either Taoism or Confucianism" (p. 212). Yet in the present perspective what stands out is not a difference in respect of shallowness or profundity, but the similarity of what few supporting reasons are offered. When Mo Tzu speaks, for instance, of the Will of Heaven, or when he repudiates fatalism, he does not analyse these concepts; and what he offers by way of confirmation for his preferred doctrines is either an appeal to either his own authority or that of the Sage Kings, or else an indication of the evil consequences of people's holding alternative views. "If the gentlemen . . . really want the world to be rich and dislike it to be poor . . . they must condemn the doctrine of fatalism. It is a great harm to the world" (Quoted, p. 226).

This is, as we shall be seeing more fully later, quite a different ball game from that played by Aristotle in Chapter IX of his *Interpretation*. Aristotle presents and criticises an argument which proceeds, from the Law of the Excluded Middle, to fatalism. He dismisses that argument, not as socially harmful, but as logically unsound. (The Law of the Excluded Middle states that anything, any X, which could significantly be said to be Φ must be *either* Φ or not-Φ: there is no third and intermediate possibility. The Law of

19

Non-contradiction, by contrast, states that nothing, no X, can be at the same time and in the same aspect *both Φ and* not-*Φ*. The Greek letter *Φ*, pronounced phi, is employed to symbolise any characteristic; thus permitting the reservation of the capital Latin letter X for the quite different function of symbolising that to which the characteristic is attributed. *Interpretation*, usually known by the Latin title *de Interpretatione*, is – along with *Categories, Topics, Sophistical Refutions, Prior Analytics* and *Posterior Analytics* – one of the six elements in Aristotle's *Organon*, or instrument. The *Organon* was a fundamental of university education in the Middle Ages. It is to the subject of the last two of its components, that Marlowe's Dr Faustus refers when he cries: "Sweet analytics, tis thou hast ravished me.")

Again, Chu Hsi writes: "Take a pot of flowers, for example. . . . Can they be said to be without consciousness? Chou Mao-shu (Chou Tun-i) did not cut the grass growing outside his window, and said that he felt towards the grass as he felt toward himself. That shows that plants have consciousness" (p. 623). Of course it shows nothing of the kind; although to some it may suggest a fine fey new excuse for not acceding to wifely pressures to mow the lawn. For us the remarkable fact is that neither Chu Hsi nor Chou Mao-shu shows any interest in either finding or assessing reasons for or against believing that this bizarre pronouncement is actually true. It appears that no one at all in their culture circle was racked by the modern philosophical Problem of Other Minds; to answer, that is, the epistemological question of how we can know – indeed whether we can know – that others are conscious.

(b)   The case with Marxism-Leninism is similar but not the same. This is no product of an alien culture, separated from ours by some chasm of incomprehension. Yet relatively few of the items in its scriptural canon are works of philosophy. This few includes some of the early writings of Marx, the *Dialectics of Nature* by Engels, Lenin's *Philosophical Notebooks*, Lenin's *Materialism and Empirio-Criticism*, and one or two short statements by Stalin and Mao Tse-tung. The list could be extended, but not all that much. Certainly it does not add up to a contribution to philosophy in any way comparable with the work of Marx in sociology, or with the sinister achievement of Lenin in developing the theory and practice of the totalitarian party.

The difficulty of getting and keeping everything in place here is increased both by the constantly realised possibility of confounding philosophy as world-outlook with philosophy as an intellectual discipline, and by the desire of the devout to believe that their heroes must have been number one in everything they touched. Shining eyed converts to a Marxist-Leninist world-outlook will assure us that Plato and Aristotle, Descartes and Kant, are all, as philosophers, put in the shade by Marx; just as a Jehovah's Witness carpenter once revealed to me that Jesus bar Joseph was the only man who ever made a perfect mortice-and-tenon joint. Others again are more or less clearheaded in their determination to transform philosophical institutions into political bases, replacing philosophy by something else: "The philosophers have only *interpreted* the world, in various ways; the point, however, is to *change* it" (Marx 1845, p. 647: italics orginal).

(ii)   It may indeed now seem obvious: that Socratic definition is not a precondition of knowledge; that the power to give new meanings to any vocable to which we choose to give new meanings is not, at the same time, a capability to make tautological or any other truths false; and that, from the fact that there can be no knowledge without concepts, it does not follow, what is not so, that there is no such thing as "knowledge of a reality independent of language". I hope it does seem obvious. For I shall have failed in my teaching task if it does not, and these particular illustrations were selected for Chapter I in part just because they do make it easy to get the points. If these points do now seem obvious, or even if they do not, it still remains important to take on board the insight that obviousness really is, what many other things nowadays are falsely assumed to be, essentially relative. It makes no more sense to say that something is obvious absolutely, without reference to particular places and persons, than it does to say that a thing is in motion absolutely, not relative to any other place or object. In fact what is obvious to one person now may seem obviously untrue to another, and may at an earlier stage have seemed either altogether obscure and uncertain or even obviously untrue to that first person.

That it now seems obvious is, therefore, no good reason for dismissing an insight as worthless; nor for believing that it did not have to be acquired, and perhaps acquired first at the cost of much toil and the exercise of unusual talent. Certainly I have never met any previously untutored students who without help seized and stated the crucial points about the Socratic quest for definitions, while the sharper views of their tutors were themselves obtained mainly by climbing onto other men's shoulders. One of the chief rewards for plunging into the history of ideas is to learn what an extraordinary variety of things have appeared to different people in different periods unquestionable or unthinkable. It is to recognise how many propositions believed even by very clever people, perhaps in their own day for the very best of reasons, can later, even by much lesser men, be known and shown to be untrue. After, and looking down over, the intervening centuries it is at last to us obvious.

Yet to the genius of Plato it seemed equally manifest that without first answering the questions set by Socrates there could be no knowledge.

The point about the essential relativity of obviousness applies generally. But there is another, particular to philosophy. For, as we saw in Section 2, a philosophical advance must be an increase, not in information about the universe around us, but in awareness of the logical relations between concepts. What in this case we become aware of must, therefore, already have been in some way implicit in those concepts themselves; and, were we creatures of unlimited intellectual capacity, would always have been obvious to us. It was with reason that Plato contended that such awareness, to which alone was he prepared to award the diploma title 'knowledge', constituted a kind of remembering; albeit, as he believed, from a timeless time before conception. (Plato argued for not only the immortality but also the pre-existence of the soul. But of both these matters more later.)

5. *Progress in philosophy*. The rest of the present book consists of chapters broaching some of the problems which arise in various often not easily or unequivocally separable areas. These particular areas have been selected partly in order to provide the widest possible conspectus and partly with an eye to their importance. This importance is itself partly internal but mainly external. For, although it is necessary from the beginning to distinguish philosophy as the study of certain logical problems about concepts from philosophy as world-outlook, some possible answers to some of the former do have a definite bearing upon some questions of the latter sort. If, for instance, the Incompatibilist is right about the freedom of the will then it seems that we shall have to choose: whether to abandon hope for a science of man; or whether to undertake the surely impossible task of persuading ourselves and everybody else – and living consistently by the persuasion – that no one ever has had, has, or will have any real alternative.

What kind of progress can the attentive and lively reader expect to make? That is a question which he has – you have – every right to put. It demands an answer. The first kind is in appreciating what the problems are; which is not to be despised. It is to this in general that Chapter I has been devoted, while its particular account of the nature of the philosophical problems of the freedom of the will has rectified a set of extremely popular misconceptions.

But, although it is better to know what the problems are than not to know, it is not enough. Are philosophical problems, as is sometimes suggested, essentially insoluble? Certainly there are in many other fields problems which are in practice insoluble: there are, for instance, many questions about human history which will never be answered; simply because there are no longer sufficient traces — whether documentary or otherwise — to serve as evidence revealing what actually happened. Other questions may be in some subtle way senseless or incoherent, or may be based upon some false assumption. The stock illustration of the latter, traditionally but unfortunately described as the Fallacy of Many Questions (Flew, 1975, §§ 7.3 – 7.7), is the question – shot at someone who in fact is either not married or, if married, has either not started or not stopped – 'When did you stop beating your wife?'

Such crooked questions, or such pseudo-questions, have in principle no answers which are at the same time both correct and direct. It would be silly anywhere to try to solve problems known to be in practice insoluble, or to propose direct answers to questions known to be in principle not susceptible to such. Philosophy, however, is not, or, at any rate, does not have to be, like that. Where the questions are, as indeed sometimes they are, either pseudo-questions or crooked questions then the problem is to recognise and to reveal that this is the case. Precisely that recognition, and that demonstration, is the solution.

Since philosophical problems are what they are, real progress is bound to be both piecemeal and pedestrian. It is nevertheless possible. Progress is a matter of finding a good question to press, of becoming seized of some crucial distinction, of appreciating that and why this or that is relevant, of seeing and showing that this or that does or does not follow. For many the temptation is to try to discuss and to settle all the great problems, or at the very least the whole of one range of them, all at once. The result for those who have thus:

> ". . . reason'd high
> Of Providence, Foreknowledge, Will, and Fate,
> Fixt Fate, free will, foreknowledge absolute,"

is, that, like the fallen angels in the Pandemonium of Milton's *Paradise Lost*, they have:

> ". . . found no end, in wand'ring mazes lost" (II 558–61).

It was, one may suggest, pandemonium in Pandemonium precisely because everyone did insist on reasoning high. The misguided devils attempted to do everything at once; never explaining, and testing, the sweeping abstract generalisation in terms of, and against, homely, concrete, familiar

23

instances. Certainly the student of philosophy, like his colleagues in many other fields, is best advised to eschew the high, wide and wholesale; and to insist on taking at last one step forward, however short, in every engagement.

Proceeding with such small, firm steps it is possible to know that the movement is in the correct direction; even when – to change the image – the final pattern into which all these pieces are to fit is either vehemently disputatious or entirely mysterious. Ludwig Wittgenstein (1889–1951) offered a helpful analogy. It is the analogy of sorting out a library of books lying higgledy-piggledy on the floor. It would be progress, slight no doubt but absolutely solid, to spot volumes two and five of *The Decline and Fall of the Roman Empire*, and to put them both together on a shelf with the latter immediately to the right of the former, notwithstanding that their ultimate position is to be on another shelf, and separated by volumes three and four.

With all this in mind it is useful to repeat that the Index of Notions, like the Index of Names, is intended for use. It constitutes a test list of distinctions made, of terms explained, of fallacies identified and labelled. To check through this index is to review progress; while the whole business of making such progress can be seen, encouragingly, as the salutary and diametric opposite of what was planned by the ideologists of Ingsoc (English Socialism) in George Orwell's prophetic nightmare *1984*: "Newspeak was designed not to extend but to *diminish* the range of thought, and this purpose was indirectly assisted by cutting the choice of words down to a minimum . . . . It was intended that when Newspeak had been adopted once and for all and Oldspeak forgotten, a heretical thought – that is, a thought diverging from the principles of Ingsoc – should be literally unthinkable . . ." (pp. 306 and 305: italics original).

CHAPTER II

The elements of ethics

Something has been made already of the concluding words of Book I of *The Republic*. The questions pursued may have seemed altogether theoretical, removed from the urgencies of practical life, and – in a once fashionable word – irrelevant. The same could not be said of the development in the nine later books of Plato's proposals for absolute rule by an elite order of communist Guardians. These golden men, since they alone are acquainted with the realities of value, have a right and a duty to rule the unenlightened and uncommunist masses. These realities are supposed to be integral to, indeed in part to constitute, the invisible infrastructure of the universe. The Guardians are Plato's notorious "philosopher kings". They have access to the fundamental realities – they know what truth, courage, temperance, justice and so on really are – thanks to a lifetime of physical and intellectual training, an education imposed upon and possible to the rarest of natural talents only. The details of Plato's proposals of course are not, and never were, practical politics. But the presuppositions and implications of the general ideas behind that dream city-state – the first Utopia – have been and remain the stuff of ideological conflicts in the twentieth century: "Plato was the child of a time which is still our own" (Popper 1945, Vol. I, p. 173).

Book I begins quietly, with Socrates and others gathering at the house of Cephalus in Peiraeus, the port of Athens. Socrates starts to discuss justice with the son of Cephalus, an eager and agreeable young man. The first suggestion, is, in effect, that justice is to ensure that everyone has their due, what they either deserve or are otherwise entitled to have and to hold. This traditional and, surely, in substance correct suggestion is dismissed on the basis of arguments which in truth only undermine the here unquestioned shared Socratic assumption that justice, along with all other virtues, must be a sort of skill. Things come alive dramatically a third of the way through, with the angry and abusive intervention of Thrasymachus. (These books, by the way, are only as long as average chapters; about thirty pages in the Everyman edition. Plato himself was not responsible either for the book division or for the marginal numbers and lettered subsections. The former is a result of scribes employing a standard size of papyrus roll. The latter derives from the original printing by the house of Étienne and Son, and makes possible precise and convenient edition-neutral references).

Thrasymachus is a hardboiled political cynic, or may be realist. He has no time for all this pussyfooting around, which, he says, wantonly ignores the fact that people and classes in power describe whatever suits them as just. Pressed to provide his own definition, he responds: "Listen then, I assert that justice is nothing else but the advantage of the stronger" (338c).

1. *What Socrates should have said to Thrasymachus*. The critique deployed in the remainder of Book I finally silences Thrasymachus. It should satisfy no one. Thrasymachus wants to keep on urging that in fact the just man, the good man, is by his very justice and goodness the destined victim of exploitation. Morality demands sacrifices from individuals. Being moral, therefore, is not to the advantage of the individual who makes the sacrifices, but only to that of those who continue to profit therefrom. Justice is thus a good thing not for oneself but for other people. It is, as Thrasymachus might have said had he had access to the vocabulary of P. T. Barnum, strictly for suckers.

In Book II the same challenge is renewed by Glaucon and Adeimantus. These two are well-born and well-bred young men, with none of the hacking cynicism of Thrasymachus. Already in Book I, when Socrates turned to him for support, Glaucon has given the firm reply: "I, for my part, believe that the life of the just man is more profitable." (347E.) Now, supported by his brother Adeimantus, and while still insisting that he himself has no doubt but that this is the truth, Glaucon proceeds — *con brio*! — to build up the most powerful possible opposing case. The whole of the rest of *The Republic* is presented as the attempt of a Socrates now presumably only a mouthpiece for Plato, to show, what is surely not true, that justice must after all always be advantageous to the just man himself. It is in response to this Glauconian challenge that Plato develops his dream of a Dorian city, austere and stately as a Dorian temple, subject to the absolute rule of the highly intellectual yet physically fit order of Guardians. Plato's response includes the first systematic presentation of the thesis, now commonplace yet still paradoxical, that all delinquency is an expression of psychological disease. The inclusion is altogether appropriate. For, if all delinquency is indeed an expression of psychological disease, then all delinquency surely must be against the interests of the patient. Even where my unfitness enables me to escape some dangerous or disagreeable duty it would still be better for me to escape that duty without being unfit at all (Flew 1973, Part I and passim).

(i)   One vitiating fault of the whole treatment in *The Republic* of questions about duty and interest is a failure to appreciate and to come to terms with the fundamental distinction between what is the case and what ought to be. Thus Thrasymachus appeals to his own excessively hard-bitten view of how things actually are, whereas Socrates rests a large part of his case upon claims which are more or less explicitly about what ought to be. No one seems to say or to see that this difference is crucial. Yet suppose we were to allow that Plato was right about what would be true in the supposedly ideal world of his visionary city-state. Still this all must be and is enormously different from this world, which is the world in and about which Thrasymachus launched his original challenge. Even the successive formulations of the Socratic counter-thesis appear to be infected to some extent with the same ruinous ambiguity. It is, surely, one thing to say "that the life of the just man is more profitable", and rather another to affirm that being just is "among those things which he who would be blessed must love both for their own sake and for their consequences" (358A).

This crucial and fundamental distinction between *is* and *ought* was most famously formulated by the Scot David Hume (1711–1776), in *A Treatise of Human Nature*. His words are characteristically ironic, and should not be misread as implying that what needs to be done always is done. Hume's point is, rather, that, though the distinction always ought to be made, usually it is not. This is substantially what Aristotle (384–322 BC) said in the *Nicomachean Ethics*, in a passage curiously overlooked during recent discussions: "Deductive inferences about matters of conduct always have a major premise of the form 'Since the end or supreme good is so and so' . . ." (1144 A31–3). Hume wrote:

"I cannot forbear adding to these reasonings an observation, which may, perhaps, be found of some importance. In every system of morality, which I have hitherto met with, I have always remark'd, that the author proceeds for some time in the ordinary way of reasoning, and establishes the being of a God, or makes observations concerning human affairs; when of a sudden I am surpriz'd to find, that instead of the usual copulations of propositions, *is*, and *is not*, I meet with no proposition that is not connected with an *ought*, or an *ought not*. This change is imperceptible; but

27

is, however, of the last consequence. For as this *ought*, or *ought not*, expresses some new relation or affirmation, 'tis necessary that it shou'd be observ'd and explain'd; and at the same time that a reason should be given, for what seems altogether inconceivable, how this new relation can be a deduction from others, which are altogether different from it" (III (i)1).

Hume's successors have made much of the notion of a Naturalistic Fallacy. This fallacy, so christened first by G. E. Moore, consists in inferring conclusions wholly or partly of the one sort from premises exclusively of the other. The label is tolerably apt. For, as Hume proceeded to show, the term 'natural', and its derivatives and associates, is frequently pivotal in committing this fallacy: from the premise that all or most of us are thus or thus inclined, and hence that it is natural to us so to behave; it is immediately, but invalidly, inferred that such action is at best morally licit, if not obligatory. Having explained this I am perhaps in academic duty bound to mention that among those best qualified to have an opinion there are some who deny that Hume was really saying what he appears to be saying, and/or insist that this Naturalistic Fallacy is somehow not really a fallacy. But even they do not, I think, deny that an is/ought distinction can be made in most of the places where the rest of us believe it can and should be pressed; nor yet that most of the examples actually offered as instances of the Naturalistic Fallacy are indeed fallacious. Whatever truth these recalcitrants may or may not have grasped it will not require us to fault Einstein's announcement: "As long as we remain within the realm of science proper, we can never meet with a sentence of the type: 'Thou shalt not kill' . . . Scientific statements of facts and relations . . . cannot produce ethical directives" (Einstein 1935, p. 114).

This insistence upon distinguishing between *is* and *ought* is now echoed by every well-instructed first year student. Yet in *The Republic*, where it is crucially relevant, no such distinction is ever made. Clearly that it is both relevant and crucial was not in his day obvious even to Plato. It is a good moment to quote a judgement made with Hume particularly in mind: ". . . the great philosophical discoveries are discoveries of the obvious. The great philosopher is the man who first formulates in clear and unmistakable words, and in as general a form as possible, something which has always been hazily familar to everybody in particular instances. If we say afterwards that he has told us nothing new, that only shows how right he was" (Price, p. 12).

(ii)   A second and at least equally important fault of Plato's treatment is that it never ever begins to show that and why what Thrasymachus offers as a definition, as a definition simply will not do. "Justice", he said, "is nothing else but the advantage of the stronger". But think: the expression 'the advantage of the stronger' (the *definiens*) transparently is not equivalent to the word 'justice' (the *definiendum*). Suppose, for instance, that someone maintains, as some people will, that the one-party regime in some newly emerging country is energetically and effectively engaged in building a just society. Such a tribute will no doubt be welcome at the top. It might even help to earn the writer his slice of the fat cake of official hospitality. But this popularity could not, surely, long survive his explanation that for him, if not according to standard usage, the phrase 'a just society' does just mean a society in which the interests of the stronger (here, presumably, the all-powerful Central Committee) prevail over all other claims and claimants. This may be, and no doubt is, the truth about many regimes in emerging countries — as well as about plenty in emerged countries too. It most certainly is not the truth about the accepted meaning of the word 'justice'.

The mistake of Thrasymachus is, however, no dull and lumpish gaffe. What on the present most natural interpretation he is saying is not just wrong, period. To define the word 'justice' as 'the advantage of the stronger' is not to say something which merely happens to be mistaken. It is to make a move which is radically, spectacularly, diametrically, and hence most illuminatingly, wrong. For it is central to the notion of justice that to appeal to justice must be to appeal to standards and principles logically independent of all particular individual and group interests. Only and precisely insofar as the standards and principles of justice are thus independent of all particular interests can it be in principle possible for such standards and principles to provide independent and impartial adjudication when those particular interests conflict. And, even where there is no immediate question of conflict of interest, it is only and precisely insofar as the standards and principles of justice are thus independent of all particular interests that it can be in principle possible to assess any and every claim of any such interest by reference to these very standards and principles.

Certainly there are many other contentions which a debunking Thrasymachus might wish to urge, and which are not touched by this appeal to established usages. He might, for example, want to say that the whole notion of such impartial standards logically independent of — not, that is to say, definable in terms of — any particular individual or group interest is somehow baseless, or even internally incoherent. Or, alternatively or additionally, he might want to say that there is a deal of hypocrisy and mendacity around, with lots of bad hats pretending to a concern for justice when this pretence is nothing but a fig leaf over something less attractive. Indeed there

29

is, and are. But do not fail to notice that the second of these alternative contentions scarcely consists with the first. Hypocrisy, notoriously, is the tribute which vice pays to virtues. There can, therefore, be little point in or possibility of pretending to a justice which you do not possess if the very idea is either baseless or incoherent.

Consideration of the wrongness of the Thrasymachean definition of 'justice' is thus beginning to give insight into the essential meaning of moral terms, and hence into the nature of morality. No doubt this insight needs to be further explained and enforced. So notice first two relevant idioms, which belong to contemporary English rather than Classical Greek. One of these is that in which an epigram is offered as a definition. If someone says, boringly, that the word 'uncle' means 'parents' brother or brother-in-law', then he really is offering a definition, and correct at that. But when, maybe in a rather smug way, you give us your favourite definition of the Roman genius as an infinite capacity for making drains, or of tanks as being armoured and mechanised fire-power, then you are in truth making remarks about the Roman genius and about tanks, and quite good ones too. You certainly are not explicating the meanings of the expression 'the Roman genius' or of the word 'tank'. Your remarks could not even be understood by anyone who did not already know who the Romans were, and what the words 'genius' and 'tank' mean. Nor could your shrewd sayings be relished as informative by anyone mistakenly believing them to provide, as a good descriptive definition should, a tautological equivalence.

The relevance of all this is that it can be made to bring out the irrelevance of so much that is said by both Thrasymachus and Socrates. For to a discussion which, though conducted largely in a material mode of speech, is certainly supposed to be about the correct definition of the word 'justice', Thrasymachus insists on contributing fierce generalisations about the invariably exploitative behaviour of every ruling class. In reply Socrates neither protests that this is all irrelevant anyway nor cites actual cases in order to disprove the generalisations. Instead both parties are at one in trying to establish or upset claims about the putative facts of human behaviour by purely verbal manoeuvres. Both respond to possible counter-examples to generalisations about actual rulers by insisting that at any rate *true* rulers would or would not behave so.

This disreputable response has the useful pillory-name 'The No-true-Scotsman Move' (Flew 1975, 3.1 – 3.7): instead of admitting that even Scotsmen sometimes do, the slippery spokesman insists that no *true* Scotsman would. He thus replaces a substantial but false generalisation about

THE ELEMENTS OF ETHICS

flesh and blood Scots by a new but empty tautological truth. When the new definition thus increases — so to speak — the membership qualifications, it is called a high redefinition; in the opposite case, a low redefinition. A descriptive definition describes the existing meaning of a word; the contrast being with a prescriptive definiton, prescribing what meaning it is to have in future. The term 'counter-example' is, surely, sufficiently explained by the context of its first employment, above.

The other relevant English idiom is a favourite with debunkers and cynics. Someone says, with a sneer, that when that playboy talks about a spiritual and purely Platonic relationship what he really means is four legs in a bed, or that when those capitalist imperialists speak about safeguarding the rights of small Asian peoples to self-determination, what they really mean is defending their own investments. The statements made in this idiom have point only and precisely insofar as what their subjects are said really to mean is not the meaning of what they are said to be saying. For, if it were, then the debunker's occupation would be gone. There would be no mask of hypocrisy to tear off.

The main point of this second subsection, that the language of morals precisely is not and cannot be that of any particular individual or group interest or affection, can now be finally confirmed in another decisive, classic statement. Again it comes from Hume, but this time from the second of his two *Inquiries, An Inquiry concerning the Principles of Morals*. The punctuation has been made to conform with the style of the present book:

"When a man denominates another his 'enemy,' his 'rival,' his 'antagonist,' his 'adversary,' he is understood to speak the language of self-love and to express sentiments peculiar to himself and arising from his particular circumstances and situation. But when he bestows on any man the epithets of 'vicious' or 'odious' or 'depraved,' he then speaks another language and expresses sentiments in which he expects all his audience are to concur with him. He must here, therefore, depart from his private and particular situation and must choose a point of view common to him with others: he must move some universal principle of the human frame and touch a string to which all mankind have an accord and symphony" (IX (i)).

2. *Objective values and Plato's Ideas.* The previous subsection suggested one thing which Thrasymachus might have been made to say, but was

not: "that the whole notion of such impartial standards logically independent of – not, that is to say, definable in terms of – any particular individual or group interest is somehow baseless, or even internally incoherent." Philosophical theses of this kind, about logical dependence or independence, need always to be distinguished from similar-sounding psychological or sociological contentions. It is one thing to maintain that there is room for some kind of scientific explanation why people accept the standards which they do in fact accept. It is quite another to hold that the very meanings of their appraisal words refer essentially to individual or group interests.

Try as an exercise applying such a distinction to a test-passage supplied by a leading behavioural psychologist, B. F. Skinner. It comes from a widely circulated book, with the chilling title *Beyond Freedom and Dignity*. Skinner quotes a Humian statement by the formerly Austrian and since by adoption British philosopher Sir Karl Popper (1902-   ): "It is impossible to derive a sentence stating a norm or decision from a sentence stating a fact. . . ." Skinner comments: "The conclusion is valid only if indeed it is 'possible to adopt a norm or its opposite'. . . . But, whether or not a person obeys the norm 'Thou shalt not steal' depends upon supporting contingencies, which must not be overlooked" (p. 114). That there are causes why someone does or does not obey a rule has no tendency to show that this does or does not follow logically from that.

Although his attempts to demolish what Thrasymachus offered as a definition were ill-starred, Plato does have an original and distinctive answer to the question of baselessness. It was indeed a main part of his own private master question. For, born and raised in a period of both unprecedented intellectual innovation and what amounted to international civil war, his chief aim as a thinker was to re-establish standards and certainties upon a firmer new foundation. Plato's answer appeals to his Theory of Forms or Ideas. (Initial capitals will be employed always and only when referring to the objects postulated by this theory. The inaudible discrimination between Ideas and ideas will thus parallel those between Classical and classical, Conservative and conservative, and all the many others in which the capital indicates the specific and the particular, the lower case the general).

(i)   The Theory of Ideas was Plato's systematic answer to all questions of the characteristically Socratic type. Wherever you have an adjective, such as 'just', applicable in many actual or imaginable instances, it is possible to ask a corresponding Socratic question; in this case 'What is justice?' Often of course your language will lack an appropriate ready-made abstract noun. But in Classical Greek substitutes could be created at will by attaching the neuter

THE ELEMENTS OF ETHICS

form of the adjective to the neuter form of the definite article – 'the just (thing)'; a little local grammatical idiosyncracy which surely did its mite to ease the way for Plato's theory construction. In the first and boldest version of that theory, found in *The Republic*, it is applied to all such words: "Wherever a number of individuals have a common name, we assume them to have a corresponding Idea or Form" (596A).

If Plato had meant only our (lower case) idea, then there would have been no call for any excitement or further explanation. But those postulated Platonic Ideas are objects of a very special sort. In the first place, Ideas are – introducing a more modern technical expression – (logical) substances: defined as whatever can significantly be said to exist separately, and in its own right. This notion is best appreciated by contemplating illustrations supplied by Lewis Carroll. When the Red Queen in *Through the Looking Glass* triumphantly concludes her subtraction sum, "Then if the dog went away, its temper would remain!", and when Alice was so rightly unable to help thinking to herself, "What dreadful nonsense we *are* talking!", the reason why it is nonsense is that the Red Queen is talking as if 'temper' was, as 'dog' is, a word for a logical substance (Ch. IX). Compare also, in *Alice's Adventures in Wonderland*, the grin of the Cheshire Cat; which, albeit temporarily, was supposed to survive the disappearance of its grinner (Ch. VI).

It is only if the soul in question is in this sense a substance that a doctrine of its survival or immortality can even make sense. If, for instance, by 'soul' we mean personality; and if 'personality' is then defined, as the *Oxford English Dictionary* defines it, as "that quality or assemblage of qualities which makes a person what he is as distinct from other persons": then the suggestion of the soul surviving the dissolution of the person whose qualities it is makes no more sense than the just quoted, calculated nonsenses of Lewis Carroll. Plato himself, when he labours in *Phaedo* to prove the immortality of the soul, is at pains to contend, albeit in another terminology, that both his souls and his Ideas are (logical) substances (Flew 1964, pp. 1–28 and 34–71).

In the second place, these Ideas are in every way egregious (logical) substances. They are, for a start, incorporeal; hence invisible, intangible, inaudible, and – generally – insensible. As such they are accessible only to the intellect, not to the senses. This point can be memorised better with the help of a sharp story. The story is preserved in a scholiasts' annotation of one of the manuscripts. (A scholiast is a person who just writes something in the margin. So most of us have been scholiasts at one time or another!) Antisthenes the Cynic complained that while he could see horses he could not see Horseness, or the Form or Idea of Horse. Plato responded, nastily, by saying

33

that while Antisthenes possessed what it takes to see horses – namely, eyes – he had in the distribution of intelligence – let's face it – been passed over. Besides being incorporeal Ideals are unchanging and eternal. Somehow also they make all the instances of whatever it is they are the Ideas of have the characteristic in question; they are themselves more real and more excellent than any of those instances; and they constitute the ultimately authoritative standard for the correct employment of the corresponding word.

In the course of a long and intellectually active life Plato certainly retreated and qualified a little. He saw, for instance, that negative terms would have to be dealt with separately: the Greek original of our word 'barbarian' was substantially equivalent to our 'foreigner', and hence referred to the not-Greek. The negative characteristic of not-Greekness must presumably be in some sort of special dependent relationship upon the Idea of Greekness. More interestingly, Plato in the later dialogue *Parmenides* presents a young Socrates flummoxed by an argument showing that a vicious infinite regress is generated by the insistence that every Idea must itself possess, in preeminent and exemplary degree, that characteristic of which it is the Idea. But the version of the Theory of Ideas summarised here is the first, the boldest and the most comprehensive. It is these Ideas to which the Guardians have, thanks to their special education and the special talents which alone make that education possible, privileged access. It is this access, for Plato the defining characteristic of the *true* philosopher, which reveals the ideally objective and authoritative bases of all proper standards. So Plato's Socrates asks, again in *The Republic*:

"Then do you think there is any difference between the blind and those who are deprived of knowledge of the real nature of everything, those who have no clear standards in their minds, and who cannot look away – like painters at their models – at the perfect truth, and, always with reference to and in the exactest possible contemplation of it, establish in this world too the norms of the beautiful, the just and the good, when that is needed; and, when these are established, as Guardians keep them safe?" (484 C-D).

(ii)   No philosophical spokesman for the objectivity of value has ever been more thoroughly entrenched: indeed this is the perfect paradigm case of what the longing for such objectivity is a longing for. Before calling counsel to speak for an opposite tradition, we must see the sort of arguments with which Plato supported his theory. For he was, though also a brilliant writer and a visionary, above all, the philosopher. Here is no guru teaching his ashram to accept accounts of unseen, eternal, incorporeal realities simply on his own unevidenced sayso. Nor are these arguments specific to morals. That they are relevant in a chapter on 'The Elements of Ethics' is one more sign of how hard it is to compartmentalise philosophy.

(a) The first, called the One over Many Argument, concerns the presuppositions of predication. There are innumerable cases in which we can apply the same word in – predicate the same of – many, many instances. Socrates kept wanting: not to be given lists of such instances; but to discover what any characteristic thus predicated essentially is. Thus in the dialogue *Meno* Socrates quickly and characteristically moves from the question whether virtue or excellence can be taught to the supposedly prior question of what it is; and, when Meno provides a varied list of instances of such excellence, dismisses these as irrelevant. Plato argued that for every collection of instances in which the same word is applicable – every Many – there must be something – some One – which makes them all instances of whatever it may be; and these Ones are the Ideas.

Plato further realises that if this argument applies at all it must apply again to the Ideas themselves, as he describes them. For every Idea is supposed to be – whatever this may mean – more real and more excellent than any of its many instances. But to say this is to imply that the Ideas in turn constitute another Many, which must presuppose another One, the super-Form or super-Idea of the Good, which is at the same time the Real. This is for Plato always a high and mysterious subject. He speaks of the Idea of the Good in many of the phrases which theists apply to God. It would nevertheless be wrong to identify the two. The Idea of the Good is not a personal or any other sort of agent, capable of acting at a particular time or at all times; and all other realities depend upon it rather as a logical presupposition than as a sustaining cause. It is in another dialogue *Timaeus*, vastly popular in the Middle Ages, that Plato introduces his own super-Agent. This is the powerful but not almighty Demiurge, who fashions rather than creates the world. But for more on the fascinating connections and conflicts between the Greek theological tradition, stemming from *The Republic*, and that of the Mosaic God of Abraham, Isaac and Israel, you had best go to that classic of the history of ideas, A. O. Lovejoy *The Great Chain of Being*.

The other necessary footnote to an account of the One over Many Argument must explain that the Theory of Forms constitutes the most spectacular illustration of one of the three sorts of answer to the desperately difficult and contested Problem of Universals. Any crisp, precisely determinate formulation is bound to misrepresent this foggy field. But to be going on with it should be enough to say that, if you think that predication presupposes the existence of exotic (logical) substances like Plato's Ideas, then you are committed to – in yet one more sense of that outrageously overworked word – realism. If with Peter Abelard (1079–1142) and John Locke (1632–1704) you believe that it is all done through mental images or perhaps concepts, then you are a conceptualist. Norminalists, such as Thomas Hobbes (1588–1679) in his *Leviathan*, insist that there is and can be "Nothing in the world universal but names" [words] "for the things . . . are every one of them individual and singular. One universal name is imposed on many things, for their similitude . . ." (Ch.IV).

(b) The other arguments can be marketed wholesale: the most important thing is to know that Plato has arguments, and to recognise of what kind they are. Although these can be distinguished as an Argument from Meaning, an Argument from the Sciences, and an Argument from Reminiscence, they are all united in being arguments about and to the putative presuppositions of knowledge. Knowledge for Plato, *true* knowledge, where it was not simply an unpropositional face to face acquaintance with the Ideas, was always knowledge of what we should call logically necessary truths. For where else could knowledge be found when in the physical universe, as Heracleitus had taught, "All things are in a state of flux"?

A logically necessary proposition is defined as one of which the contradiction – the denial – would be self-contradictory, and which can itself be known to be true without reference to how things actually are under the Sun. The contrast is with logically contingent propositions. The tautological truth that 'There's ne'er a villain living in all Denmark, but he's an arrant knave' is one example of the former sort. To deny, however, the contingent proposition that 'There's ne'er a villain living in all Denmark but he's the underprivileged product of a broken home' would not be self-contradictory. That proposition could be known to be true, if it were true, only through some actual study of the home background of Danish criminals.

Knowledge of unchanging necessary truths (which in the beginning Plato found mainly in geometry) surely could not be derived from our everyday, everchanging, Heracleitean world: in that world, indeed, "All things are in a state of flux". So this true knowledge must, Plato went on, have been learned and always in us from a previous existence; and be a kind of remembered knowledge of the Ideas. Had Plato noticed a point discussed in Chapter I, that the same truths may be formulated indifferently in innumerable different word patterns, he would have seen that as yet one more reason for insisting that eternal truths presuppose eternal and unchanging realities.

36

Perplexed by the same problem of the nature and possibility of such knowledge Gottfried Leibniz (1646–1716) and others postulated not preexistence but, in a studiously circumscribed sense, innate ideas; while Leibniz himself also urged that the logically necessary eternal truths had to be grounded in and validated by a reality that is both eternal and unchanging. But this ground was now not Plato's Ideas but the rather unMosaic God of Leibniz. It is perhaps just worth mentioning too that Plato's Argument from Reminiscence appears in two forms: in one, in *Meno*, what is supposed to be being remembered is a proposition, namely, the conclusion of the Theorem of Pythagoras; in the other, in *Phaedo*, the thesis is that operating with the concept of strict equality presupposes a remembered acquaintance with the Idea of Equality.

In that second move Plato – ever the Founding Father – was to become the ancestor of many who have maintained that at least some key concepts must be somehow underivable from experience. For example: the Frenchman René Descartes (1596–1650) asserted that the concept of God as the Perfect Being could not be constructed by so imperfect a creature as man; inferring that this concept must be stamped in our souls as the trademark of their Maker. Again: Immanuel Kant (1724–1804), in what was then German Königsberg in East Prussia and is now Kaliningrad in the Russian Soviet Federated Socialist Republic, contended that several key notions are apriori concepts, applicable to, but not abstractable from, experience. (The terms 'apriori' and 'aposteriori' derive from pairs of Latin words meaning, respectively, from what comes before and from what comes after. An apriori proposition, argument or concept is one which is in some appropriate way independent of experience. Their aposteriori opposite numbers are, correspondingly, dependent. Here and throughout both terms are printed as single unitalicised words.)

3. *The man-centredness of Hume.* The previous section was variously rich in both philosophy and the history of philosophy. But its direct relevance to the present chapter was to display Plato's Theory of Ideas as an attempt to satisfy a craving for inexpugnably authentic standards and objective values. The next business is to confront Plato with Hume. Hume provides the first inspiration in modern times for all those who believe that value cannot be, and is not, embedded in the structure of things, but instead is, and must be, some sort of projection of human desires and human needs. These two fundamentally different sorts of view about value in general, and moral value

in particular, may be labelled, respectively, Objectivist and Subjectivist. But if we do employ these labels in this way then we must never forget: first, that they were not employed by Plato, or by Hume, or by any of those other classical philosophers whom we may want to categorise thus; and, second and more important, that both words are also commonly used in other and narrower senses. So no classical philosopher would have recognised himself as either an Objectivist or a Subjectivist. It is also easy, but wrong, to assume that someone who is one or the other in these broad senses must also be whatever the word means in some narrower sense.

(i) The Humian weapon unmasked in the first subsection of Section 1 already threatens the security of Plato's Objectivism. For the Guardians are supposed to be able to settle all questions about what *ought* or *ought not* to be done by an appropriately intellectual inspection of the incorporeal Ideas; realities which are in Plato's own words, "a pattern laid up in heaven" (592B). Yet what else can result from any such inspection but reports about what, albeit in another and aetherial world, *is* the case?

It is fundamentally this same point, albeit seen from another angle, which Plato himself had pressed in *Euthyphro*. *Euthyphro* discusses what is usually rendered holiness of piety. Its eponymous anti-hero Euthyphro, of whom Plato clearly thinks rather ill, is about to bring a private prosecution against his own father for manslaughter: the victim was a hired man who had died from exposure, having been bound and thrown into a ditch by the father for killing one of the father's slaves in a drunken quarrel. Socrates accepts Euthyphro, on his own valuation, as an expert on holiness. The key question in the ensuing cross-examination is: "Is the holy loved by the gods because it is holy, or is it holy because it is loved by the gods?" (9E).

This is put here as a very particular question about holiness and about the many gods of Classical Greek polytheism. Its significance for philosophical ethics is absolutely general. The implications to be drawn concern every possible moral virtue and every possible authority, personal or non-personal, human or divine. For instance: suppose that some pious person proposes that good things are good *because they are approved by an almighty God*. This implies that the word 'good' is to be defined in terms of this God's will and this God's approval; and hence that whatever an almighty Being might choose to will or to approve must, by the fact alone, become good. This option has been grasped by many clear-headed and tough-minded theists. Others equally clear-headed reject it with horror. Among the classical philosophers Hobbes accepted while Leibniz rejected.

A possible attraction is the promise of a simple drastic, Gordian response to the challenge of The Problem of Evil. The Problem of Evil is the theist's or would be theist's problem of squaring the claim that the Universe is the work of an almighty and perfect God with the concession, indeed the insistence, that it contains a deal of evil. The Gordian response is to say that, since everything is either immediately or ultimately the work of the perfect God, therefore there can be no evil. This wildly paradoxical conclusion is of course logically incompatible with, that is to say it contradicts, any kind of Mosaic theism. (This last expression is introduced to characterise Judaism, Christianity and Islam, the three great religions springing from and sharing the monotheism of Moses.)

Quite apart from any indirect implications for The Problem of Evil, for the theist the main direct cost of choosing the present option is that any such choice abandons all possibility of any well-grounded praise of God's goodness. For, taking this alternative, to say that what God does or what God approves is good is to say no less and no more than that this is what God does and this is what God approves. Since these two statements would remain equally true whatever any almighty Being might choose to do or choose to approve, they cannot constitute grounds for praising as perfect and good whatever it is supposed that that Being does in fact happen to choose.

The alternative option proposes that God, like ordinarily good people, loves the things which are good *because they are good*. This leaves open the possibility of praising God for in fact doing and approving what is good, but without emancipating the theist from that old intractable Problem of Evil. It also leaves him aware that he is no more able than anyone else to deduce conclusions about what ought to be from premises stating only what is. In particular, from the mere fact that an almighty Being wants this or approves that, it cannot be deduced that this or that ought to be done.

To master the essentials here, and to appreciate their wide and general significance, it is necessary to work through the same moves with other and secular cases. Everywhere the attempt to define moral goodness or moral obligation in terms of the will or interest or approval of any individual or group incurs parallel costs. If once we stipulate that whatever is in some way requested and required by the nation, or the working class, or the party, or what have you, is and must be as such good; then that chosen authority is at once raised above either grounded reproach or grounded praise. Yet it is, surely, an essential feature of morality that everything else, including the prescriptions of every system of positive law, should be subject to moral criticism. 'Yes, I know that is the law of England, or of Massachussetts, or of the Medes and Persians, but ought it to be, is it right?' (The adjective

39

'positive' is here equivalent to 'normative', 'prescriptive', or 'imperative': the contrast is with the laws of nature, which describe what cannot in fact be prevented from happening.)

In a legal sense the word 'justice' can indeed be defined in terms of the prescriptions and proscriptions of one particular system, whether human or divine. So in this sense it is tautological to assert, and incoherent to deny, that the system is just. But what Socrates and Thrasymachus were labouring to define was the moral sense, the sense in which all agents and all systems of law can in principle be sensibly appraised as just or unjust. This point, and the earlier conclusion that any definition on Thrasymachean lines must be irreparably wrong, can be elegantly underlined by citing a passage from the Melian Dialogue. This comes in the *History* of Thucydides, a senior contemporary of Plato. It is a dramatic reconstruction of exchanges between the representatives of a great power – Athens – and those of a tiny island state – Melos. The Athenians, compatriots of Socrates and Plato, wished to subjugate with as little fuss as possible this neutralist state. It fell unambiguously within their tradition sphere of influence. In fact they did, when the talking had to stop, 'normalise' the situation by an exercise of overwhelming military force. (The Melian Dialogue was, one might say, an account of the Cierna nad Tisou of the Great Athenian Empire; Cierna nad Tisou being the name of the railway halt to which in 1968 Czech representatives were summoned for a browbeating before the Soviet reoccupation of their country.)

It is often and with reason suggested that Thrasymachus and Cleitophon in *The Republic*, and similar characters in other Platonic dialogues, are spokesmen for cynical contemporary ideas of power politics. Yet notice what the Athenian representatives say to the Melians when both are supposed to be speaking frankly and off the record. They begin:

"We on our side will not offer a lengthy speech which no one would believe, with a lot of fine talk about how it is our right to have an empire because we defeated the Persians, or that we are coming against you now because we have been wronged; and we do not expect you to think to persuade us that the reason why you did not join our camp was that you are kith and kin of the Spartans who originally settled Melos, or that you have done us no injury."

After this 400's BC equivalent of dismissing appeals to services rendered in the Great Anti-Facist War, and of eschewing calls for the promotion of 'socialism with a human face', the Athenians go on:

"Rather we expect you to try to do what is possible on the basis of the true thoughts of both parties, since you know and we know that it is part of the human condition to choose justice only when the balance of power is even, and those who have the advantage do what they have the power to do while the weak acquiesce."

The Melians accept that they cannot here appeal to justice as such:

"Well, we consider that it is expedient that you should not destroy something which is for the general good. (The word has to be 'expedient' since you have in this way laid down that we must speak of advantage rather than justice)" (V89).

(ii)   Hume was the first major thinker of the modern period to develop a world-outlook which was through and through secular, this-worldly, and man-centred. But to claim, as Hume did, that moral values are rooted in fundamental needs and responses of our universal human nature is not at all to say that they are unimportant. This is a moment to reiterate an earlier warning against The It-is-merely Fallacy. For many will be inclined to think, as indeed the young Hume of the *Treatise* sometimes momentarily suggested, that any rejection of Objectivism must necessarily depreciate the authority and significance of morals. But in his second *Inquiry*, which he himself thought to be of all his mature writings "incomparably the best", Hume insisted that what was thus rooted in our basic needs and nature must matter to us as much as anything possibly could. He expressed this insight through a memorable political image: ". . . these principles, we must remark, are social and universal; they form, in a manner, the party of humankind against vice or disorder, its common enemy . . ." (IX (i)).

Hume's first and longest work in philosophy is *A Treatise of Human Nature*. (His longest work by far was a *History of England*, which dominated its field until overtaken by Macaulay. It was a best-seller going continually into new editions for over a century.) The title of the *Treatise* is significant, for Hume's central aim was to conduct a kind of Copernican Revolution in reverse. Whereas the astronomy of Copernicus had shifted the earth – and hence, apparently, man – from the centre of the Universe, the new human science to which Hume saw himself as a major contributor promised to restore humanity to the middle of the map of knowledge. " 'Tis impossible to tell", he declared in his Introduction, "what changes and improvements we might make in these sciences were we thoroughly acquainted with the extent and force of human understanding, and cou'd explain the nature

41

of the ideas we employ, and of the operations we perform in our reasonings."

The project of studying the nature, and especially the limitations, of the human understanding had been invented by Locke. It was the original and structuring idea of his *Essay concerning Human Understanding*. Hume's *Treatise* and the two Inquiries were essays in the same genre: he gave the first of those the deliberately allusive title *An Inquiry concerning Human Understanding*. The three major works of Immanuel Kant (1724–1804), who was after Hume the second of the two great philosophical figures of the Age of Enlightenment, fit into the same tradition: *A Critique of Pure Reason, A Critique of Practical Reason* and *A Critique of Judgement*.

Hume's own special model for the way in which the discoveries of a new science of man might reshape the map of knowledge was contributed by what he, and everybody else, took to be the physical discovery of a fundamental difference between Primary and Secondary Qualities. This distinction, or family of distinctions, has had a long history and taken a variety of forms. Its core is a contrast between, on the one hand, those qualities (called primary) which objects in themselves are supposed truly to have and, on the other hand, those other so-called qualities (termed secondary) where there are in the external objects only powers to produce their distinctive kinds of sensory experiences. These experiences we ourselves then unwittingly project onto a world to which they are altogether alien.

The memberships of these two contrasting groups seemed happily to correspond to those marked out by two other most practical dichotomies: that between measurable and non-measurable characteristics; and that between those characteristics of which classical mechanics did and did not take account. Colour, smell, taste, and sound were the stock examples of secondary qualities. Newton explains the distinction in the *Opticks*. (His Latin word 'sensorium' means literally thing of sensing, but no harm will come of taking it here as a synonym of 'mind'.):

" . . . if at any time I speak of light and rays as coloured or endued with colours, I would be understood to speak not philosophically and properly, but grossly, and according to such conceptions as vulgar people in seeing all these experiments would be wont to frame. For the rays, to speak properly, are not coloured. In them there is nothing else than a certain power and disposition to stir up a sensation of this or that colour. For as sound in a bell, or musical string, or other sounding body, is nothing but a trembling motion, and in the air nothing but that motion propagated from the object, and in the sensorium it is a sense of that motion under the form of sound; so colours in the object are nothing but a disposition to reflect this or that sort of rays more copiously than the rest" (pp. 124–5).

This then is Hume's very scientific, very Newtonian, model of valuation. Certainly it is in our broad sense Subjectivist as opposed to Objectivist. Certainly too it is centred upon man rather than either God or nature. The crux is not in the natural order itself but in a human response; while, to the scandal of his contemporaries in the middle 1700's, when God appears at all in Hume's moral writing it is only in connection with perverse and unhealthy aberrations. In terms of the Classical Greek distinction between *phusis* (nature; as in our word 'physics') and *nomos* (law, custom, convention; as in our words 'autonomy', 'heteronomy', 'nomothetic', and 'nomological') Hume puts moral and every other sort of valuation into the second category.

Yet, equally certainly, it is not by that token arbitrary, trivial, or 'a mere matter of personal taste'. If I am looking at an orange I cannot choose what colour I see it as having. Also, if this is the right sort of analogy, the presumption will be in favour of a predominant uniformity. For though some people cannot see at all, and others are afflicted with various disorders of colour vision, the vast majority see the same things as having the same colours. In fact Hume, who was from his Classical studies well aware of the diversity of moral opinion, argued nevertheless for some fundamental community of commitment; while, in general, he contended that a basic uniformity of human nature is both a presupposition and a finding of both the human sciences and ordinary experience. How, after all, could or can any historian proceed if not on the assumption that the people of the past were, beneath all the differences brought about by the different circumstances of their lives, people?

I will end the present Section 3 by quoting two passages, the first from the *Treatise* and the second from the second *Inquiry*, in which Hume applies this model first to moral and then to aesthetic valuation:

'Take any action allowed to be vicious: wilful murder, for instance. Examine it in all lights, and see if you can find that matter of fact, or real existence, which you call vice. In whichever way you take it, you find only certain passions, motives, volitions and thoughts. There is no other matter of fact in the case. The vice entirely escapes you, as long as you consider the object. You can never find it, till you turn your reflexion into your own breast, and find a sentiment of disapprobation, which arises in you, towards this action. . . . Vice and virtue, therefore, may be compared

43

to sounds, colours, heat and cold, which, according to modern philosophy, are not qualities in objects, but perceptions in the mind" (III(i)1).

"Euclid has explained fully the qualities of the circle; but has not in any proposition said a word of its beauty. The reason is evident. The beauty is not a quality of the circle. It lies not in any part of the line, whose parts are equally distant from a common centre. It is only the effect which that figure produces on the mind, whose peculiar fabric or structure renders it susceptible of such sentiments. . . . Attend to Palladio and Perrault, while they explain all the parts and proportions of a pillar. They talk of the cornice, and frieze, and base, and entablature, and shaft, and architrave. . . . But should you ask the description and position of its beauty, they would readily reply that the beauty . . . results from the whole, when that complicated figure is presented to an intelligent mind, susceptible to those finer sensations" (App. I).

4. *Subjective or relative, conventional and expressive.*   The previous Section 3 ended by quoting two passages in which Hume maintains that moral value and disvalue are not intrinsic characteristics of conduct, but projections of human reactions to it; and that beauty is not a property of the objects which we call beautiful, but a matter of the response to them of a "mind susceptible to those finer sensations". Suppose that we allow, as today perhaps most philosophers would allow, that this Subjectivist thesis is at bottom correct. Then the next questions are: 'What is the content of (the various sorts of) moral utterance?'; and 'What room is now left for what sorts of reasonings?'

(i)   The last of the three sentences omitted from the first of the two Hume quotations reads: "So that when you pronounce any action or character to be vicious, you mean nothing, but that from the constitution of your nature you have a feeling or sentiment of blame from the contemplation of it." Suppose that we interpret this — as the French would say, if only they spoke English — at the foot of the letter. Then Hume is saying that the word 'vicious' means no more and no less than 'disapproved by the speaker or writer'. Precisely that is the view which comes to many minds when they hear tell of subjectivism. They therefore tend to tar everything called subjectivism, including what is only subjectivist in the much wider sense explained in the two previous sections, with one very particular brush. This is important since subjectivism, in the sense defined by that sentence of Hume as construed here, can be quite simply and decisively refuted. (Throughout this book the word 'refute' is, of course, employed in the rich traditional sense now being lost to English through sloppy or dishonest abusage. It is not equivalent, simply, to 'deny'; but to 'deny, and show to be false by reasons given.') To go through the necessary moves here, and to appreciate what they decide and why, is an elementary but at the same time illuminating exercise.

To say that conduct is vicious is, on the definition proposed, to report a (certain kind of) reaction in onself. The first objection to this is that any such report reports what allegedly *is* the case, whereas the term 'vice' as usually understood implies that something *ought not* to be done or to have been done. The definition proposed, therefore, can be squared with established usage only at the altogether unacceptable price of confounding a basic distinction; and that one which Hume himself is going to say in the very next paragraph is "of the last importance".

The second objection to this definition, a definition which makes what looks like a statement about his vice a report of my reactions to such conduct, is also and by itself decisive. For say what you like about either what is going on in the sayer or what and all that the sayer is really entitled to say. Still it is just not true that, in the established interpretation of the words, to assert that conduct is vicious is to assert that the assertor himself is reacting in a certain way. The phrase 'He is vicious', when uttered ingenuously by me, no more means that I am reacting in such and such a way than the sentence 'It is just', employed mendaciously by some mighty hypocrite, means that it is in his own interests. If what he says meant this thing, which is surely true, then he would not be the hypocritical liar he so scandalously is.

Third, since to assert a proposition p is equivalent to denying the denial of p, it is often a good tactic, in order to bring out what p means, to ask what would contradict p. So consider two persons disputing whether the conduct of a third is vicious. On the definition proposed neither of the two is speaking of the third. Each speaks only of himself. The dispute is thus at ludicrous cross-purposes. It is as if one man announced, 'I went to London yesterday,' and the other responded, 'It is not true, I did no such thing!'

(ii)   The demonstrably false analysis examined in the previous subsection is in fact quite commonly combined with the assertion that value and, in particular, moral judgements are essentially relative; which assertion is in turn mistaken to entail the conclusion that they are, and can only be, 'arbitrary matters of purely personal taste'.

The main source of such ideas is an awareness of the actual diversity of opinion, even among intelligent and disinterested persons, as to what is and is not proper conduct. The Greek historian Herodotus, whose work was well-known to Plato and Plato's contemporaries, records a confrontation organised by King Darius of Persia, who:

". . . summoned those Greeks who were with him and asked them what sum of money would induce them to make a meal of their dead fathers. And they said that nothing would induce them to do this. Darius then summoned the so-called Callatian Indians, who do eat their parents, and, in the presence of the Greeks (who understood what was said through an interpreter) asked them how much money they would take to burn their dead fathers in a fire. And they raised a great uproar, telling him not to speak of such a thing" (III 37–8).

Herodotus thus provided for his generation material of a kind which ours finds in such deservedly popular books as Ruth Benedict's *Patterns of Culture* or Margaret Mead's *Growing up in New Guinea, Coming of Age in Samoa*, and *Sex and Temperament in three Primitive Societies*. Two morals are often drawn from such – as it is sometimes called – Herodotage; of which neither follows. First, it is taken that from the mere fact of a diversity of opinion in some area we may immediately infer that there is in that area no correct or incorrect opinion. The invalidity of any such inference becomes obvious the moment its general character is clearly described. Furthermore and in particular we need to notice that much, though surely not all, of the actual diversity of the conduct recommended is to be understood by reference to differences between the situations to which the agents are seen or see themselves as responding: some of these differences will correspond to actual differences between these situations; while others will be a matter of disagreements in beliefs about what is the case and how things work. This suggestion is taken up by Hume in an essay called simply 'A Dialogue', reprinted as an appendix in some editions of his second *Inquiry*. It has been in our own century pursued more thoroughly, and with the benefit of much greater anthropological knowledge, by among others Edward Westermarck and Morris Ginsberg.

The second moral drawn is that such diversity shows that morality must be essentially relative; and, furthermore, that this relativity means that it is all merely subjective and a matter of arbitrary personal taste. Certainly there is some truth in this: everyone must allow that what people ought to do will to a greater or lesser extent depend on what their situations are. What is entirely wrong is the identification of the relative with the subjective, and that in turn with the neither correct nor incorrect. It can, therefore, be salutary to notice that this identification has been urged as manifest truth by some great philosophers. That most brilliant of Irishmen George Berkeley (1685–1753) declared, in *The Principles of Human Knowledge*, that "*great* and *small*, *swift* and *slow*, are allowed to exist nowhere without the mind, being entirely relative, and changing as the frame or position of the organs of sense varies" (I § 11).

Of course these four terms are relative or, better, comparative; in as much as it would make no sense to say that something was greater than, or slower than, save in more or less explicit comparison with something else supposed to be smaller or faster. But that does not mean that comparative statements cannot be true or false, nor that the relations involved are entirely subjective. Motion is, thanks to Einstein, the modern paradigm of the essentially relative. It is a notorious nonsense to suggest that anything might be in motion absolutely; and without any reference at all, either explicit or implicit, to that relative to which it moves. It is no doubt for us to decide what to compare with what, and what frames of reference to use in measuring motions. But, these decisions once made, it is the straightest of straight matters of objective fact whether this is bigger than that, or whether one thing is in motion relative to another. There is, for instance, nothing subjective about the issues: first, whether the Metroliner is now moving from New York to Philadelphia; and then whether some of its passengers are at the same time at rest relative to their seats.

Apply these conclusions to conduct. Is there anything subjective about that most relativistic of maxims, 'When in Rome do as the Romans do'? It cannot be obeyed at all if the Romans, or whoever else, happen to be more or less evenly divided in their practice or their principles. But, wherever it can yield unambiguous directions, the sense of those directions must be as independent of the visitor's will as are the movements of the stars; while questions about what that sense must be will be no more and no less susceptible of categorically correct or incorrect answers than the corresponding prior and determining questions as to what practices or principles are in fact, in this particular region, established.

(iii) The comment of Herodotus on the passage quoted in the previous subsection reads: "So firmly rooted are these matters of habitual usage; and I consider that the poet Pindar was quite right to say that custom is the universal king." The historian was not at all inclined to commit the It-is-merely Fallacy; by inferring the conclusion that the issue in dispute between "those Greeks who were with him" and the "so-called Callatian Indians" must be trivial, from the premise that it is a matter of *nomos* rather than *phusis*. Any such conclusion would be, not only invalidly derived, but

47

also utterly wrong. For what is, in the broadest senses of those terms, conventional as opposed to natural can be quite literally a matter of life and death. Again, although this is not the same point at all, there can be decisive good reasons both for having some convention rather than none, and for having one particular convention as opposed to others.

No one could bring themselves to deny that to have some universally accepted rule of the road is a matter of life and death; although any such rule falls into the category of *nomos* rather than *phusis*. It is a prescriptive law commanding this or forbidding that rather than a descriptive law saying that certain things are as a matter of fact either necessary or impossible. Suppose that you were the first people to adopt a rule of the road. Then there would appear to be no very strong reason to choose a right hand rather than a left hand rule, or the other way about. It is, however, very different with other cases. Those sets of norms and practices which both shape and constitute social structures have vast and wide-ranging consequences, often unintended and perhaps unrecognised as such. Any of these consequences can provide a reason for adopting or maintaining one convention or system of conventions, and rejecting alternatives.

Take, as an explosively disputatious example, that set of norms and practices which shape and constitute the most powerful of all British social institutions – the trades unions. These laws and practices, belonging one and all to the comprehensive category of *nomos* as opposed to *phusis*, include: both the legal privileges – such as immunity from prosecution for tort; and the more informal norms – such as the ban on crossing picket lines ('scabbing') or the tabu against speaking ill of these institutions ('union-bashing'). There is, in Britain, no universal agreement on whether, as their spokesmen assert, they alone have saved their members from far lower wages and less tolerable working conditions, or whether, as is contended by those few who have dared publicly to question the actual effects of union power, they are the most important single cause of Britain's relative, and soon perhaps absolute, national impoverishment. There is, nevertheless, complete agreement: both about the enormous importance of these particular issues of *nomos* as opposed to *phusis*; and that there are overwhelmingly strong reasons either for or against these institutions, and hence either for or against having the corresponding norms and practices!

(iv)   The first subsection of the present Section 4 deployed two decisive reasons for rejecting the thesis that an utterance such as 'His conduct is vicious' is a report that the speaker is reacting in a certain way. The first reason was that an utterance which was nothing but a report, whether about the speaker or about anyone or anything else, would by that token be purely descriptive; and could not, therefore, entail the prescriptive conclusion that that conduct ought to have been other than it was. It is this insight which opens the way for an insistence that any adequate analysis of the meaning of such utterances must make room for at least some element of the non-descriptive, the not fact-stating. Once again Hume was in part seized of this truth. Thus in the first Appendix to his second *Inquiry* he wrote: "But after every circumstance, every relation is known, the understanding has no further room to operate, nor any object on which it could employ itself. The approbation or blame which then ensues cannot be the work of the judgement but of the heart; and it is not a speculative proposition or affirmation, but an active feeling or sentiment."

It is this suggestion which was developed by Sir Alfred Ayer in his alltime philosophical best-seller *Language, Truth and Logic*. His thesis was that the essentially ethical element in the meaning of such an utterance, an element which might in some cases be the whole, was not a report that the speaker was reacting in a certain way; but an expression of that reaction. It constituted an ejaculation rather than a statement. This position earned the apt nickname 'The Boo-Hooray Theory of Morals'.

An alternative suggestion is surely more plausible and certainly less scandalous. It is that any non-descriptive element is not so much expressive and ejaculatory as imperative. This has been developed in the books *Freedom and Reason* and *The Language of Morals* as well as in many articles, by the White's Professor of Moral Philosophy in the University of Oxford, R. M. Hare. He took his cue immediately from Kant, for whom the supreme principle of morality is a categorical imperative; although another more distant ancestor must have been Aristotle, who sponsored an enigmatic doctrine of the practical syllogism yielding an imperative conclusion. (The term 'syllogism' itself was introduced by Aristotle, to refer to any argument in which a conclusion is deduced as following necessarily from two premises. The stock example, hallowed by immemorial tradition, runs: 'All men are mortal' and 'Socrates is a man'; therefore 'Socrates is mortal'.) If, as we heard Whitehead saying, all philosophy is indeed a series of footnotes to Plato, that we might now add that all modern moral philosophy is more immediately a series of footnotes to Hume and Kant; or rather, to Hume and to the Kant of the critical period after Hume had — in Kant's generous and delightful words — "woken me from my dogmatic slumbers."

5. *Making room for moral argument*. The contrast with a categorical is a hypothetical imperative. Kant develops this contrast first in a short work uncompromisingly entitled *The Foundations of the Metaphysics of Morals*: "All imperatives command either hypothetically or categorically. Hypothetical imperatives declare a possible action to be practically necessary as a means to the attainment of something else that one wills (or that one may will). A categorical imperative would be one which represented an action as objectively necessary in itself apart from its relation to a further end" (II, p. 82). An example of the former is 'If you want to arrive in Whitehorse by train you must ride the White Pass and Yukon Railroad from Skagway.' To illustrate the latter take one of the ten commandments without promise; such as "Thou shalt do no murder", or "Thou shalt not commit adultery." Whereas imperatives of the first kind are directed only at those who happen to harbour the desire indicated in the protasis – the *if* bit – the second sort are unconditional and universal: regardless of what anyone may or may not want, these are categorically to be obeyed.

Kant connects the imperative with the idea of law, the unconditional and the universal with that of reason. His aim, as stated in the Preface, "is to seek out and establish the supreme principle of morality" (p. 60); and, as this is there explained, it seems that what is to be found should be a formal essence rather than a substantial supreme good.

Kant's master question, therefore, is of an altogether different kind from that of John Stuart Mill (1806–1873). In his *Utilitarianism* Mill saw "the main problem" of moral philosophy "as the question concerning the summum bonum [supreme good], or, what is the same thing, concerning the foundation of morality" (p. 1). This, following Jeremy Bentham (1748–1832) and James Mill his father, he took to be "the Greatest Happiness Principle"; that the ultimate objective of all moral conduct must be the greatest happiness of the greatest number; "that actions are right in proportion as they tend to promote happiness, wrong as they tend to produce the reverse of happiness" (p. 6).

The official aim of Kant's inquiries is fundamentally different. He talks in his Preface of "the utmost necessity to work out for once a pure moral philosophy completely cleansed of everything that can only be empirical" (p. 57). Kant's "supreme principle of morality", quite unlike Mill's "foundation of morality", should therefore be thought of as an account of what makes a moral imperative moral, of what the word 'moral' means. This remains the master question notwithstanding that we are later disappointed to discover that Kant, in treating his illustrations in Chapter II, so far forgets himself as

THE ELEMENTS OF ETHICS

to attempt to derive from purely formal premises very substantial concrete conclusions on what ought and ought not to be done. In particular these include the conclusion, so repugnant to libertarians, that suicide is at every stage of life and in all circumstances wrong.

(i) In that second Chapter Kant introduces, what he never really examines, the notion of a maxim. The maxim of my proposal or actual conduct on a particular occasion is the general principle under which I subsume that conduct. Suppose that someone "feels sick of life as the result of a series of misfortunes that has mounted to the point of despair", and contemplates suicide. Their maxim, Kant tells us, must be: " 'From self-love I make it my principle to shorten my life if its continuance threatens more evil than it promises pleasure' " (p. 89). Again: "Another finds himself driven to borrowing money because of need." Suppose that he proposes to promise to repay, well knowing "that he will not be able". Then "the maxim of his action would run thus: 'Whenever I believe myself short of money, I will borrow money and promise to pay it back, though I know that this will never be done' " (pp. 89 and 90). The investigation proceeds:

> "In this task we wish to inquire whether the mere concept of a categorical imperative may not also provide us with the formula containing the only proposition that can be a categorical imperative. . . .[If] I conceive a categorical imperative, I know at once what it contains. For since besides the law this imperative contains only the necessity that our maxim should conform to this law . . . there remains nothing over to which the maxim has to conform except the universality of a law as such. . . . There is therefore only a single categorical imperative, and it is this: 'Act only on the maxim through which you can at the same time will that it should become a universal law' " (pp. 88: italics removed).

Whatever the difficulties in detail we do surely have to concede that Kant here has put his finger on something essential to morality. The challenge 'Suppose everybody did it' always is relevant. It is too a most important element in the meaning of maintaining that some protest, or stand, or attitude is moral that the protest, or stand or attitude, appeals to general principles; which have to be applied consistently, impartially, and universally. When this necessary, though not of course sufficient condition is not met; then what we have is personal and partisan, not moral. That is why we impugn the moral sincerity of the selective 'moralist'. The expressions of animosity or enthusiasm may well be heartfelt. It is the blinkered selectivity which rules out their claim to be moral. Someone professes a moral objection to — say — the use of poison gas. But when gas is employed by a party which they happen to favour — CS by white, capitalist, Americans against Communists in Vietnam or Lewisite by brownish, socialist Egyptians in the Yemen — then, as the Greek tragedians were wont to say — a great ox sits on their tongues.

(ii)   Before going on, time spent rereading and reconsidering the final paragraph of Section 1 of the present chapter would not be wasted. It is one of the passages in which Hume approached his nearest to this first Kantian insight, a realisation of the essential universality of morals. A second suggestion is provided by what Kant counts as his third formula, The Formula of Autonomy. This he thinks to derive from his second, The Formula of the End in Itself; the first being The Formula of Universal Law, quoted already. Of the second formula it suffices for the moment to say that it requires everyone to respect themselves and everyone else as equally persons: "'Act in such a way that you always treat humanity, whether in your own person or in the person of any other, never simply as a means, but always at the same time as an end'". Kant proceeds:

". . . the ground for every enactment of practical law lies . . . in the form of universality which (according to our first principle) makes the rule capable of being a law . . . but (according to our second principle) the subject of all ends is to be found in every rational being as an end in himself. From this there now follows our third practical principle for the will . . . the idea of the will of every rational being as a will which makes universal law" (pp. 96 and 98: I have, as usual, subdued Kant's exuberant typography).

Whatever difficulties may be felt about the derivation — difficulties which would only be exacerbated by more extensive quotation — we must not fail to recognise that Kant is once again onto something of the first importance. He boasts of being the first philosopher to appreciate that a moral agent "is subject only to laws which are made by himself and yet are universal" (p. 100).

This is a tricky business. Perhaps it is best to adopt a strategy of indirect approach. Two questions were raised back at the end of the first paragraph of Section 4: 'What is the content of . . . moral utterance?'; and 'What room is now left for what sorts of reasoning?' Hume concluded that there could be no distinctive form of moral reasoning. There is room only for the agent to discover what the situation is, and what will be the consequences of various alternative courses of action: "But after every circumstance, every relation is known, the understanding has no further room to operate, nor any object on which it could employ itself".

(a) In a famous, or notorious, passage of the *Treatise* Hume earlier had pronounced:

"Since reason alone can never produce any action, or give rise to volition, I infer, that the same faculty is as incapable of preventing volition, or of disputing the preference with any passion or emotion. This consequence is necessary. . . . Nothing can oppose or retard the impulse of passion, but a contrary impulse. . . . Thus it appears, that the principle which opposes our passion, cannot be the same with reason, and is only called so in an improper sense. We speak not strictly and philosophically when we talk of the combat of passion and of reason. Reason is, and ought only to be the slave of the passions, and can never pretend to any other office than to serve and obey them" (II(iii)3).

There is no doubt but that the young Hume relished making so shocking a pronouncement; nor that, had it come to his attention, Kant would have been one of those most shocked. There is a question whether it did, and he was, because the *Treatise* was not translated into German until after Kant's death. Yet much of what Kant writes about reason and conduct reads like a reaction to Hume. Thus Kant is determined to maintain that the will to do moral duty is not just one more ordinary and particular volition. It has to spring from universal and necessary reason, not wayward and contingent individual psychology. In the Preface, for instance, he faults his predecessors: "they do not distinguish motives which, as such, are conceived completely apriori by reason alone and are genuinely moral from empirical motives. . . . On the contrary, without taking into account differences in their origin they consider motives only as regards their relative strength or weakness (looking upon all of them as homogeneous) . . ." (p. 59). In spite of all this, at the end of the final Chapter III, Kant is forced to a despairing confession. After all, how could pure reason generate a motive for action? His last word is: "But how pure reason can be practical in itself without further motives drawn from another source . . . or, in other words, how pure reason can be practical – all human reason is totally incapable of explaining this, and all the effort and labour to seek such an explanation is wasted" (p. 129: italics removed).

Kant here is indeed banging his head against an adamantine wall. For Hume's conclusion is, properly understood, a tautology dramatised. By dismissing any other uses of the word 'reason' and its derivatives as improper, he is in effect urging that words such as 'reason' and 'passion' ought only to be so employed that every conceivable motive to action must count as a passion. Correspondingly reason by itself – which is a matter of discovering what is the case, what logically follows from what, and what is the causal consequence of what – cannot without absurdity be said to generate motives. If we allow Hume his sense of 'reason', then it is not possible: either to deny him his exultant and dramatic inference that reason is the slave of the passions; or to concede to Kant that this pure reason can be, by generating its own peculiar motive, practical.

(b)   What it is still possible to do is to notice: both that there are other established uses, which Hume wants to outlaw; and that there is a distinctive kind of moral reasoning, for which he should – and could – find a place in his scheme. Just such another use is recognised and rejected in the next paragraph but one, in another notorious passage:

"Where a passion is neither founded or false suppositions, nor chuses means insufficient for the end, the understanding can neither justify nor condemn it. 'Tis not contrary to reason to prefer the destruction of the whole world to the scratching of my finger. 'Tis not contrary to reason for me to chuse my total ruin, to prevent the last uneasiness of an *Indian* or person wholly unknown to me. . . . In short, a passion must be accompany'd with some false judgement, in order to its being unreasonable; and even then it is not the passion, properly speaking, which is unreasonable, but the judgement" (II (iii) 3: italics original).

Kant might with both relevance and truth have replied that except in their most selfconsciously Humian moments everyone would in fact, notwithstanding the lack of any accompanying false judgement, describe these choices as unreasonable. Recall now Kant's second formula, The Formula of the End in Itself. Certainly its actual wording leaves Kant wide open to the forceful and forthright objection urged by his younger compatriot Arthur Schopenhauer (1788–1860). In his essay *On the Basis of Morality* this usually sympathetic and respectful critic puts down the key concept as simply and flagrantly incoherent: "But I must say frankly that 'to exist as an end in oneself' is an unthinkable expression. . . . To be an end or aim means to be willed. Every aim or end in view exists only in reference to a will, and is the end of the will. . . . Only in this relation has the concept . . . any meaning . . ." (p. 95).

Yes indeed, it cannot be denied. Nevertheless, as in each of the other two formulae, Kant is onto something crucial. The full nature of this something must be for future moral philosophers to labour to explicate. It has already been suggested, however, that the second formula "requires everyone to respect themselves and everyone else as equally persons." So, although it certainly makes no sense to speak of anything as being an end in itself all on its own, it is completely to the point to ask people to recognise that all persons have their own ends – ends which are ends relative to their own wishes and plans. All persons are as such themselves agents, capable of forming and fulfilling purposes. We surely must permit some sort of concern about and respect for everyone's wishes to provide another of the defining characteristics of morality. Imperatives with no such reference could scarcely count as moral. And, turning to the outrageous possible choices which Hume lists, a possible justification for the rejected description of these as 'unreasonable' would be that the choosers fail to give equal attention to all those concerned who are equally persons. They make in favour of one individual or group and against another discriminations which, because they are arbitrary, must be accounted, in a traditional and mainstream sense, unreasonable.

It was just such an idea and ideal of equality as this which led Bentham to qualify his Greatest Happiness Principle by adding the gloss: "Everybody to count for one, nobody for more than one." This qualification was later reformulated by Henry Sidgwick (1828–1900), the most subtle and sophisticated of all ethical utilitarians, in a way which nicely underlines that point about the essentially impartial and universal character of morality made in Subsection (i). An ethical utilitarian, by the way, is someone who holds that actions are morally obligatory to the extent that they (tend to) promote the greatest something or other of the greatest number: what has to be thus maximised may be – as with such classical Utilitarians as Bentham, Mill, and Sidgwick – pleasure or happiness; or it may be something else. Sidgwick's way of making the point about the essential impartiality and universality of morality was to say: "The good of any one individual is of no more importance, from the point of view (if I may say so) of the Universe, than the good of any other" (p. 382). The individuals of the ethical utilitarians, however, are thought of primarily as enjoyers and sufferers, rather than as agents capable of forming and fulfilling plans and purposes.

One way in which this difference matters is in its implications for the status and treatment of subhuman animals – the creatures known to the old religion as the brutes. No one thinks of these as moral agents, subject themselves to moral obligations. But those who stress rational agency rather than passibility are apt to forbid cruelty to the brutes only on account of its possible indirect consequences for people, whereas utilitarians are likely to allow that even the brutes have rights which must be taken into account. (The word 'passibility', often met in this kind of context, means liability to enjoy and to suffer.)

St Thomas Aquinas (c. 1225–1274) and Kant, who both put enormous emphasis on rationality, both argue in the first way. Thus, Kant, in one of his *Lectures on Ethics*, maintains that we "must practise kindness towards animals, for he who is cruel to animals becomes hard also in his dealings with man. . . . Our duties towards animals . . . are indirect duties towards mankind" (pp. 239 and 240). But Bentham insists in his *Principles of Morals and Legislation*: "the question is not, 'Can they *reason?*' nor, 'Can they *talk?* but, Can they *suffer?*'" (p. 412n: italics his. On the whole subject of *Animal Rights and Human Obligations*, compare Regan and Singer).

(c)   You may well have forgotten by now that the present Subsection (iii) took off from Kant's third formula, The Formula of Autonomy. This asserts that a moral agent "is subject only to laws which are made by himself and yet are universal." Because the explanation of what this means is going eventually to display the distinctive form of moral argument, the task was postponed to make room: first, in (ii)(a), for a preliminary confrontation of Kant with Hume about the impossibility of pure reason being practical; and, second, in (ii)(b), for uncovering another apparent essential of morality – the non-arbitrary and perhaps, in that sense, rational principle of considering all persons as equally persons. Having dealt with the first formula in Subsection (i), and the second in (ii)(b), it is now time in (ii)(c) to treat the third. (Kant himself had a fourth, but if you want to learn about that you will have to read something else – preferably *The Foundations of the Metaphysics of Morals*; which is at least, though hard, short!)

Suppose that someone says that a Callatian Indian ought to eat the dead body of a parent. It is an utterance which can be construed in two fundamentally different ways. If it comes from an anthropologist then the chances are that he is speaking with professional scientific detachment. In that case it is equivalent to the completely non-partisan assertion that the Callation Indians believe, whether rightly or wrongly, that offspring ought to eat the dead bodies of their parents. In Humian terms this is not an *ought* but an *is* assertion, notwithstanding that it contains the actual word 'ought'. For that word is here neutralised by its inclusion in non-committal reported speech: the speaker is not expressing his own views of what ought to be done; only reporting the relevant beliefs cherished by others. If, alternatively, the original claims was made by a Callatian Indian, or perhaps by an anthropologist committed to some demanding doctrine of participant observation, then the speaker has to be construed as by these words taking a side. He is now in his own person expressing a principle of conduct to which he is thereby himself committed. This is unequivocally an *ought* not an *is* assertion. As such it neither entails nor presupposes that this is in truth what Callatian Indians believe or how they act: "It is," as Popper said, "impossible to derive a sentence stating a norm or a decision from a sentence stating a fact."

As it stands this example is, maybe misleadingly, rather particular. If the principle of conduct involved here is to rate as moral it must be universal, applying to every person finding themselves in some situation of a particular kind, not to Callatian Indians only. So let us assume that our speaker was making a particular application of something much more general: all off-spring ought to eat the dead bodies of their parents, perhaps; or – still wider – everyone ought to observe the customs of their own people.

But now, once someone adopts a norm as one of his own moral principles he makes himself subject to one of these Kantian "laws which are made by himself and yet are universal." He thus imposes upon himself the obligation, both to apply this principle – this law – on all appropriate occasions, and to reconcile it with his other moral and other commitments. If he did not want to get involved in this way, if he was not prepared to extend his commitments over so broad a front, then he should not have ventured any moral utterance. The right course for him – his own made-to-measure hypothetical imperative – was to make only remarks of kinds to which moral assertions are so commonly but so wrongly assimilated. These are the autobiographical – 'I love to see Callatian Indians eating the dead bodies of their parents'; or the ejaculatory – 'Callatian Indians eating the dead bodies of their parents; hooray!'

If moral utterance was in truth reducible to something like this and nothing more, then there would indeed be no room for any distinctively moral argument. The situation would be as in *Language, Truth and Logic* Ayer informed us that it is: " . . . one really never does dispute about questions of value. . . . It is because argument fails us when we come to deal with pure questions of value, as distinct from questions of fact, that we finally resort to mere abuse" (pp. 110 and 111). "When every circumstance, every relation is known", when it is agreed what actions will in fact have what consequences, then the reasoning has to stop: there is nothing for it but confrontation, non-rational rhetoric, and – ultimately – force.

"I know," wrote Einstein *Out of My Later Years*, "that it is a hopeless

AN INTRODUCTION TO PHILOSOPHY

undertaking to debate about fundamental value judgements. . . . [Although] if there is agreement on certain goals and values, one can argue rationally about the means by which these objectives may be obtained" (p. 12). Yet there may be, and usually is, another possibility. Suppose that one of the parties has made some moral claims, as most of us find it impossible not to do. Then the party will by so doing have accepted the authority of certain "laws which are made by himself and yet are universal." These laws, whatever they may be, will carry consequences. But "that party" is, like the rest of us, fallibly human: often it will actually be us! So he will surely not have recognised all these consequences. Nor will he have appreciated that his commitment to the particular principle of conduct which carries these consequences can with difficulty, if at all, be reconciled with others of his own moral and other commitments. The distinctive form of moral argument consists in educing such consequences, and pointing out such incompatibilities.

This form of argument is essentially *ad hominem*; although the man to which it is directed should of course, both embrace women, and include ourselves as well as other people. The expression '*argumentum ad hominem*' is Latin for argument directed to, or at, a man. Such an argument takes as a premise something which is accepted by the other party but not, or not necessarily, by the arguer himself. It then deduces some consequence unacceptable to that other party. This form of argument is sometimes rejected as fallacious or otherwise improper. But this is quite wrong. For there is no fallacy, no mistake in argument, in drawing from a premise a conclusion which does indeed follow. Nor is there anything improper about showing someone that they cannot consistently both hold that and reject this. What is wrong, and what is also sometimes wrongly called the *ad hominem* fallacy, is to pretend to refute an argument by irrelevantly abusing the arguer.

These misconceptions are popular. For instance: there are nowadays many above average prosperous and powerful people who miss no opportunity of telling the world that we ought all to be very much more equal in wealth, income, and welfare than we in fact are. Some indeed have achieved their own unusually high levels of both prosperity and power as a direct consequence of actively promoting and enforcing the very egalitarian measures which are, they maintain, morally imperative. To ask such a person how, if at all, their own excessive abundance is to be reconciled with, as they themselves say they see it, the moral imperative of equality, is to argue *ad hominem*. In such an argument one party points some consequence of a premise or premises assumed or asserted by the other. The force of the argument is in no way diminished by the fact, if this does happen to be the fact, that the person who draws out the logical consequences of that premise, or those premises, does not accept it, or them. There is neither unfairness, nor hypocrisy, nor any other impropriety in my pointing to the uncomfortable consequences of principles which you profess; while I myself all the time repudiate those principles — insisting perhaps that equality is not to be identified with justice, nor justice itself mistaken for the whole of virtue.

The truth is that arguments *ad hominem* are as such neither fallacious nor improper. They owe their bad name to the fact that even, or perhaps especially, when they are valid their conclusions are likely to embarrass those to, or at, whom they are directed. Yet precisely to the extent that we are striving to be honest, sincere, and rational — if we are — such arguments should be welcome. They show us that there is an inconsistency in our present body of beliefs, commitments, and practices. Therefore, if we are to approach a little nearer to realising our ideals, there has to be some change somewhere.

This is a personally challenging point, which may therefore be characterised as being, in a modest sense, existential. Both this general point, and the more particular conclusion that this is the distinctive form of moral argument, are unforgettably illustrated by the story of Nathan's rebuke to King David for his treatment of Uriah the Hittite:

"And it came to pass in an evening tide, that David arose from off his bed, and walked upon the roof of the king's house: and from the roof he saw a woman washing herself; and the woman was very beautiful to look upon. And David sent and enquired after the woman. And one said, 'Is not this Bathsheba, the daughter of Eliam, the wife of Uriah the Hittite?' And David sent messengers, and took her, and she came in unto him, and he lay with her. . . . And it came to pass in the morning, that David wrote a letter to Joab, and sent it by the hand of Uriah. And he wrote in the letter, saying, 'Set ye Uriah in the forefront of the hottest battle, and retire ye from him, that he may be smitten, and die. . . .

And the Lord sent Nathan unto David. And he came unto him, and said unto him, 'There were two men in one city; the one rich, and the other poor. The rich man had exceeding many flocks and herds. But the poor man had nothing, save one little ewe lamb which he had bought and nourished up: and it grew together with him, and with his children. . . . And there came a traveller unto the rich man, and he spared to take of his own flock and of his own herd, to dress for the wayfaring man that was come unto him; but took the poor man's lamb. . . . And David's anger was greatly kindled against the man, and he said to Nathan, 'As the Lord liveth, the man that hath done this thing shall surely die: and he shall restore the lamb fourfold, because he did this thing, and because he had no pity.' And Nathan said to David, 'Thou art the man!'" (II *Samuel*, 11–2).

CHAPTER III

Scepticism and the external world

One element in his popular image presents the philosopher as seeking for the meaning of certain wholly familiar words. This element we owe in the first instance, as Chapter I showed, to Socrates. Another element in that same popular image makes the philosopher out to be a person professionally committed to doubting what everyone else thinks they know perfectly well. This second element is primarily a legacy from Descartes. The main original vehicle of the Cartesian inheritance is his brief yet devastating *Discourse on the Method*. ('Cartesian' is the adjective from 'Descartes' – des Cartes; just as 'Thomist' is the adjective from 'St Thomas Aquinas'.)

Almost every syllabus, you will find, dates the effective beginning of Modern Philosophy from 1637, the year of its – and his – first publication. This date gives a precise periodic dividing line much less arbitrary than most. After Descartes, and very largely thanks to him, the main centres of interest had become entirely different. The chief of these was epistemological inquiry; inquiry, that is to say, into whether we can know, what we can know, and how we can know. Here for all of three centuries most even of the greatest of his successors continued to think within a framework constructed by Descartes, striving to find their answers to questions he had set.

The *Discourse* is both accessible and exciting. It is addressed to the general not a specialist public. The author tries to eschew, even if he does not wholly succeed, all the medieval technicalities which he had been taught in the crack Jesuit college of La Flèche. He also chose to publish first in French not Latin, which was only just beginning to lose its status as the international language of learning. (In 1628 William Harvey's epoch-making *de Motu Cordis* had appeared only in Latin.) Then again the *Discourse* is remarkable for its autobiography and its individualism. A single paragraph may tell you more about the life and hopes of Descartes than you could learn about Aquinas from the entire *Summa Theologica*. And always, as in this instance

61

from Part II, there is with its not quite ingenuous disclaimer the stress on individual reason: "My design has never extended further than an attempt to reform my own opinions, and to build upon a foundation which is entirely my own."

Much of this is just putting on the style. But if we are really to understand Descartes, as well as to appreciate the enormous impact of the *Discourse*, we have to recognise and never to forget that the method which he sought, and believed that he had found, was the method for extending our knowledge in mathematics and the natural sciences. When the *Discourse* was first published it was bound up with three other essays which were supposed both to illustrate and to vindicate this new method. Of these the second – *Dioptric* – was a treatise on optics, exploiting the recent invention of the telescope. The third – misleadingly entitled *Meteorology* – developed Descartes' radically and comprehensively mechanical view of material reality. But it was the first – called simply *Geometry* – which put everything else in the shade. For here Descartes presented his new creation, analytical geometry: it is in his honour that we speak still of Cartesian co-ordinates. "The possibilities", as one historian of science has written, "were too immense for his generation. . . ." Nevertheless, before the century was out, "One element in the Newtonian synthesis would be to unite an abstract and continuous conception of space with a concrete and atomistic conception of matter. Even without that hidden implication, however, the invention of analytical geometry was the most momentous contribution to mathematics since Euclid" (Gillispie, pp. 87–8).

1. *Systematic doubts and an unshakable certainty*. The *Discourse* starts quiet and slow. In Part I Descartes reviews the various subjects of his education, both in and out of, school. Like so many others of the great philosophers he was fascinated by mathematics, seeing in it the ideal model for all true knowledge: "I was attracted above all by mathematics, because of the certitude and the evidence of the arguments there. . . . I was astonished by the fact that when foundations are so firm and solid no one should have built anything taller on top." In feeling this fascination, and in harbouring consequent hopes, Descartes takes his place in a long philosophical succession. It began with Pythagoras and the Pythagorean Plato of *The Republic*. It continued after Descartes, in Leibniz and in Spinoza, and it goes on through to include, in our own century, the Bertrand Russell of that classic introduction *The Problems of Philosophy*.

Such certitude and evidence appears especially attractive against a background of disagreement and confusion. In Part II Descartes provides this background, and draws the moral that he must make his own discovery of a legitimate basis for certainty. The disagreement and confusion to which he attends now is over conduct and ideology: ". . . how very different the self-same man, identical in mind and spirit, may become according as he is brought up from childhood amongst the French or Germans, or has passed his whole life amongst Chinese or cannibals."

One thing which no one could infer from reading only his account, even when the *Discourse* is supplemented by the later *Meditations*, is that arguments for a radical and wholesale scepticism had been familiar to intellectual France since the publication in the 1560's of Latin translations of the works of Sextus Empiricus. Sextus was himself undistinguished as a thinker. He is important only because, by the accidents of loss and survival, he happens to be our main source for the ideas of the original Greek Sceptics, above all Pyrrho of Elis (c. 360 – c. 270 BC). The finest example of the influence of such ideas before Descartes is found in the *Essays* of the captivating and admirable Michel de Montaigne (1533–1592). Another and more significant point which no one could infer from the published works of Descartes is that, since Luther's great challenge at the Diet of Worms in 1521, the most fundamental issue in dispute between Reformers and Roman Catholics had been that of the correct criterion of religious knowledge – the authority of the Bible or the authority of the traditional teaching Church.

Still in Part II Descartes goes on to tell us how he met and overcame his own personal crisis of scepticism. (These parts by the way, are extremely brief: the entire *Discourse* occupies a mere 60 pages in the Everyman edition.) "I was then in Germany", he writes, "brought there by the wars which have not yet finished; and, as I was returning to the army from the coronation of the Emperor, the beginning of winter held me up in a place where – having no conversation to divert me, and having besides, fortunately, no cares or passions to trouble me – I stayed all day shut up in a room with a stove where I had complete leisure to occupy myself with my thoughts. . . ." It was in 1619. "The wars which have not yet finished" were what we now know as the Thirty Years War of 1618 to 1648. But Descartes was so fortunate as to be able to discharge himself unharmed in 1621, shortly after he had participated, on the winning side, in the Battle of Prague ("the White Mountain") – the battle which finally subjected Bohemia to the Counter-Reformation.

In what remains of Part II Descartes lays down four principles of method. These appear almost unbearably trite and pedestrian. The first was "never to accept anything as true which I did not clearly know to be such"; the second "to divide each difficulty which I examined into as many parts as was possible and as was required for its best resolution"; the third to deal with problems in order of difficulty, starting with the simplest and easiest; and the fourth to make exhaustive general reviews to ensure that nothing had been left out. All this sounds just about as fresh and arresting as the advice poured out onto all comers by Polonius in *Hamlet*. The only hint of more exciting things to come is a suggestion of the vast possibilities of suitably disciplined quasi-mathematical deduction. In Part III Descartes expounds the conservative principles by which it is right for him to live while the work of demolition and reconstruction is in progress. By the beginning of Part IV he is ready. Suddenly, in a few overwhelming paragraphs, he outlines what was to become the luminously obvious new frame of reference:

Because "I wished to give myself entirely to the search after truth I thought that I must . . . reject as if it were absolutely false everything about which I could suppose there was the least doubt, in order to see if after that there remained anything which I believed which was entirely indubitable. So, on the grounds that our senses sometimes deceive us, I wanted to suppose that there was not anything corresponding to what they make us imagine. And, because some men make mistakes in reasoning — even with regard to the simplest matters of geometry — and fall into fallacies, I judged that I was as much subject to error as anyone else, and I rejected as unsound all the reasonings which I had hitherto taken for demonstrations. Finally, taking account of the fact that all the same experiences which we have when we are awake can also come to us when we are asleep without there being one of them which is veridical, I resolved to pretend that everything which had ever entered into my mind was no more veridical than the illusions of my dreams."

This is the celebrated systematic doubt. But, sure enough, amidst the almost universal ruin one thing stands out "entirely indubitable". Descartes strides forward:

"But at once I noticed that while I was wishing in this way to think that everything was false it followed necessarily that I who was thinking must be something. And I observed that this truth, 'I think, therefore I am', was so solid and certain that all the most extravagant suppositions of the sceptics were unable to upset it. I judged that I could receive it without hesitation as the first principle of the philosophy which I was seeking."

For some unknown but surely insufficient reason this principle, first stated in French, is often by an extraordinary miscegenation of English and Latin called 'the *cogito*'. (*'Cogito, ergo sum'* is Latin for 'I think, therefore I am'.) Often too it is urged that, notwithstanding the 'therefore', it should not be construed as embodying an inference. Certainly it is primarily an expression of immediate and indubitable awareness of present consciousness, or perhaps self-consciousness. From this starting point Descartes goes on so to define 'thinking' that it includes all and only modes of this consciousness. Since such a move precludes all the usual ratiocinative implications, this official definition cuts against the grain of our established verbal habits. Readers, and Descartes himself, must now find it hard to remember what in the new sense proposed the old word does and does not imply. In the final Part V of the *Discourse*, for instance, Descartes offers as "two most certain tests" for the presence of a thinking substance criteria which refer directly to rationality; but not at all, it would seem, to consciousness. He thus seems himself to have been the first to overlook implications of his own redefinition.

Another perhaps even more misguided essay in redefining against the bias of established verbal habit is seen in the insistence upon a usage in which such words as 'experience' have to be interpreted as specifically excluding their most important ordinary entailment. The experiences mentioned at the end of the first of the two passages just quoted are thus experiences without prejudice to all questions of veridicality. Yet ordinarily – when, for instance, books about *Woman's Experience of the Male* are read or people with experience of computers are sought – it is essential to their really having had the experience in question that they should have been, and should have known that they were, in contact with whatever it was that the experience was experience of. So let the former and more technical sense be distinguished as subjective or private, the latter as objective or public. Some philosophers introduced the label 'sense-data' for some of these private experiences. The idea was to include all but only those which either are or might mistakenly be thought to be perceptual. But this label has much the same disadvantages as the word 'experience'. For our perception words ordinarily carry the implication that what is said to be sensed is something which is actually there, and which the senser is aware of as actually there. If the alcoholic during his lost weekend claims to see pink rats which do not in fact exist, then, while it is true to say that he 'saw' (in snigger quotes), it is false to say that he saw (without qualification), pink rats.

Descartes gives the best account of the prime and inexpugnable Cartesian certainty in Principle IX of Part I of his *Principles of Philosophy*:

"By the word 'thought' I mean everything in us which is the object of our own immediate awareness. That is why not only understanding, wishing and supposing, but also feeling are here the same thing as thinking. For if I say that I can see or that I am walking, and from this I infer that I am, and if by this I intend to speak of the action of my eyes or my legs, then this conclusion is not so infallible that I have no basis for doubt about it. The reason is that it is possible for me to believe that I see or am walking, notwithstanding that I do not open my eyes and do not stir from my place. For that does sometimes occur when I am asleep, and the same thing could perhaps happen if I had no body. But if instead I intend to refer only to the occurrence of my thoughts and feelings – to the knowledge which is inside me, that is, makes it seem to me that I see or that I am walking – then that same conclusion is so absolutely true that I cannot doubt it. . . ."

2.   *Reconstruction after the cataclysm*.   Having established the unshakable certainty of immediate consciousness as "the first principle of the philosophy I was seeking", Descartes in the next paragraph asked himself what the I was which is thus conscious and certain. He answered: "I, that is to say my mind – what makes me what I am – am entirely distinct from the body; and, furthermore, the former is more easily known than the latter, while if the latter did not exist the former could be all that it is." It was in these terms that Descartes set what his successors were to accept as the problem of *Our Knowledge of the External World*. (In 1914 that last phrase served as the title of one of Bertrand Russell's books.)

The problem was how a person so conceived could know, indeed whether such a person could know, either anything about a world outside himself, or even that there is such a world. The most heroic answer to that problem is, of course, solipsism: the doctrine that I am the only one there is. Like so many philosophical doctrines this might be defended in either an epistemological or a metaphysical version. The epistemological solipsist would argue only that it must be impossible for him to know about anyone or anything else; whereas the metaphysical solipsist would maintain that there just is not anyone or anything else to know about. (Russell used to tell a characteristic story about the professed solipsist writing to say how surprised he was that there seemed to be so few of them!)

In Part V of the *Discourse*, having to his own satisfaction set and solved the Problem of the External World in Part IV, Descartes begins to sketch the mechanical conception of nature which he claims to be able to deduce from his new foundations. From physics he quickly proceeds to physiology. After recommending those who may lack his own familiarity with the subject to attend a few anatomical demonstrations, and after paying to William Harvey one of his very rare tributes to a predecessor, Descartes recommends that the body (not exactly is but) should be "regarded as a machine which having been made by the hands of God, is incomparably better arranged, and possesses in itself movements which are much more admirable, than any of those which can be invented by man." In the case of the brutes that is that: brutes have no souls or minds. But in the case of humans the bodily machine is occupied by something incorporeal: "I, that is to say my mind — what makes me what I am — am entirely distinct from the body . . .". So Gilbert Ryle (1900–1976) in *The Concept of Mind* had good reason to describe Cartesian man as "the ghost in the machine". It is this ghost which the Cartesian external world is external to.

Attempting to solve his problem of our knowledge of that world Descartes seeks a criterion:

> "After that I examined in general the question of what is required in a proposition for it to be true and certain. For since I had just discovered one which I knew to be such I thought I should also know in what this certitude consists. So, after observing that there was nothing at all in this 'I think, therefore I am' which assures me that I am speaking the truth except that I can see very clearly that in order to think it is necessary to exist, I concluded that I could take it as a general rule that the things which we conceive quite clearly and quite distinctly are all true; but just remembering that there is some difficulty about distinguishing properly which are cases which we do conceive distinctly."

You may need to pause for a moment here, to recover breath or to make sure that that statement really says what it seems to be saying. Take advantage of that pause to recognise that, for better or for worse, what Descartes has found is a generalised and secularised version of the ultimate criterion of religious knowledge defended by the Reformers. He himself was raised, and throughout his life remained, within the Roman Catholic fold. Yet compare what he has just said about the infallible illumination of clear and distinct conception with Calvin in the *Institutes of the Christian Religion* on what were supposed to be similarly infallible illuminations from the Holy Spirit: "It is . . . a persuasion of a kind which requires no reasons; and at the same time a knowledge of a sort which is based on a very good reason. It is a matter of knowing in as much as our mind rests more certain and assured than in any reasons. Finally, it is an experience which could only be the product of a revelation from heaven" (I (vii)).

Having found his criterion, the next step for Descartes is to employ this to test, and to vindicate, some arguments for the existence of God. The members of this group are selected for their suitability to the Cartesian starting-point. Thus, whereas all the Five Ways of Aquinas take off from supposed very general features of the universe around us, these are intended to provide a "knowledge of God which is easier and more certain than our knowledge of the things of the world". Indeed, by an elegant inversion which must have appealed most strongly to his mathematician's spirit, Descartes undertakes to prove that the latter cannot provide a basis for, but instead presupposes, the former. (The quoted phrase comes from the Dedication of the *Meditations* to "the Dean and Doctors of the Sacred Faculty of Theology at Paris" – part of the Sorbonne. The Five Ways are what Aquinas offers in the *Summa Theologica* (IQ2A3) as five demonstrations: "We must say that it is possible to prove the existence of God in five ways.")

Having got his own proofs, which studiously do not appeal to any premises drawn from the external world, Descartes now argues that it is the existence of the good God, "who is no deceiver" which alone can and does guarantee that, always provided they are directed rightly, our faculties are fundamentally reliable. Without this assurance there is no defence against the systematic, all-corroding scepticism: "And though the wisest minds may study the matter as much as they will, I do not believe that they will be able to give any sufficient reason for removing this doubt, unless they presuppose the existence of God."

3. *Three responses to the Cartesian challenge (i) Locke.* Having as he believed made sure of this sufficient guarantee, Descartes put aside his original wholesale scepticism, accepted most commonsense knowledge of things and people, and proceeded with his scientific investigations. But his philosophical successors, with reason, refused to concede that he had solved the problem.

(i)   Consider first an archetypal Englishman. Locke's *An Essay concerning Human Understanding* was, as we had occasion to remark in Chapter II, an inquiry into the nature and limitations of the cognitive apparatus; Locke's object being, as he puts it in his Epistle to the Reader, to "see what objects our understandings were, or were not, fitted to deal with". He starts from the basic Cartesian certainty, presented now in terms of what Locke likes to call "the new way of ideas": his catchall word 'ideas' covers not only sense-data but also private experiences of every other variety. So, "Since the mind in all its thoughts and reasonings, hath no other immediate object but its own ideas, which alone it does or can contemplate, it is evident that our knowledge is only conversant about them" (IV (i)1).

But Locke cannot resign himself to stopping there. He is a man not only of great common sense but also of science: he studied medicine at Oxford, though he never actually qualified as a doctor; and he became a Fellow of the Royal Society, though he did not always remember to pay his subscription. He develops a Causal, and in part a Representative Theory of Perception. In this context a causal theorist is one who maintains that we can from the occurrence of our sense-data infer the existence and something about the nature of objects in the external world. A causal theorist can be, and almost always is, a representative theorist as well. He will be a representative theorist to the extent that he maintains that some or all of these sense-data are faithful representations of those objects. Locke is a causal theorist about all sense-data, or, at any rate, about all non-hallucinatory sense-data. He is a representative theorist only with regard to the sense-data of what he allows as the primary qualities, not the secondary: ". . . the ideas of primary qualities of bodies are resemblances of them, and their patterns do really exist in the bodies themselves, but the ideas produced in us by . . . secondary qualities have no resemblance of them at all" (II (viii) 15).

Locke paints a haunting picture of our human situation. All our ideas are and must be derived from our experience. For "external and internal sensation are the only passages I can find of knowledge to the understanding. These alone, as far as I can discover, are the windows by which light is let into this dark room. For, methinks, the understanding is not much unlike a closet wholly shut from light, with only some little openings left, to let in external visible resemblances, or ideas of things without . . ." (II (xi) 17).

This is a thoroughly Cartesian picture, though sketches for it can be found before Descartes. Shakespeare's Prince Henry in *King John*, for instance, mentions "his pure brain — Which some suppose the soul's frail dwelling house" (V (vii)). But it is also a picture still possessing an almost irresistible appeal both for working scientists and for scientifically informed laymen. The analogies and the vocabulary change, the emphases vary, but the essentials remain hardy perennials. The only objects of my immediate awareness are my subjective experiences; including my sense-data or — in other terminologies — my percepts or (perceptual) sensations. In this my awareness I am irremediably removed from the world outside — confined to the isolated Dark Room of the Understanding, solitary is my own private Sensorium Cinema, or trapped in a one-person Operations Control; a place which is, in a most literal sense, a nerve centre.

To Einstein, for instance, in *The World as I See it* this Cartesian picture appeared just obvious: "The belief in an external world independent of the perceiving subject is the basis of all natural science. Since, however, sense perception only gives information of this external world of 'physical reality' indirectly, we can only grasp the latter by speculative means " (p. 60). Again, in an essay on 'The Neurophysiological Basis of Experience' the Nobel Prizewinning Australian physiologist J. C. Eccles explains how in perception "the sequence of events is that of a stimulus to a sense organ causing the discharge of impulses along the afferent nerve fibres which, after various synaptic relays, eventually evoke specific spatio-temporal patterns of impulses in the neuronal network of the cerebral cortex. . . . Yet, as a consequence, . . . I experience sensations . . . which in my private perceptual world are 'projected' to somewhere outside the cortex" (p. 268). Eccles, being a Roman Catholic, both recognises and welcomes the presupposition that the subject of these sense-data is an incorporeal substance. That could not have been true of our third spokesman. As a professional revolutionary he will serve as a representative of the scientifically informed layman. In 1908 Lenin took time off to write *Materialism and Empirio-Criticism*, a polemic directed against certain "revisionists" of orthodox Marxist materialism. They are excoriated for offering "something incredibly muddled, confused, and reactionary", as well as — perhaps worst of all — ultimately religious. Yet, without one qualm of hesitation, Lenin writes: "Matter is . . . copied, photographed and reflected by our sensations, while existing independently of them" (pp. 9, 11 and 127).

(ii)   The first objection to this picture is simple yet decisive. If I really am so confined to my own private experiences, having no direct access to any public world, then I cannot ever be in a position to confirm the hypothesis that some of my sense-data are caused by public objects, or to discover whether or not any of these are or are not faithful representations of those objects. The second objection is perhaps a little more difficult, yet equally decisive. This second, though logically prior objection is that a being in the situation assumed could not even make sense of the Causal and the Representative Theories of Perception. Any word which anyone has to be somehow explicable in terms of their own experience. But a person whose experience was exclusively private could at best understand only words definable in terms of that private experience. Such a person could not, surely, have the needed concepts: neither the concept of objects necessarily and for ever outwith his own private experience; nor the concept of comparing one of his sense-data – his essentially private photographs – with such an object? The force of this second and more sophisticated objection should become clearer as we go further.

The main reason why the decisiveness of these objections is so often not appreciated is that people cheat. Surreptitiously, and without on their stated principles any warrant, they reintroduce crucial items of rejected common-sense knowledge. The fundamental certainty surviving all the systematic Cartesian doubt is that of one person, conceived as an incorporeal substance, immediately aware of his own present private experience. Good and sufficient reason is needed to get from there to knowledge that there are other people. That adequate rationale, as Descartes himself recognised, must include: both, first, reasons for believing that there are objects external to and independent of that particular individual; and, second, reasons for believing that some of those objects – human bodies – are, so to speak, occupied by other incorporeal substances. For, even allowing that people are a kind of such substances and not creatures of flesh and blood, there is no way for one to know another save through the mediation of their bodies. What we nearly always find is a quick step, made with no justification given, from the individualistic premise that my one unchallengeable certainty is my own immediate consciousness, to the collectivist conclusion that we are all of us collectively in the same boat. This conclusion then becomes a premise from which to launch inquiries into the possibility, extent, and foundations of our knowledge of the external world. Yet if I already know that there are other people to share an investigative task, then I already know that there is a populated public world.

The more scientifically minded you are the greater the temptation now to think that Causal and Representative Theories of Perception, as philosophical contentions, can be and are experimentally established. After all, is it not possible and indeed common for experimenters to present objects to subjects, thus causing those subjects to have sense-data, and then to compare the reports on those sense-data given by the subjects with the objects as observed by the experimenters? Yes it is. But every such experiment presupposes that perception, involving awareness of public objects, both occurs and is known to occur. Yet that generally unexceptionable presupposition is flat incompatible with the basic assumption shared by both these philosophical theories; the assumption, namely, that no one can ever be directly aware of anything other than their own private experiences.

71

(iii)   If we are to repudiate this assumption, as we surely must, then we shall have at some stage to try to come to terms with what to so many of the ablest philosophers has seemed the compelling case for making it. The immediate, briefer task is to suggest that something may yet be salvaged from the wreckage of these theories. The difficulty is to distinguish: logically contingent, scientific truths about the mechanisms of perception; from logically necessary, philosophical truths forming part of an analysis of the meaning of the word 'perception'. Particular propositions about "the afferent nerve fibres" and "various synaptic relays" clearly belong in the former category. It is a general and more philosophical truth that I cannot be correctly said to have seen this or tasted that unless the presence of this or that was a causally necessary condition for my having the appropriate sense-data. Suppose that I am blind and that I turn my blind eyes towards some scene, while some super science-fiction neuro-physiologist causes me by direct manipulations of my brain to have the sense-data which someone seeing that scene would have. It would still, surely, be false to say that I saw that scene? If this is right, then it certainly follows that the idea of causation is an essential element in the idea of perception.

Salvage operations on the Representative Theory of Perception would be much harder and more protracted. But, if there really is that difference between two sorts of qualities which Locke and his scientific contemporaries believed that they had found, then it must be a matter of contingent fact that the sense-data produced in us by the primary qualities of objects are more faithfully representative of their actual physical characteristics than those produced by the secondary qualities; a possible discovery presumably to be both made and vindicated by relying on some senses, aided by instruments, to provide the check on the others. (For high level discussion of the issue see Campbell and Armstrong in Brown and Rollins.) It might also prove possible to make something of the suggestion that some sort of resemblance between perceptual experiences and their physical causes is perhaps essential to the distinction between perceptual experiences and non-perceptual bodily sensations.

Be all this as it may. The main lessons of the present subsection are: first, that the Representative Theory of Perception is a natural first response to the Cartesian problem of the external world; second, that pictures illustrating this theory are perennially tempting and fascinating; and third, that it is nevertheless exposed to decisive objections. A piquant way of underlining the first and easier of these two objections is to quote a single sentence from one of Locke's minor works. In his *Examination of Father Malebranche's Opinion*

Locke makes the point himself: "This I cannot comprehend, for how can I know that the picture of anything is like that thing, when I never see that which it represents?" (§52).

4. *Three responses to the Cartesian challenge (ii) Berkeley.* A second response is idealism. In the philosophical sense the word 'idealism' does not refer, as ordinarily it does, to elevated and perhaps unrealistic aspirations. Instead it characterises a metaphysical position; a contention about the ultimate nature of existence, about what in the last analysis there is or is not. Philosophical idealism is the view that there are and can be no such things as physical objects existing independently of all consciousness. It is in this sense that Lenin in *Materialism and Empirio-Criticism* contrasts idealism with materialism: "Materialism is the recognition of 'objects in themselves', or outside the mind . . . . The opposite doctrine (idealism) claims that objects do not exist 'without the mind', objects are 'combinations of sensations' " (p. 17). Both words are often extended to include other more general theses about primacy: for instance, that on the one hand matter, or on the other hand mind or spirit or consciousness, is either ontologically dependent, or ontologically prior; that is, that the one either does or does not depend for its existence upon the other.

(i) The classical spokesman for philosophical idealism in the strict interpretation is that most brilliant of Irishmen George Berkeley. Berkeley later became a practically minded bishop within the Anglican communion. Like Hume but unlike Locke and Kant he was philosophically precocious. Most of his main philosophical works were published before he turned thirty; while his most distinctive and original thoughts seem to have occurred to him first in his early twenties, in the course of studies of Locke made at Trinity College, Dublin. The very first sentence of *The Principles of Human Knowledge* is a restatement of Locke's reformulation of the basic Cartesian certainty: "It is evident to anyone who takes a survey of the objects of human knowledge, that they are either ideas actually imprinted on the senses; or else such as are perceived by attending to the passions and operations of the mind; or lastly, ideas formed by help of memory and imagination – either compounding, dividing or barely representing those originally percieved in the aforesaid ways" (§1). But Berkeley has no intention of proceeding, with Locke, to an inconsistently materialist conclusion. Even before his first paragraph is out he is telling us that what we uninstructedly think of as material objects – existing prior to, independently of, and after any observation — just are collections of ideas: "Thus, for example, a certain colour, taste, smell figure, and consistence having been observed to go together, we account it one distinct thing, signified by the name 'apple'; other collections of ideas constitute a stone, a tree, a book, and the like sensible things. . . ."

Hume was later to offer a terminological improvement here: replacing the 'ideas' of Locke and Berkeley by 'perceptions of the mind'; introducing 'impressions' as a label for the first two sorts of ideas on Berkeley's list; and restricting the word 'ideas' to Berkeley's third sort only. The expression 'perceptions of the mind' is open to the same objection as the compound word 'sense-data'. Both were specifically coined to refer to private experience without commitment on whether or not that experience corresponded to anything in the external world. Yet both incorporate perceptual terms which in their ordinary non-technical employments categorically imply awareness of some independent and external reality.

Especially in the *Treatise* Hume remembers his Cartesian commitment, and tries to make his distinction between impressions and ideas purely phenomenological. He tries, that is to say, to make it solely by reference to differences within his private experience and without appeal to beliefs about any independent objects to which some of that private experience may or may not correspond. Impressions, Hume suggests, may be identified by their greater vivacity, "the force and liveliness with which they strike upon the mind". But this strictly phenomenological enterprise soon collapses. He has to admit that "in sleep, in a fever, in madness . . . our ideas may approach to our impressions"; while "sometimes . . . our impressions are so faint and low, that we cannot distinguish them from our ideas" (I (i) 1). He is, in order to make his first and most fundamental distinction, forced to appeal to the perceptual knowledge which he is supposed not to have. Hume's impressions include, and cannot be identified without reference to, Berkeley's "ideas actually imprinted on the senses".

(ii)   The next move for Berkeley was to argue that in addition to ideas there must always be someone to have them. Ideas are like pains or thrills; indeed for Berkeley pains and thrills are two kinds of ideas. It makes no sense to speak of a lost pain or of a lost thrill as if a pain or a thrill could, like a lost wallet, exist without anyone having it in their possession. Pains and thrills, and ideas of all kinds, are not logical substances. They must be had by someone who has them: "This perceiving, active being is what I call 'mind', 'spirit', 'soul', or 'myself'. By which words I do not denote any one of my ideas, but a thing entirely distinct from them, wherein they exist, or, which is the same thing, whereby they are perceived; for the existence of an idea consists in being perceived" (§2).

The often quoted Latin slogan *"Esse est percipi"* (To be is to be perceived) can be misleading. It is only ideas the existence of which "consists in being perceived". For Berkeley the full metaphysical truth is encapsulated only in the slightly longer slogan *"Esse est aut percipere aut percipi"* (To be is either to perceive or to be perceived). What there is is spirits and their ideas, and that is all; while of these two categories of being only spirits are substances. There are no corporeal substances. Indeed Berkeley argues, and in *Three Dialogues* between Hylas and Philonous with especial verve and vigour, that we have and can have no idea of material substance existing "without the mind;" all such talk is so much insignificant verbiage. How could we, he urges, have an idea of something which is not an idea in the mind; or an idea which is a sensible representation of something itself insensible; or an idea of some sort of a substratum defined as different from all the sensible ideas to which it gives rise? (The names of the two partisans derive from Greek roots: Philonous is a lover of mind; while Hylas stands for stuff. The word 'sensible' here means not having good sense but being able to be sensed.)

(iii)   Now Berkeley considers an objection. It is the objection which was to be put by common sense incarnate, in the bulky shape of Dr Samuel Johnson. Boswell tells how once after coming out of church they fell to discussing "Bishop Berkeley's ingenious sophistry to prove the non-existence of matter and that everything in the Universe is merely ideal." Boswell opined that though we are all satisfied that this doctrine is not true, it is impossible to refute it: "Johnson answered, striking his foot with mighty force against a large stone, till he rebounded from it, 'I refute it *thus*'." (6 VIII 73: italics original.)

Surely the Doctor is right? How can anyone say that apples, stones, trees, books, and all the rest of the visible and tangible furniture of the world is nothing else but so many more or less arbitrary collections of sense-data? But Berkeley, a master of intellectual judo, has seen him coming. Although always in a mind ideas are not always creatures of that mind's will. The *Principles* proceeds:

"When in broad daylight I open my eyes, it is not in my power to choose whether I shall see or no, or to determine what particular objects shall present themselves to my view; and so likewise as to the hearing and other senses, the ideas imprinted on them are not creatures of my will. There is, therefore, some other will or spirit that produces them.

75

The ideas of sense are more strong, lively, and distinct than those of the imagination; they have likewise a steadiness, order and coherence, and are not excited at random, as those which are the effects of human wills often are, but in a regular train or series, the admirable connexion whereof sufficiently testifies the wisdom and benevolence of its Author. Now the set rules or established methods, wherein the Mind we depend on excites in us the ideas of sense, are called the Laws of Nature: and these we learn by experience, which teaches that such and such ideas are attended with such and such other ideas, in the ordinary course of things. . . .

The ideas imprinted on the senses by the Author of Nature are called 'real things': and those excited in the imagination – being less regular, vivid and constant, – are more properly termed 'ideas', or 'images of' things, which they copy or represent. But then our sensations, be they never so vivid and distinct are nevertheless ideas, that is, they exist in the mind, or are perceived by it, as truly as the ideas of its own framing" (§§29, 30, and 33).

Thus, with superb confidence, Berkeley elegantly diverts the impetus of his opponents into what he sees as a new demonstration of the continual presence and activity of God. Certainly the fact that my sense-data are not, like the phantasms of my imagination, creatures of my will requires some causal explanation. But that cause or those causes cannot be independently existing material objects: first, because, as he considers that he has shown, talk of such objects makes no sense; and, second, because the only possible causes are in any cases active and personal beings – which, he takes for granted, must be incorporeal. The second of these two points seems obvious to Berkeley because he thinks of all causation as necessarily agency: how could inert and senseless stuff do anything? His is, it has to be said, an infantile and atavistic view; although, once this has been said, it then has also to be said – and much louder – that simply to describe a view in such a way is not to show sufficient reason for putting it down as mistaken. The point is that we surely do all derive our concepts of cause from experience of our own and other people's agency, and could not have such concepts if we were not ourselves agents; even though most of us later come to employ a notion which allows for impersonal and inanimate causes as well as animate and personal (Flew 1978, passim).

(iv) (a)   Before moving on to a third type of response to the Cartesian challenge, consider two objections to Berkeley's position. One, which he noticed, is that he collapses all distinctions between illusion and reality, reducing the familiar material world to a vast hallucination. "If anyone thinks", Berkeley replies, that this account:

". . . detracts from the existence or reality of things, he is very far from understanding what hath been premised in the plainest terms I could think of. . . . There are spiritual substances, minds, or human souls, which will or excite ideas on themselves at pleasure: but these are faint, weak and unsteady in respect of others they perceive by sense, which being impressed upon them according to certain rules or laws of nature, speak themselves of a mind more powerful and wise than human spirits. These latter are said to have more reality in them than the former: by which is meant that they are more affecting, orderly, and distinct, and that they are not fictions of the mind perceiving them . . . . Whether others mean anything by the term 'reality' different from what I do, I entreat them to look into their own thoughts and see" (§ 36).

Certainly Berkeley can provide for a distinction. But what he can provide is, equally certainly, not enough to warrant the curious claim, made in the early private *Philosophical Commentaries* and reiterated in public print, that he is throughout "recalling men to common sense" (§ 751). For it is one of his main purposes to deny that we are in perception aware of sensible objects which can and do exist unperceived: what and all we are in contact with – though, until instructed by Berkeley, not aware of – is the Producer of our orderly and systematic hallucinations. The nearest which Berkeley ever comes to allowing that sensible objects may exist unperceived, and this nearest is still a very long way off, is to suggest that something may be going on in God even when God is not producing human or other animal sense-data: ". . . all the choir of heaven and furniture of the earth, in a word all those bodies which compose the mighty frame of the world, have not any subsistence without a mind – that their being is to be perceived or known; and that consequently so long as they are not actually perceived by me and do not exist in my mind or that of any other created spirit, they must either have no existence at all, or else subsist in the mind of some Eternal Spirit . . ." (§ 6).

This is a suggestion which Berkeley never developed. Had he done so he would have needed to take account of the point that God could not have my sense-data, any more than anyone else can have my pains. The most which it could make sense to hint is that God might have similar sense-data, but not numerically the same. This nice distinction matters. For Berkeley here is rather carelessly talking as if he was going back upon what he most wanted to say. Yet in truth there is for him no question of conceding that there could be objects perceived by first one perceiver and then another. Such objects would be logical substances, meaning that they can significantly be said to exist independently, notwithstanding that it might in fact also be the case that they were being kept in existence by one of their perceivers. Every theist believes that the entire Universe, defined as everything there is (with the exception of God, if God there be), is in fact kept in existence by God as its sustaining cause. The theist believes that without this ontological support it would all – in a striking phrase of Archbishop William Temple – "collapse into non-existence". This belief is the doctrine of creation, which is itself crucial to the definition of the word 'theism'. What distinguishes the theist Berkeley as also a philosophical idealist is his conviction that the Universe consists in nothing else but created incorporeal substances and their ideas.

(b)   The second of our two present objections he did not himself see as a difficulty. This objection is that he has made no adequate provision for our knowledge of one another. There is an argument in the *Principles* from which he triumphantly concludes that "it is evident, that God is known as certainly and immediately as any other mind or spirit whatsoever, distinct from ourselves. We may even assert, that the existence of God is far more evidently perceived than the existence of men . . ." (§ 147).

Certainly we may assert this. Indeed, if we accept Berkeley's framework, we must: it is far, far more evident. What he himself has to say about his knowledge of other people is cursory and lame: "I perceive several motions, changes and combinations of ideas, that inform me that there are several particular agents like myself, which accompany them, and concur in their production" (§ 145). Before offering "two most certain tests" of whether or not a bodily machine is occupied and run by an incorporeal soul, Descartes was scrupulous to deploy some if not sufficient arguments for the general reliability of his senses, and hence to show warrant for his belief that there are such sensible objects. But now Berkeley – who starts from the same fundamental Cartesian certainty, "I think, therefore I am" – denies that there even could be such objects. He then recruits all the sensory experience which he finds not to be subject to his own will as the basis for his proud demonstration of the immediate and constant presence of another and supreme Will. If that demonstration is accepted then the true outcome must be the extreme limiting case of radical Protestantism. The individual – not all individuals, but one absolutely solitary individual – confronts his God; and, if God does

78

in fact create other souls, then Berkeley can know of these only by grace of some special Divine revelation.

5. *Three responses to the Cartesian challenge (iii) Hume and Kant.* A third response is some kind of agnosticism. This is the resort of both the Scot Hume and the German Kant. Though there are of course important differences between the two, both accept as fundamental the original Cartesian certainty. Both maintain that all efforts to reason from there to knowledge of a public world outside our own private consciousness have been and must be unsuccessful. Both believe that the only positive task for the philosopher here is to produce some sort of study of the structure imposed upon experience by the workings of our own minds. Yet neither is prepared to deny that there is such a world. For Hume this is a matter of natural belief. We just cannot help believing that there is an external world; and we neither can, nor should attempt to, act as if there could be any real doubt about this. Nevertheless it is impossible to excogitate any rationale for such belief sufficient to justify awarding to it the diploma title 'knowledge'. Kant too was always keen to rebut charges of philosophical idealism. He insisted that he could not properly be so classed since he believed that there is an external world, albeit in itself unknowable.

(i)   The best summary of Hume's position comes in the *Treatise*, in a rebuke to "scepticism with regard to the senses". The sceptic, Hume says:

". . . must assent to the principle concerning the existence of body, tho' he cannot pretend by any arguments of philosophy to maintain its veracity. Nature has not left this to his choice, and doubtless esteem'd it an affair of too great importance to be trusted to our uncertain reasonings and speculations. We may well ask, 'What causes induce us to believe in the existence of body?' but 'tis in vain to ask, 'Whether there be body or not?' That is a point which we must take for granted in all our reasonings" (I (iv) 2).

Kant explains his position in the *Prolegomena to any Future Metaphysics* – a helpful short work written for the benefit of possible readers who, with reason, find the *Critique of Pure Reason* impossibly difficult. Kant is no idealist, he says, for he holds that "things are given to us as objects of our senses situated outside us, but of what they may be in themselves we know nothing; we only know their appearances. . . . I do indeed admit that there are bodies outside us, i.e. things which, although wholly unknown to us as to what they may be in themselves, we know through the representations which their influence . . . provides for us, and to which we give the name of bodies" (p. 45). This is the origin of the phrase 'thing-in-itself', which is sometimes even by English writers left in the original German, *'ding an sich'*; as, for instance, in the *Autumn Journal* of Louis Macneice (p. 51).

(ii)   What the starting point is, and that it is unquestioned, is made very clear by such throwaway statements in the *Treatise* as: ". . . 'tis universally allow'd by philosophers, and is besides pretty obvious of itself, that nothing is ever really present with the mind but its perceptions, or impressions and ideas . . ." (I (ii) 6). In the first *Inquiry* Hume spells it out a little further, in a curiously close anticipation of the just quoted passage from Kant:

> "the slightest philosophy . . . teaches us that nothing can ever be present to the mind but an image or perception, and that the senses are only the inlets through which these images are conveyed, without being able to produce any immediate intercourse between the mind and the object. . . . These are the obvious dictates of reason; and no man who reflects ever doubted that the existences which we consider when we say 'this house' or 'that tree' are nothing but perceptions in the mind . . ." (XII (i)).

(a)   The first thing to notice is that once again a giant tacit stride has been taken: "from the individualistic premise that my one unchallengable certainty is my own immediate consciousness; to the collectivist conclusion that we are all of us collectively in the same boat." Once we have remarked that there is a big gap here we are bound to find it perfectly extraordinary, and almost incomprehensible, that so many able philosophers in so many generations should have crossed this gap without, apparently, noticing what they were doing, and certainly without tendering any argument in support of the move. Presumably Hume, had he ever been challenged, would have replied that for each and every one of us the conviction that we are not alone, that solipsism is false, is an unevidenced but irresistible natural belief. But this reply would still have required him drastically to recast statements of the sort quoted in the present Section 5. It is not we as a collective who should be said to be confronted with the question whether, in addition to all these incorporeal beings, there are also material things. It is each and every solitary individual who has to ask himself alone whether solipsism is true, whether he − or, since it is bodiless, it − is all there is.

It is − credit where credit is due − one of the great merits of Lenin's contribution to philosophy that he hammers away at the scandalous lack of any warrant for the move from I to we. Thus Lenin quotes Ernst Mach

(1838–1916), a main precursor of the Vienna Circle of Logical Positivists between the wars: "It is then correct that the world consists only of our sensations. In which case we have knowledge *only* of sensations . . .". Lenin comments: "From which there is only one possible inference, namely, that the world consists only of *my* sensations. The word 'our' employed by Mach instead of 'my' is employed illegitimately." Again: "If bodies are 'complexes of sensations', as Mach says, or 'combinations of sensible ideas', as Berkeley said, it inevitably follows that the whole world is but my idea. Starting from such a premise it is impossible to arrive at the existence of other people besides oneself: it is the purest solipsism" (pp. 36 and 34: italics original. Compare Flew 1978, Ch. 10).

(b)   The second cause for comment is provided by Kant's reference to "the representations . . . to which we give the name of bodies" and by Hume's claim "that the existences which we consider when we say 'this house' or 'that tree' are nothing but perceptions in the mind". Whether or not they themselves completely appreciated the implications, Hume and Kant by employing these phrases commit themselves to phenomenalism. This is not to be confused, though it is connected, with phenomenology. The phenomenalist holds that talk about material things can be completely reduced to talk about the actual or possible occurrence of sense-data.

In the heyday of phenomenalism a favourite associated phrase was 'logical construction', and the stock example of a logical construction was the average man. The point of this stock example was that the expression 'the average man' is not the name of one particular nondescript. To make an assertion about the average man is to say something the truth of which depends entirely upon the corresponding facts about particular flesh-and-blood men. To say, for instance, that the average resident in Windsor Hall has a one metre waistline, is to say – a shade more tersely – that the sum of the waistlines of all these residents divided by their total number is one metre. So the contention that these are logical constructions out of those says that statements about these are some sort of function of statements about those. Such contentions are characteristic of the deflationary metaphysician: his aim, opposed to that of the inflationary metaphysician, is to show, not that there are more things in heaven and earth, but that there are fewer, than are dreamt of in your philosophy. Among many other candidates considered have been nations and social classes. In these cases there have been strong practical concerns: both methodological, to secure proper procedures of sociological inquiry; and political, to display the fraudulence of those

AN INTRODUCTION TO PHILOSOPHY

spokesmen and would be masters who pretend to represent such groups without reference to the actual wishes of their flesh-and-blood members.

The phenomenalist maintains that material things are logical constructions out of sense-data, and hence that all exoteric talk about such favourite philosophical objects as chairs and tables is somehow reducible to esoteric talk about the categorical or hypothetical occurrence of appropriate sense-data. Interpreted straightforwardly this is an extremely unpromising thesis. So it has sometimes been construed less heroically. It then refers: not to actual present vernacular significance; but to the outlandish meanings which words would have if we so reconstructed our language as to enable ourselves to say no more than the most which, granted the assumptions of the phenomenalists, we could have good evidence for saying.

Interpreted in the straightforward way it at once falls down before the objection that the claims made by asserting 'This is a house' or 'That is a tree' are, whether true or not true, claims about possible objects of perception. Material things, such as those chairs and tables, as well as other less tangible objects of perception, like rainbows and sonic bangs, are as such things which conceivably can, and of course often do, exist unperceived. This possibility of existence unperceived, this essential independence of the logical substance, is part, and a very large part, of what is at stake when someone says, within the framework of one of the most fundamental of all antitheses: that he did not dream the incident, but saw it with his own eyes; or that this is no hallucination – these are real rats. It is essential to material things and other objects of perception, just as, as we have already recognised, it is necessary to perception itself, that it must involve awareness of such objects. It may be instructive to argue, with Berkeley, that the very suggestion of sensible objects existing unperceived is incoherent and absurd, or, with Hume, that we can never know, but only believe, that there is a world beyond our (collective) private consciousness. But it can only obfuscate to speak of sense-data or collections of sense-data as if these could, whether individually or collectively, constitute either a material thing or any other possible object of perception. For sense-data cannot exist unhad, cannot occur save as the sense-data of some person or some brute; whereas possible objects of perception must be able, conceivably, to exist unperceived.

Another and, surely, equally decisive objection to the phenomenalist thesis as straightforwardly interpreted is that it is committed to reducing categorical assertions about mind-independent possible objects of perception to hypothetical assertions about the occurrence of mind-dependent sense-

SCEPTICISM AND THE EXTERNAL WORLD

data. Consider assertions about the present state of what is at present not perceived: the example which my teachers gave, back in the pre-Sputnik days when I was young, was the other side of the moon. The unreconstructed phenomenalist has to maintain that what such assertions do actually mean is something about what would be experienced if anyone were to get into position to have the appropriate experiences.

It is important to realise that the word 'experience' in that last sentence has to be read in the private not the public sense. It would be hard enough to defend a phenomenalist thesis if the contention was only that the meaning of categorical assertions about the presently unobserved boils down to some set of hypothetical claims about what would be observed if anyone were to get within range for some sort of observation. But that milder yet still highly artificial contention cannot suffice. All these references to observation carry implications about material things and other possible objects of perception; whereas the whole purpose of the phenomenalist exercise is to cash all this supposedly more sophisticated and speculative verbalising about material things into the brass tacks of immediate private experience.

The image of cashing, of demanding the cash-value, which appeals at once to the tough-minded, was, like the contrast itself between tough- and tender-mindedness, introduced into philosophy by William James (1842–1910). This American psychologist was, notoriously, the far better writer than his novelist younger brother Henry. The reason for bringing in these fine images is to remind ourselves that few, if any, of those who have entertained phenomenalist views have really wanted to defend a thesis only about the established meanings of words. Even where they have written, as they so often have, as if this were the point, their actual concerns have usually been tough-minded and radical. They have in their own eyes – though visual imagery is, for reasons already more than once explained, inept – been people who have seen through. Maybe material things, as material thing words are vulgarly understood, are not after all logical constructions out of sense-data. Nevertheless, once you have acquired the slightest tincture of philosophy, once you begin to realise what is what; then you must appreciate that the only evidence available, that all we can or could ever be justified in making any assertions about, is sense-data; and nothing else whatsoever but.

To which the right reply is to fire the first ranging shots on the Cartesian citadel. This citadel has two aspects. On the forward-looking, positive side there is the absolute security that the individual can know present private experience. On the backward-looking, negative side there is the strong insistence that there can be no such thing as immediate awareness of anything else but that present private awareness. If the assault is to succeed it will need to overwhelm the defences on both sides. The weakness on the positive side is that it is only possible to know present private experience upon certain assumptions; and, although these assumptions are both correct and commonsense, they are in fact inconsistent with the defence of the negative aspect. The crux is this. If the present private experience is to be known and not, as it might be by some poor dumb brute, just passively had; then there must be some possibility of articulation, of somehow — whether aloud or to oneself — saying something about the occurrence and characteristics of that experience. Inert immediacy, looking neither before nor behind, is not enough. If the illumination, "I think, therefore I am", is to be an item and foundation of knowledge; then there has to be active response and intellectual organisation. So what the attackers have to do is to show that this necessity itself logically presupposes perceptual knowledge of a public world.

That qualifying adverb 'logically' is important. It would not be sufficient to make out, what is no doubt perfectly true, that no one could be in a position to perform or even to follow Cartesian *Meditations* without living in a developed and sophisticated society. For, since this is supposed to be a contingent fact, which could conceivably have been otherwise, it too lies open to all-subverting systematic doubt. What the attackers have to establish is that it is subtly, yet nonetheless fundamentally, self-contradictory for the sceptic to suggest: both that he can and does know something about his private experience; and that he might never have perceived, or be going to perceive, anything in a public world.

Confronting the phenomenalist such an adversary latches onto fatal phrases. First, how are the demonstrative 'this house' and 'that tree' supposed to be understood? Surely Hume is silently taking it for granted that he can after all straightforwardly point to certain public objects; objects, that is, which others too can perceive, with or without instrumental aids; and at which they can see Hume himself pointing? The private Kantian "representations . . . to which we give the name of bodies", the private Humian impressions which are indeed "nothing but . . . in the mind", can be identified, it seems, only by reference to their supposedly forever inaccessible public causes. Second, in the *Principles*, Berkeley maintains: "The table I write on, I say, exists, that is, I see and feel it; and, if I were out of my study I should say it existed, meaning thereby that if I was in my study I might perceive it . . ." (§ 3). It is, notoriously, essential to phenomenalism thus to appeal to hypotheticals in order to explicate categorical assertions about what is not at present observed. But how are such hypotheticals to be interpreted if not as referring, in a way quite inconsistent with phenomenalism, to the possible movements from place to place of one kind of body among others?

6. *The Arguments from Illusion.* The quotation from Hume's first *Inquiry* at the beginning of Subsection (ii) of the previous Section 5 omitted one sentence: "The table, which we see, seems to diminish, as we remove farther from it. But the real table, which exists independent of us, suffers no alteration. It was, therefore, nothing but its image, which was present to the mind." This is one of an arsenal of similar considerations, known as the Arguments from Illusion. What these have in common is: not that they all start from something which the philosophical layman would ordinarily put down as an illusion; but that they are all intended to end in the conclusion that we are necessarily and for ever separated from any realities in the external world by an impenetrable Veil of Appearance. This is the conclusion described in more pedestrian terms by Hume: "that nothing can ever be present to the mind but an image . . . , and that the senses are only the inlets through which these images are conveyed, without being able to produce any immediate intercourse between the mind and the object . . .". Those who hold that, on the contrary, we do in perception have intercourse with mind-independent public objects are often, by those priding themselves on "the slightest philosophy", dismissed as Naïve Realists. If we are going to preserve this label, then perhaps we should confine its application to those who have never entertained the Arguments from Illusion. We could then introduce, if that were not felt to be equally prejudicial in the opposite direction, the new label 'Sophisticated Realists". It would describe those who have returned to a commonsense view of perceptual knowledge after examining and rejecting those arguments.

(i) Besides the Case of the Diminishing Table there are many many others, some being of great antiquity. Several of the phenomena which became and remained favourite starting-points were noticed already by Plato; and these, and lots more, were later lovingly listed by Sextus Empiricus. Thus there is, for example, mention in *The Republic* of the straight stick which when plunged partly into water appears through refraction bent (602C); while the towers "frequently observed" by Descartes in *Meditation VI* may well have been borrowed from the *Outlines of Pyrrhonism* (I (xiii) 32). The argument in Descartes runs: "that towers which from a distance had looked round to me appeared from close to to be square; and that

85

colossi raised on the topmost summits of these towers appeared to me like statuettes when I looked at them from below. So, in an infinity of other instances, I discovered error in judgements based upon the external senses" (I (xiii) 32).

This statement is instructively typical in that it fails to make a distinction vital to any attempt to prove the Veil of Appearance doctrine. This is the distinction: between cases in which I am, or may be, mistaken about what I am in fact perceiving; and cases in which the mistake is, or would be, to believe that I am perceiving anything at all. The Cases of the Diminishing Table, the Bent Stick, the Square Tower, the Colossal Statuettes, and such other longtime favourites as the round coin which when viewed askew allegedly looks elliptical, fall into the first of these two categories. But they are for that very reason inadequate grounds for drawing the conclusion proposed. For they all accept and appeal to our knowledge of what is really there. Hume says in so many words that "the real table, which exists independent of us, suffers no alteration". Fair enough, of course: but, this once granted, he cannot consistently proceed to prove that tables, if they exist at all, must be forever hidden from us.

And, furthermore, is the fact that my (private) images of tables or colossi occupy a diminishing proportion of my (private) visual field while I withdraw progressively further away, a reason for believing that it was not really a table or a colossus which I saw; and can still see? Suppose that – to my disquiet and astonishment – I find that wherever I go, and in whatever direction I turn my eyes, the images remain, still occupying the same proportion of my visual field. Then these outré phenomena constitute decisive good reason for concluding: not that I have been uniquely privileged to tear off the Veil of Appearance; but that I have become subject to a peculiar and tiresome hallucination. Much the same applies with the Bent Stick and the Elliptical Coin. If I direct my eyes at a circular coin, but find that however I twist and turn that coin I still have a circle of constant size in my visual field, then once again I can only conclude that I am victim of an hallucination. If I put a straight stick into water, yet observe no diffraction phenomena, then there must be something wrong with either me or the stick or the water.

One general moral to draw from all these cases is the perception, and in particular visual perception, involves skills which have to be acquired. It may be – it surely is – true that when we succeed in perceiving something we are engaged in "immediate intercourse" with a perceptual object. It is nevertheless a kind of intercourse requiring practice and technique. It is easy to miss this moral. For the fundamentals – the learning to take account of the effects of distance, perspective, lighting, and so on – are usually mastered in infancy. Most of us are forced to recognise that acquired skills are involved here only if we have in adult life to practice some previously unfamiliar form of observation – seeing through a microscope, for instance – or if – a much rarer occasion, unfortunately – we come across someone who having been blind from birth suddenly gains their sight. As William James once said, wearing his psychologist's hat, the truth seems to be that the private experience of the infant must be "a big, blooming, buzzing confusion".

(ii)   The best sort of Argument from Illusion falls into the second of the two categories distinguished in Subsection (i) – "cases in which the mistake is, or would be, to believe that I am perceiving anything at all". These include mainly dreams and waking hallucinations, but also such disturbing peripheral phenomena as the sensations felt as being in the vacant place of limbs which have in fact been amputated. (These last particularly caught the attention of that sometime soldier Descartes.) In all such cases we are thought to enjoy subjective or private experiences phenomenologically indistinguishable from those which occur in authentic perception. This suggests that perhaps all we ever are directly acquainted with is our own subjective or private experiences; and hence that perception, if there really is such a thing, must be an indirect matter of inference from these as evidence. "Finally", as Descartes had it in the *Discourse*, "taking account of the fact that all the same experiences which we have when we are awake can also come to us when we are asleep without there being one of them which is then veridical, I resolved to pretend that everything which had ever entered into my mind was no more veridical than the illusions of my dreams."

(a)   The first and more superficial objection to these seductive proceedings is that the justifying reasons offered not merely do not support, but are inconsistent with, the proposed pretence. Earlier in the same paragraph Descartes has argued: "So, on the grounds that our sense sometimes deceive us, I wanted to suppose that there was not anything corresponding to what they make us imagine". To which I want to reply that, if this is what you are proposing to suppose, then the last thing which you should blurt out is that you know that your senses sometimes deceive you. For how can you claim to know that, without thereby conceding that you also know that sometimes they do not? How can anyone come by means neither immediately nor ultimately sensory to know, for instance, that some of what look like superfine apples are really surrogates in soap? Someone, somewhere along the line, has got to have scratched some, and seen the soap beneath the skin; or –

preferably – to have taken a good big bite, only to find themselves foaming at the mouth! Descartes makes the same mistake in reasoning in his parallel argument about mistakes in reasoning, albeit with this time a significant and endearing moment of hesitation: "because some men make mistakes in reasoning . . . I judged that I was as much subject to error as anyone else, and I rejected as unsound all the reasonings which I had hitherto taken for demonstrations".

(b) The second and more profound objection to even the best sort of Argument from Illusion develops suggestions hinted at the end of the previous Section 5. The first and more superficial objection is, it seems to me, decisive against any Argument from Illusion which appeals to the (known fact of) discovered error in order to conclude that there is, perhaps or certainly, no known perceptual truth. But it can get no purchase at all on another version. This different version employs ordinary beliefs about discovered error simply as illustrations for the thesis that all our perceptual beliefs, these included, conceivably might be wrong. In the one case the argument assumes that some such beliefs are knowledge. In the other it assumed only that they, and the constitutive notion of perceptual error, are intelligible and free of self-contradiction. The crux then is: not that I know that I have often been wrong; but that I realise that in every case it makes sense to suggest that I might be. Enter now, from the first of the *Meditations*, one of the most memorable characters in the philosophical literature:

> "I shall suppose then that there is, not a true God who is the sovereign source of truth, but a certain Evil Demon, who is as clever and deceitful as he is powerful, and who has employed all his energies to deceive me. I shall consider that the sky, the air, the Earth, colours, shapes, sounds, and everything which we see in the external world are nothing but illusions and tricks which he employs to gull my credulity."

Descartes may have been stimulated to this alarming invention by pondering the implications of an affair much discussed in the 1630's; the trial of Father Grandier, who was accused of infesting a convent with demons. In our century this was dramatised by Aldous Huxley in his novel *The Devils of Loudun*. Alarming this Cartesian invention certainly is. Yet is it ultimately coherent? Of course it makes sense to suggest of every proposed perceptual belief, separately and in succession, that it may perhaps be wholly mistaken and unfounded: perceptual beliefs must embrace logically contingent propositions, the contradictories of which cannot be self-contradictory. But it does not follow from this that it is possible without inconsistency or incoherence to suggest that the whole lot, taken together, might be erroneous.

That it does not follow, and why, is best appreciated by looking first at the different problem of radical scepticism about arguments: "I rejected as unsound all the reasonings which I had hitherto taken for demonstrations." Can Descartes say this, and understand what he is saying, without at the same time and by the same token knowing that he has been acquainted with at least some recognisably valid and at least some recognisably invalid arguments? Well, maybe some sceptical ultra wants to suggest that Descartes, or indeed anyone else, might conceivably have come into existence suddenly and abruptly, without having had any past. There is, this sceptic suggests, no logical contradiction in such a wildly counterfactual speculation. He might then remind us of the legend that the goddess Athena originally arose fully armed out of the head of the god Zeus – equipped too, no doubt, with a perfect fluency in Attic Greek. Be that as it may. It is still certain that Descartes cannot say what he does say, and know what he is talking about, unless he knows the difference between validity and invalidity in argument, knows the meanings of the expressions 'valid argument' and 'invalid argument'. Yet how can this condition be satisfied if he really is altogether incapable of identifying any specimens, however elementary? Would you, as a teacher testing vocabulary and comprehension, give a pass mark to a candidate who really was as conceptually incompetent as that?

Now apply the same ideas to the professed inability to distinguish the "experiences which we have when we are awake" from those "which come to us when we are asleep". Can this profession consist with the suggestion that perhaps it is all a dream, that perhaps we never actually perceive anything? One reason for urging that it cannot is that all notions of dreaming and hallucination seem to be parasitical upon the concepts of straightforward perception: to understand what is meant, for instance, by a dream of fair women or a mirage of an oasis you must already understand what is meant by talk of (actual) fair women or (actual) oases. Seeing in a dream, like the 'seeing' (in snigger quotes) of pink rats, is a sort of failed seeing. It is not a positive achievement in its own right. There is no question but that we do in fact acquire such secondary notions after we have already acquired, and by contrast with, the primary concepts of perception. Yet, remembering the sceptic's suggestion of a person without a past, we still have to ask whether such a person, or anyone else, could be said now to be master of the notions of dreaming and hallucination if he is now unable to identify any object of perception as being such, and to know that he is neither dreaming nor victim

89

of an hallucination. Once again, would you, as a teacher testing vocabulary and comprehension, pass this candidate as one who has satisfied the examiners that he knows what an object of perception is?

To make the abstract and indirect criticism of the last three paragraphs come alive, take a direct look at the project proposed in full Cartesian colour. Notice first that the Evil Demon is hypothesised, not as one more inhabitant of the created Universe, but as a sort of Black Creator: that is why the ever prudent Descartes is stepping so delicately. If the suggestion were of an enormously intelligent and competent yet still finite disinformer, then his products, presumably, would be more and better of a kind with some specimens of which we are already familiar: the lump of soap cunningly fashioned to look like a luscious apple; the realistic dummy aircraft deployed on the abandoned airfield; and so on. But nothing of this kind is good enough for the Black Creator. For, however impossible it may become to distinguish the soap apples or the dummy aircraft by purely visual inspection or by photographic reconnaissance, all illusions must be definitively shattered the moment anyone tries to eat the apples or to fly the aircraft. So the Evil Demon "as clever and deceitful as he is powerful, and who has employed all his energies to deceive me", must produce: trick apples which are indistinguishable from real apples, even when dissected or put under the microscope, even when being eaten or afterwards; and dummy aircraft which can be flown and in every other way treated for real; and so on. In these triumphs the Evil Demon overreaches himself, effectively recreating the same old familiar Universe.

In the fourth of his contributions to *The Leibniz-Clarke Correspondence* the bold and brilliant Leibniz formulated two "great principles" to "change the condition of metaphysics, which becomes through them genuine and demonstrative where before it consisted of little but empty words." The second was the Principle of the Identity of Indiscernibles: "To postulate two indiscernible things is to postulate the same thing under two names." Applying the substance of this in the style of Damon Runyon, that much-loved master of Broadway picaresque, can we not say that, if the apple which I am munching is not a real apple, if the machine which I am piloting is not a real aircraft, then both will at least do until real apples and real aircraft come along?

(iii)   Besides such Arguments from Illusion as have already been considered in the present Section 6, there are also arguments from the sciences of a kind indicated earlier, in Section 3. These arguments, mainly from physiology but some from psychology and other sciences too, may be classified as a kind of Arguments from Illusion. For they are all deployed to demonstrate the same conclusion; the conclusion that the doctrine of the Veil of Appearance is true. Discussion of these arguments, being discussion of the wider logical presuppositions and logical implications of scientific work, is part of the philosophy of science. Consider, as an epitome of such science-based arguments, a characteristic passage from *Human Knowledge* by Bertrand Russell (1872–1970). To believe "that a man can see matter" is, he urges, totally mistaken:

> "Not even the ablest physiologist can perform this feat. His percept when he looks at a brain is an event in his own mind, and has only a causal connection which he fancies that he is seeing. When, in a powerful telescope, he sees a tiny luminous dot, and interprets it as a vast nebula existing a million years ago, he realises that what he sees is different from what he infers. The difference from the case of a brain looked at through a microscope is only one of degree: there is exactly the same need of inference by means of the laws of physics, from the visual datum to its physical cause. And just as no one supposes that the nebula has any close resemblance to a luminous dot, so no one should suppose that the brain has any close resemblance to what the physiologist sees" (p. 245).

(a)   Such a picture of our cognitive condition has enormous fascination. Before launching into further lessons you would do well to return for a few minutes to Section 3, in order to make sure that you really are firmly seized of the points made there about what must be, what cannot be, and what may be true in the Causal and Representative Theories of Perception. Upon one certain truth we can and must stand unshakable. Unless sometimes, some-where along the line, we are all in perception immediately aware of the existence and some characteristics of some public objects, including espe-cially other people, we can have no warrant for any assertions about a world consisting of such objects, nor yet for talking of ourselves as members of it. Without the possibility and the actuality of some immediate awareness in perception of public objects, the scientists have no basis for any of their inferences and assurances. So let us as we leave this point revolve in our mouths, and relish, an exultant statement from one of 'The Heterodox Systems' in India: "Thus we fasten on our opponents as with adamantine glue the thunderbolt-like fallacy of reasoning in a circle" (Quoted Radhákrish-nan, p. 233).

But now, what are the true implications? How should we view the physiological work? It is so very tempting to interpret this as showing that we never really perceive anything; although and at best we may perhaps, from our visual and tactual sense-data, infer the hidden powers and presence of objects forever unfelt and unseen. The secret is to press a distinction broached already: between scientific investigations of the mechanisms of perception; and philosophical explorations of the concept. The temptation, to which Russell and so many others have succumbed, is to mistake an account of the one for a demonstration that there can be no application for the other.

It is one thing, as Locke said long ago in the *Essay* (III (iv) 10), to elucidate the meaning of colour words. It is quite another to explore the physics and physiology of visual perception. One remark to make in the former context is that the primary colour terms have to be given in ostensive definition: the meaning (the *definiendum*) of such a term can, that is to say, only be shown by some sort of pointing; not stated in a synonymous form of words (the *definiens*). There are two relevant consequences. First, you and I together can know that we are both separately employing the same word 'yellow' in the same sense in describing our peculiar and private sense-data, only in so far as we share access to yellow public objects which can serve as our known and steady common standard. Second, neither of us separately can know that our own usage is from day to day stable and consistent, unless we as individuals have such access to yellow public objects: seeming memories of fleeting private experiences are too weak a foundation for any assurance that our verbal practice is regular.

From none of these semantic and philosophical considerations about colour words are we entitled to infer anything about rods and cones in the retina, or about whether light is a matter of waves or of particles. Equally, discoveries of the second are not rivals to findings of the first sort: my ignorance of physics and physiology does not disqualify me from having an adequate knowledge of the established meanings of ordinary colour words; as well, perhaps, as a rather less commonplace realisation of philosophical presuppositions and implications.

So the problem is to apply our fundamental distinction to the more difficult case of the nature of perception, emphasising as we go that this 'the nature of' terminology is ambiguous as between the two categories of inquiry now being distinguished. Suppose that we ask, 'What is the nature of perception?', construing this question as equivalent to, 'What criteria does something have to satisfy in order to score as a case of perception?'. Then it should be clear, from all that has gone before, that any sufficient answer must include references to an immediate awareness of mind-independent public objects; and to the role of those objects as causally necessary conditions of the awareness. Suppose, that we ask next, 'What is the nature of perception?'; but this time construing that same form of words as synonymous with 'What are the physical and physiological mechanisms through which perception occurs?'. Then it becomes odd indeed either to offer or to accept an answer implying that perception, as previously understood, simply does not, and perhaps could not, occur at all.

What such an answer does is to identify experiences of perceiving with objects of perception. This is the canker at its heart. From a sober recognition that the occurrence or sense-data is essential to perception, it rushes to the wild conclusion that these are its only possible objects. Thus Russell – like Berkeley and the entire Cartesian tradition – insists that "what the physiologist sees", and what everyone else sees, is and can only be sense-data: to believe "that a man can see matter" is a prephilosophical and prescientific superstition. But, on the contrary; it is plain contradictory to speak of anyone perceiving anything but public perceptual objects. When in truth I can perceive a table, or a chair, or some other traditional object of philosophical observation; then certainly I must be having tabular, chair-like, or other appropriate sense-data. But what I can perceive must be the table, the chair, or whatever there is before my senses.

It was – it is perhaps just worth mentioning – by worrying at such abuses of perceptual words, and at the accompanying collapse of the categorical distinction between perception and sensation, that Thomas Reid (1710–1796) became the founder of the Scottish Philosophy of Common Sense. Sensation, he insisted throughout his *Essays on the Intellectual Powers of Man*, is altogether different from perception, precisely because "it hath no object distinct from the act itself. . . . When I am pained, I cannot say that the pain I feel is one thing, and that my feeling is another thing. . . . Pain when not felt has no existence. . . . It cannot exist by itself, nor in any subject but a sentient being" (I (i) 12).

(b)   In the passage quoted at the beginning of this Subsection (iii) Russell employed one particular argument, spelt out earlier: ". . . though you see the Sun now, the physical object to be inferred from your seeing existed eight minutes ago; if in the intervening minutes, the Sun had gone out, you would still be seeing exactly what you are seeing. We cannot, therefore, identify the physical Sun with what we see" (p. 204).

This – recently christened the Time-lag Argument – presents a pretty philosophical puzzle. I offer only two comments. These probably will, and probably should, leave you still dissatisfied. First, our perceptual concepts evolved and are adapted to compass transactions with other people and things on earth; transactions in which the objects of perception are typically accessible to more than one sense. We must, therefore, expect some failures of adaptation when we try to apply these concepts to our dealing with enormously distant and inaccessible phenomena. Back in Section 1 of Chapter 1 I queried the unrecognised Socratic assumption that an adequate analysis of such a notion as justice must yield "a clearcut and correct determination of how it should be applied in all possible cases – including all marginal cases and cases involving unforeseen and perhaps unforeseeable novelities." Perhaps some small adjustment is called for here in order to adapt the ancient concept of seeing to what we now know, but our remote ancestors did not, about the distance and physical nature of the Sun and the stars. If we abandon the requirement that in seeing the seer is directly aware of public perceptual objects, we abandon the concept of seeing. So maybe we ought instead to allow that in, as we now say, seeing any very distant object what we do actually see is not that object but its earthly appearance.

Second, these earthly appearances, though not material things, nevertheless are public perceptual objects. It is precisely in order to allow for such aberrant entities as rainbows, flames, flashes, shadows, and appearances of heavenly bodies in the sky at night – things which presumably do not qualify as solid material things – that I have been careful often to employ the longwinded phrase 'material things and other perceptual objects'. The great, and common, mistake is to argue that, if we are somehow failing to perceive a material thing, then the only alternative is that we are perceiving a sense-datum. In general: talk about how things look or appear is not self-centred and autobiographical. If I claim to discern what looks like a three-phase rocket on its launching pad, then I am concerned with the public world rather than with my private experiences. In particular: if I am to identify that dot as being or being caused by Epsilon Eridani, then I shall no doubt have to make inferences. But those inferences will be from what everyone can see by looking through the same telescope or at the same photographs, not from anything private to myself alone.

CHAPTER IV

Rationalism and empiricism

Chapter III began by sketching the Cartesian programme of systematic doubt, and then ran through the moves by which Descartes hoped to found a new, vastly improved and extended structure of knowledge on the freshly excavated bedrock of one unshakable certainty: "I think, therefore I am." After that most of the chapter dealt with the Veil of Appearance, various attempts to come to terms with that doctrine, and the reasons offered in its support. But Descartes himself disposed of his Problem of the External World in pretty short order, proceeding promptly to develop a mechanical system of nature. Given his assurance of the existence of a good God who – unlike the imagined Evil Demon – "is no deceiver", he believed that he was entitled to conclude that all his natural faculties, and in particular his senses, must be generally reliable.

The mechanical system of nature was in Descartes a system of philosophical rationalism. The word 'rationalism', like the word 'idealism', has a special sense in philosophy. The philosophical rationalist holds that there are self-evident fundamental truths from which it is possible to deduce substantial consequences about the way things have been, are, and always will be. The contrast is with the philosophical empiricist, who holds that all our knowledge of what in fact has been, is, or will be the case must and can only be warranted by our actual experience. The layman expects anyone who calls himself a rationalist to be in religion either agnostic or atheist, whereas most philosophical rationalists have been theists, who based their systems on the conviction that some very important propositions about the existence and nature of God are of this kind which can be known without reference to or dependence upon any observation of what happens to happen in the Universe around us. The empiricist may construe the word 'experience' in either a public or a private sense: indeed, being human, he is apt to slide without noticing or notice from one interpretation to the other.

The rationalism of Descartes comes out in Part V of the *Discourse*. What he says there is clear enough, though summary and muted. It takes the form of references to a treatise called *Le Monde* [The Universe], a treatise which he had prudently suppressed on hearing of the persecution of Galileo. Descartes writes of "knowledge . . . so natural to our minds that no one could ever pretend not to know it"; and, referring to *Le Monde*, he reports that:

"I pointed out what the laws of nature are, and, without basing my arguments on any other principle than the infinite perfections of God, I tried to demonstrate all those about which there could be any doubt, and to show that these laws are such that even if God had created several universes he could not have known how to have one in which they were not observed. . . . And, furthermore, it seems to me that by attending to the logical consequences of these laws I have discovered several truths more useful and more important than everything which I had hoped to learn previously."

1. *Knowledge, error and infallibility*.   Descartes enforced that last statement, as we noticed before, by making the *Discourse* introduce three contributions to science and mathematics. Everything he achieved was supposed to be both produced and guaranteed by the newfound method. And – like almost all philosophical rationalists – he gives indications that this work was inspired by, while yet transcending, mathematics. "I have always remained firm", he wrote in the sentence immediately preceding the passage quoted above, "in my original resolution to postulate no other principle besides the one which I have just used to demonstrate the existence of God and the soul, and not to accept anything as true which did not seem clearer and more certain than the demonstrations of the geometers had done formerly".

(i)   This unique master principle is the criterion of knowledge explained in Section 2 of Chapter III. Seeking in the proposition "I think, therefore I am" for the assurance of its truth: "I concluded that I could take it as a general rule that the things which we conceive quite clearly and quite distinctly are all true . . ." Whatever else may need to be said, whether for or against, it should be obvious at once that this investigative procedure is tailor-made for the rationalist. Any empiricist seeking such a criterion would be bound to look, neither to the proposition itself nor to his own reaction to it, but to the correspondence or lack of correspondence between that proposition and some actual or possible state of affairs.

Next notice that Descartes, like so many of us, is inclined to think that knowledge presupposes infallibility. If this were granted, then indeed we should have: either to reconcile ourselves to the impossibility of knowledge; or else to seek the secret of at least some limited infallibility. Thus in *Meditation III* Descartes making this assumption chooses the second option: "In this first knowledge there is nothing but a clear and distinct perception of what I know; which would not indeed be sufficient to give me a guarantee that this is the truth if it could ever happen that something which I conceived so clearly and distinctly turned out to be false." Again, in the totally different context of his classic libertarian essay *On Liberty*, J. S. Mill agrees with Descartes, but chooses the first option: "All silencing of discussion is an assumption of infallibility. . . . We can never be sure that the opinion we are endeavouring to stifle is a false opinion . . ." (p. 79: Mill does not, however, undertake to defend this thesis of the impossibility of knowledge in his own, widely influential treatise *A System of Logic*).

Now, against the assumption that knowledge implies infallibility, put an argument from another great Victorian, Cardinal Newman (1801–1890). In *A Grammar of Assent* he describes a person who accepted all the particular doctrines taught by the Roman Church at one time, but then found some fresh dogmatic definition more than he bargained for. Such a person, Newman maintains, shows thereby that he has never really been a Catholic. For he clearly never accepted the claims of the Church to infallibility: "He was asked, before he was received, whether he held all that the Church taught, he replied that he did; but he understood the question to mean whether he held those particular doctrines 'which at that time the Church in matter of fact formally taught', whereas it really meant 'whatever the Church then or at any future time should teach'" (VII (2) 5).

The claim simply to know is thus, manifestly, weaker than, and therefore cannot imply, the claim to be infallible. Yet we still have somehow to come to terms with the seemingly compelling contention that if we know then it is not possible for us to be mistaken, that if we know then we cannot be wrong; and hence, it would appear necessarily, that knowledge must imply infallibility. Here we face a typical philosophical antinomy. (It is entirely fitting that the Greeks who first needed, should have had, and then bequeathed to us, the words 'dilemma' and 'antinomy'.) It is precisely from this kind of difficulty that philosophical questions about meanings arise. For in order to untie the knot, we have to ask what knowledge is; what is, and what is not, implied by the claim to know. The first really strenuous attempt to thrash out such questions was made not by some twentieth century Linguistic

Philosopher but by Plato, in the *Theaetetus*. I have cited J. S. Mill and Cardinal Newman here in order to bring out that what may seem remote and frivolous logic-chopping can also be relevant to big issues. To widen the ideological spectrum still further I now quote a statement by Enver Hoxha, the longtime little Stalin of Albania, made several years and one or two line-shifts ago. "Our party", he said, "has made no mistakes, because it has followed the glorious experience of the Communist Party of the Soviet Union; whose Leninist policy has been, and always will be, right."

(ii) One once popular, wrong way to answer questions about meaning is to seek with Descartes a private introspective illumination: I remember a colleague years ago wont, clasping hands over tight-shut eyes, to ask himself whether he could conceive this or that — rather as if he had been straining after a magic sex change. The right way is to examine the correct public usage of all relevant words, this being what determines their meanings in the public language. A good particular method of following this correct general course is to ask what would count as contradictory.

Every proposition must be equivalent to the denial of its contradictory. (For those who like symbolism this logical truth can be rendered as $p \equiv \sim\sim p$ (Def.): where p is any proposition; $\sim$ is read as not; $\equiv$ means is equivalent to; and the parenthesis indicates that it is all a matter of definition.) So, in order to get clearer about the meaning of 'She knows p', we can begin by asking what would show this proposition to be false. Any logically, as opposed to causally, sufficient condition of its falsity must by the same token be the contradictory of a logically, as opposed to causally, necessary condition of its truth; while the meaning of any proposition just is the sum of the logically necessary conditions of its truth.

It is well worth taking a few minutes to master the notions and the distinctions employed in the previous sentence: all are essential for theoretical thinking; while one of the key ideas is continually misunderstood and misrepresented in current practical debate. A causally necessary condition is one without which whatever it may be cannot as a matter of fact occur; notwithstanding that there would be no inconsistency or incoherence in the suggestion that, in another world, things might have been different. If, by contrast, this is a logically necessary condition of that, then to assert that while denying this must be to contradict yourself. Both sorts of necessary condition may be insufficient: this may be causally necessary, or logically necessary, but that may be similarly necessary as well. Especially in the heat of controversy the temptation is to make things so much easier for our side by attributing to an opponent, who has said only that something is necessary, the stronger thesis that it is sufficient. He says, for instance, that state ownership and control of the economy is necessary for establishing the New Jerusalem: we have a field day establishing that it is not sufficient. She maintains that without a pluralist economy there can be no political liberties: we wax irrelevantly indignant because some pluralist economies too are politically authoritarian and illiberal.

(iii)   One most obvious way of contradicting 'She knows p' is to maintain that p is false. If what she claims to know is that Lover Boy will win the Derby, and if Lover Boy does not even run, then it follows that she did not really know. She only 'knew' (in snigger quotes). The truth of the proposition alleged to be known is thus one logically necessary condition of authentic knowledge. A corollary of this is that the term 'know' – along with 'see', 'refute', 'prove', and many others – belongs to a group we might solemnly label Cognitive Achievement Words. Be always on guard against the popular abusages of allowing that these things have been achieved when in fact they have been no more than confidently claimed. Every time some sloppy journalist reports that a corporate spokesperson – liar for a living! – refuted, what in fact he simply without evidence denied, that reporter drops his little drip to erode the essentials of rational discourse. From 'She knows p', p follows necessarily; but from 'She asserted, sweating with conviction, "I know p",' it does not.

The immediate relevance of this is that the first necessary condition of the previous paragraph constitutes the sole but insufficient basis: both of the assumption that knowledge presupposes infallibility; and of the further misconception that knowledge can only be of logically necessary truths. The first of these false and invalidly drawn conclusions is usually mediated through the proposition 'If I know, then I cannot be wrong'. Eventually this is construed as involving that I must, on this condition, be infallible. But initially, when we are being given reason for believing that it is true, it is construed as no more than a less formal restatement of a totally different and much weaker claim: namely, that from 'I know p' it follows necessarily that p. The frequently realised possibility of thus misunderstanding a speech in the material mode, 'If I know, then I cannot be wrong', is, therefore, excellent reason for transposing that speech into a formal mode, 'From "I know p" it follows necessarily that p'. Such transpositions remain often worthwhile not-withstanding that the formal version is by comparison uneasy and stilted.

The second false and invalidly drawn conclusion is product of confusions about what exactly is, or is supposed to be, either necessary or impossible. To sort this out too in a second swift paragraph will be a second crisp object lesson in philosophical method. We are offered the argument: if someone knows p, then it is impossible that p is false; but, if the falsity of p is impossible and the truth of p is necessary, then p must be necessarily true; and so, if p is known, then p must be a necessary truth. Wait a minute: certainly if I know p then, it follows necessarily, p must be true; or, in other words, given that I know p, then, it follows necessarily, it is impossible that p is false. But these are the necessities and impossibilities which qualify inferences from premises to conclusions. They do not refer to the status of those propositions which happen to be serving in these roles. To say that it is impossible to assert that you know p, while denying p, without thereby contradicting yourself, is not at all the same as to say that p itself is logically necessary — that it is impossible to deny p itself without self-contradiction.

We shall later be looking more closely at the perennially persuasive sophism which, thanks to a similar misplacing and misreading of these and other related expressions, proceeds: from a purely tautological premise such as whatever will be, will be; to the formidably substantial conclusion that whatever happens, happens inevitably. Our immediate moral is that, if anyone satisfies the other necessary conditions, and is in fact right, then he does genuinely know. This is sufficient. It is not necessary to be infallible.

(iv) Descartes, however, wanted more. He searched, and searched "in this 'I think, therefore I am'", for a talisman. This talisman had to fulfil a dual specification: it must be impossible for Descartes to misidentify it; and it must be necessary that any proposition sanctified by it is true, and perhaps necessarily true. Since there can be no such cognitive Aladdin's Lamp, we should not be surprised, either that it proves elusive, or that he is unforthcoming. Put briefly, and perhaps too brutally, his "clear and distinct conception (or perception)" is synthesised by collapsing the distinction between a proposition's *being certain* and a person's *feeling certain*. If p is certain, and known; then, it follows necessarily, p is true. If I feel certain; then, about my own feelings, who can say me nay? But, of course, while I may feel as certain as certain can be, p may still be false. By all means let Descartes "take it as a general rule that the things which we conceive quite distinctly are all true". Yet, if that is how it is going to be played, then indeed we must expect "some difficulty about distinguishing properly which are cases which we do conceive distinctly".

It was perhaps some glimmering awareness of the irreparable inadequacy of clear and distinct conception as the unattainable talisman, which sometimes encouraged Descartes to derive its authority from something else: ". . .

after I have discovered that there is a God . . . and that he is no deceiver, and after I have inferred from this that nothing which I clearly and distinctly conceive can fail to be true . . . then I really do have true and certain science". Since the "two truths" which here serve as premises were themselves supposedly established only by the help of precisely this conclusion, it is a desperate manoeuvre. It was first countered by an extremely sympathetic yet no less acute critic, Antoine Arnauld (1612–1694), in the fourth set of solicited 'Objections' to the *Meditations*. Arnauld was later to become, with Pierre Nicole (1625–1695), co-author of the Port-Royal *Logic*, a famous practical treatise on 'The Art of Thinking'. Port-Royal was the Jansenist Convent with which Blaise Pascal (1623–1662) was associated too. The restraint of Arnauld's comment may remind us of James Thurber's cartoon fencer who, having decapitated his opponent, cries only "Touché":

"My one hesitation is about how it is possible to avoid circularity when our author says 'our only guarantee that the things which we clearly and distinctly conceive are true is the fact that God exists'. For our only guarantee that God exists is that we conceive very clearly and distinctly that he does exist. . . ."

2. *The Ontological Argument.* Fortunately, rationalism has no need for the impossible talisman of infallibility which the rationalist Descartes sought, and half-believed that he had found. For rationalism the appropriate criterion of truth is coherence, just as for empiricism it is correspondence. Since the rationalist hopes to deduce a complex system of consequences from a few elementary truths he will be concerned always with logical compatibilities and incompatibilities, rather than with whatever may seem to correspond with the facts of experience: to deduce this from that is, by definition, to show that it must be impossible without self-contradiction to affirm that while denying this. His first problem is to find these elementary truths – truths suitably big with implications – and to show that these basics are themselves necessary; that they are, in as much as they could not be denied without incoherence, self-authenticating.

(i) The history of philosophical rationalism begins, like so much else in philosophy, with Plato; although here we ought not to overlook entirely a prehistoric prelude. Pythagoras flourished in the low 500's BC, and therefore counts as one of the Presocratics. His school, in one of the then Greek coastal cities of Sicily, seems to have been a cross between an Eastern ashram and a

Western research institute: a tabu on the eating of beans cohabited with intellectually rigorous creative speculation. Whether or not he first proved the theorem which now bears his name it was certainly his school, and probably the Master himself, who discovered – presumably by measuring the required lengths of string on a monochord – that the chief musical intervals are expressible in simple numerical ratios between the first four integers: the octave as two to one, the fifth as three to two, and the fourth as four to three.

To us now this does not look an epoch-making discovery. In fact it was. For it was one of those – like Harvey's discovery of the circulation of the blood – which, while important enough in its particular field, was immeasurably more important in the general scope of what it suggested. What Harvey's work suggested was that all organic nature, as well as inorganic, is to be understood in mechanical terms. The suggestion of the modest discovery made – as Plato put it – "by teasing and torturing the strings" was that somehow, *somehow* the secret of the Universe lay in mathematics. The infatuated vision of Pythagoras, mediated to the Founding Fathers through the Platonists of the University of Padua, was to become, surely, one of the reasons why modern theoretical science emerged in Western Europe rather than in China; notwithstanding that China was at that time in almost every field technically more advanced. So Galileo maintains as a key truth that the Book of Nature "is written in the language of mathematics, and its letters are triangles, circles and other geometric figures; without which it is humanly impossible to understand a word of it . . ." (Burtt, p. 64).

It was mathematics which both by action and reaction inspired Plato to formulate a rationalist programme; though, where for Pythagoras it had been arithmetic, for Plato it was geometry. "God", he is said to have said, "is forever doing geometry." Legend also has it that he caused to be inscribed over the entrance of his Academy – the first university – the words: "Let no one enter who is ignorant of geometry". Its attraction for Plato was that the proofs of pure mathematics proceed without reference to the ever changing and – it seemed to him – relatively unreal world of the corporeal. Its deficiency in his eyes lay in the fact that geometry is all hypothetical. Given the various axioms and postulates it all follows necessarily. But what about these, the hypotheses themselves? In *The Republic* Plato outlines, sketchily, a new form of inqury supposedly superior to geometry. This new discipline of Dialectics is to be like mathematics in being both purely deductive and untainted by the empirical. But it is to be superior in that it will first proceed backwards from hypothesis to hypothesis until it reaches some "unhypothetical first principle". Then and only then, on this categorically secure foundation, will it go forward to develop a structure of deductive consequences.

Precisely what Plato meant by Dialectics, and whether indeed he did have any very precise programme in mind, are both, not surprisingly, matters of scholarly dispute. For us it will be enough to fix one minor point and two major. The minor point is that Plato's interest was in some pattern of argument, whereas what Friedrich Engels (1820–1895) paraded in *The Dialectics of Nature* was putative laws of universal change.

The first major point is that Plato appears to have expected that his dialecticians would eventually demonstrate the truth of geometrical hypotheses. Like all the other great philosophical rationalists he lived before the development and acceptance of any non-Euclidian systems. So it was natural for him to assume that even pure geometry must somehow correspond to, and report, facts about some reality. Maybe this reality is special mathematical objects like yet unlike his Ideas, or maybe it is the nature of space. Plato's rationalist hope was that something resembling what Euclid would later systematise, yet crucially better, could compass a far wider range of necessary truths. Only after the Russian N. I. Lobachevsky (1793–1856) and the Hungarian J. Bolyai (1802–1860) had produced their self-consistent systems of geometry, from axioms and postulates in sum inconsistent with those of Euclid, did it become at all easy to accept that a pure geometry is not a collection of true descriptions. The mathematical achievement here is another of those discoveries more important in their wider implications than in themselves. These refer not only to the main inspiration of philosophical rationalism but also to the nature of mathematics itself. Of the latter the best epitome is provided by Einstein, the first to find physical application for a non-Euclidean geometry: "As far as the laws of mathematics refer to reality, they are not certain; and as far as they are certain, they do not refer to reality" (Schilpp, p. 380).

The second important observation is that Plato fails to make clear what might serve as his "unhypothetical first principle", and how. Certainly he would like to have this key role played by his super-Form or super-Idea of the Good and the Real. Nevertheless, and very understandably, he is overcome by reverence when it is time to tell us how that could do what is required. With the benefit of hindsight we can see a gap in the works; and it is a gap shaped like the Ontological Argument.

(ii) This was in fact only invented centuries later, by St Anselm

(1033–1109). He was effectively criticised by a contemporary monk Gaunilo. Aquinas in the *Summa Theologica* in the context of his presentation of the Five Ways rejected the argument; albeit in a fashion which seems to some critics ambivalent. It was reintroduced by Descartes, making no acknowledgement to any predecessors, and it was Descartes who first put it to the rationalist use for which it might have been designed. The argument moves straight from the concept of God to the conclusion that this concept is one which necessarily must have application, that God must exist. Furthermore, this is not just a case of a conclusion which follows necessarily. That conclusion itself is taken to be self-evident and necessary. To deny the existence of the God so conceived would be, the contention is, to contradict yourself.

Suppose that you are not already inclined, whether on other grounds or on no grounds at all, to accept this conclusion. And suppose too that you meet the argument represented in a formal mode of speech. Then you will likely find it hard to feel any force in the argument, or to understand how it could have gripped minds of the calibre of Anselm and Descartes, Leibniz and Spinoza. If that is your situation, then there is nothing for it but to try to make sympathetic allowances for theirs. Nor must any of us, in any situation, ignore the enormous attraction of the premise and conclusion of the Ontological Argument for anyone of a naturally rationalist cast of mind. Given that the existence of an all-powerful, all-wise, all-perfect Being is a self-evident and necessary truth; then, surely, whether with or without the help of one or two other powerful premises, it must be possible to draw out innumerable consequences, all themselves in the last analysis similarly necessary, for how all things must have been and must be. Even for those fully persuaded that their entire enterprise is radically misconceived, the great metaphysical visions expressed in the *Monadology* of Leibniz and in Spinoza's *Ethics* can hold abiding fascination. So read now the Ontological Argument as Descartes urges it in Part IV of the *Discourse*:

"After that I wanted to seek for other truths and I put my mind to the subject matter of the geometers. . . . I saw clearly that, given a triangle, then necessarily its three angles must be equal to two right angles. But none of this gave me any reason to believe that any triangle existed in the world. However, on reverting to the examination of the idea which I had of a perfect Being I found that existence was comprised in the idea in the way that that of a triangle contains the equality of its three angles to two right angles. . . . And so, consequently, it is at least as certain that God —

this Perfect Being – is, or exists, as any demonstration of geometry could possibly be."

Something has gone very wrong. But we do not want just to know that this is so, nor even just to show that this is so. Our business is to learn whatever wider philosophical lessons there are here to be had. The first is the importance of discovering and employing a good notation. If you feel inclined to dismiss this as something trivial and insubstantial – 'a matter of mere words' – then attempt two exercises. First, write down two large numbers in Roman numerals, one below the other. Now multiply the other by the one. Second, try to give or to follow a description of an even modestly complex chemical transformation in words only, without resort to the familiar symbolism. Now, was the purely notational part of the Arab contribution to arithmetic, or of the contribution of Berzelius to chemistry, trivial and insubstantial?

Both Gaunilo and Aquinas saw the deductive move from existence in thought to actual existence as both crucial and illegitimate. Kant contrasted "100 possible thalers" (dollars) with "100 real thalers", ruefully reflecting that nothing but the latter would improve his financial position. In order to sharpen the contrast still further, and to neutralise any devout tendency to treat the mere concept of God with the uncritical respect rendered to an actual God, it is best to discuss: first, definitions of the term 'God'; then whether there is in fact anything corresponding to the term when it is defined so, or when it is defined thus. Descartes stands revealed as operating with a definition which includes existence as one of the characteristics which something has got to have if it is to qualify as, in this sense, God. Clearly, if anything satisfies this Cartesian definition, then it must be a logically necessary Being: there will, that is to say, be a contradiction between this definitional specification and the denial of the existence of the Being so defined.

This, however, does nothing to meet the point that it is wholly wrong to treat existence as on all fours with any run of the mill characteristic; to hold with Descartes, for instance, that it could be one of a series of defining "perfections". This second main lesson is one which Kant opened in the first *Critique*: "*Being* is obviously not a real predicate. . . ." (If someone says that X is Φ this performance can also be described as predicating Φ of X.) Regrettably, from the flash of insight just quoted, Kant proceeded, in a fashion which was to prove ominous, to confound the possibly redundant *is* of predication, as in 'The cat is fat', with the *is* of existence, as in 'There is a cat'.

105

(Classical Chinese seems to get by without any equivalent of the former, whereas no natural language dispenses with methods of asserting existence.) So Kant concludes: "Logically it is merely the copula of a judgement" (A598: B626).

Philosophers since Kant have adopted many devices for bringing out the fundamental difference: between existential assertions; and the ordinary attribution of predicates to subjects already presumed to exist. The most charming was G. E. Moore's contrasting of 'Some tame tigers growl, and some do not' with 'Some tame tigers exist, and some do not'. Yet for present purposes it should be enough to demand a form of presentation underlining the huge difference between definitional manoeuvres and factual investigations. Even if the manoeuvre of intruding 'and exists' into a definition of the term 'God' were to be allowed, Descartes would still be left with the old problem of showing that in fact there is a Being satisfying the complete specification — a problem inevitably made more acute by every additional requirement.

3. *Rationalist systems*.   Before passing to empiricism a brief word must be said — and it does have to be extremely brief — about some of the great rationalist systems. Plato never succeeded, nor in the end wished to succeed, in developing such a system. But his dialectics was in *The Republic* the discipline through which the Guardians were to acquire their knowledge of the Forms; and that, as we saw in Chapter II, was what was to give them authority to exercise absolute power. The parallel between this, and the appeal to the very different Marxist kind of dialectics to justify the absolute power of a ruling Leninist elite, is remarkable.

(i)   Descartes did develop a system. It was in large part a system of mathematical physics. But it was one where, he believed, all the principles are by his clear and distinct conception guaranteed as absolutely necessary: ". . . these laws are such that even if God had created several universes he could not have known how to have one in which they were not observed. . . ." No doubt Descartes was wrong about this. For, although there is plenty of room and need for deduction in any science, natural laws must be logically contingent. Being wrong about this, however, was entirely consistent with making major contributions to the growth of modern theoretical physics. However, whereas the undermining and the reconstruction of the foundations in the *Discourse* and the *Meditations* are part of philosophy, those contributions belong to the history of science.

(ii)   Like Descartes, the German Leibniz was a creative mathematician of the first rank. In a notorious controversy he was able to challenge Newton's claim to priority in the invention of the Infinitesimal Calculus. Throughout a multifariously active life Leibniz always wanted to seem, and perhaps even to be, an ecumenical Christian. He was, therefore, forever embarrassed by the difficulties of reconciling, his rationalist vision of the apriori necessity of everything, with the orthodox doctrine that the whole creation is a gratuitous expression of the Divine Will. There must be, by the Principle of Sufficient Reason, a sufficient reason for everything – including every actual Divince choice; and furthermore, by the Principle of the Identity of Indiscernibles, if there were no discernible difference between two options to provide ground for that sufficient reason, then there could not really be two options. Given, by the Ontological Argument, that it is a logically necessary truth that there must be a Being combining all perfections – all power and all goodness – then, surely, this God necessarily must create all other compossible goods; all other goods, that is to say, which could without contradiction be said to exist simultaneously?

This being so our world must be the best of all possible worlds. Manifestly it is not. But, since the existence of such a God is a necessary truth, and cannot be denied, Leibniz sets himself to demonstrate that every evil which might mislead anyone to deny it must in truth be the logically necessary precondition of some actual higher good; as the occurrence of an injury to be forgiven is the logically necessary, but not sufficient, condition of the occurrence of an act of forgiving. The *Theodicy* – a book whose title has since given a new word to several languages – was one of the few items from a mass of always lucid writing which Leibniz published in his own lifetime. The general theme of "the best of all possible worlds", and such particular movements as "The work most worthy of the wisdom of God involves . . . the eternal damnation of the majority of men" (§ 236.), provoked the finest satire of Voltaire, *Candide*.

Most distinctively, Leibniz argued that the Universe must consist of "simple substances, without parts". These are called monads; hence the *Monadology*. The idea of atoms of matter he dismissed as incoherent, arguing that anything which has any size at all must be further divisible. This argument parallels his proof that the suggestion of a fastest possible motion must be similarly incoherent. His reason there was that, whatever the speed of a spot on a revolving axle, the speed of a dot on the circumferance of the wheel must be greater. (In both cases the modern critic, as we shall be seeing later, wants to distinguish two senses of 'impossibility'.) These monads are naturally indestructible, immaterial, and without spatial or temporal position. Above all they have no relations one with another. The experience and activity of each is a necessary consequence of its own essential nature. The actual correlations between the entirely independent experience and activity of these completely non-communicating creatures is a matter of a Divinely "preestablished harmony". It sounds wild. Yet Leibniz always has a reason, sometimes several reasons, for every move.

One pervasive drive is what appears to be a primal metaphysical urge to put down anything relative or relational as ultimately unreal. We met this already in Chapter II, in Berkeley's just obvious remark that relations are by everyone "allowed to exist nowhere without the mind". For Leibniz, the outstanding logician of his day, this metaphysical conclusion must have seemed inescapable. It had been built into the structure of the traditional formal logic, as we see from the builder Aristotle's statement in the *Prior Analytics*: ". . . every premise is of the form which says that some predicate either does or must or may apply to some subject" (25A1–3).

This might be unexceptionable if it was to be construed as a grammatical remark — or should it be syntactical? — about correctly formed sentences in most Indo-European languages. Interpreted, as it was meant, as a logical thesis it must fall before the overwhelming objection that it takes no account of any propositions stating that relations obtain. For instance: the logical subject — as opposed to the grammatical or syntactical subject — of the proposition 'New York is to the north of Buenos Aires' is as much or as little Buenos Aires as it is New York. For this proposition is equivalent to, it entails and is entailed by, 'Buenos Aires is to the south of New York.' One main achievement of the great logical revolution of the nineteenth century, consolidated in the last years before World War I in the *Principia Mathematica* of Russell and Whitehead, was to provide a place in the sun for relations. Another, profiting from the development and later devastation of the Ontological Argument, was to entrench into the symbolism the radical peculiarity of existential assertions.

(iii)   Unlike Leibniz, Baruch Spinoza (1632–1677) was not inhibited by hangups of religious orthodoxy. At an early age dangerous thoughts earned his expulsion from the Synagogue of Amsterdam. His *Ethics* suppressed for posthumous publication, consists of definitions, axioms and theorems, arranged "in geometrical fashion". It contains not ethics only but a complete and rigorous intellectual world-system. He called it the *Ethics* because he saw his master problem always as the discovery of "the life of blessedness for man", yielding the supreme and eternal joy of "the intellectual love of God".

All this, however, is still misleading. The God he thought to prove by his Ontological Argument was in truth Nature: the key tag is "God or Nature", often quoted in the original Latin *"Deus sive Natura"*. What he means by "the intellectual love of God" is joyous awareness of the supposed absolute necessity of everything.

A curious mixture of profoundly religious temperament and terminology with totally secular and this-worldly doctrine runs right through Spinoza's works. It is neither surprising nor unfitting that both he and they continue to have a dual influence: hailed by some as "the God-intoxicated man", he is by others, particularly the handful of Soviet philosophical scholars, admired as one of the main sources of modern atheist materialism.

Spinoza's systematic employment of hallowed phrases from his Talmudic childhood in idiosyncratic senses will serve as a textbook example of what our American contemporary C. L. Stevenson (Born 1908) usefully labelled Persuasive Definition. There may, for example, be no question of free and contested elections in the Democratic Republic of Vietnam. Nevertheless – be persuaded – it is a true and real democracy. For does not the Leninist party ensure that what it determines to be the interests of what it recognises to be the people always prevail? Adolf Hitler too had his reasons for shouting that not international but National Socialism is true democracy! In philosophy another and Classical example is Plato's labouring effort in Book IX of *The Republic* to prove that the only true and real pleasures are those of approved activities. In a nutshell, the aim of all persuasive definition is, usually with some reason given, to redirect the favourable or, as the case may be, unfavourable responses and attitudes psychologically associated with the term so redefined.

Like Leibniz, Spinoza drew, from an analysis of his concept of God or Nature, the conclusion that every (compossible) possibility of existence must be realised. This is "the principle of plenitude" (Lovejoy, p. 52): its long history, in both philosophy and poetry, began to falter only as the word went round that innumerable species which once were are now extinct. The relevant passage from Part I of the *Ethics*, to be savoured slowly, gives a sample of the austere intellectual flavour of high rationalism. No harm will come here of equating the essence of something with the definition of the word for that something:

"Proposition XVI. From the necessity of the Divine nature must follow an infinite number of things in infinite ways – all things, in fact, which can be conceived by an infinite intellect.

Proof. This proposition should be clear to everyone who remembers that from the definition given to anything the intellect infers several properties which actually follow from it necessarily – that is, from the very essence of the thing. And it infers more properties in proportion as the essence of the thing defined contains more reality. Hence, since the Divine nature possesses absolutely infinite attributes (by Definition vi), of which each also expresses infinite essence in its own kind, from the necessity of that nature there must therefore follow necessarily an infinite number of things in infinite ways – all things in fact, which can be conceived by an infinite intellect. Q.E.D."

Especially after that it will be interesting, and perhaps helpful, to review the same ideas in a poet. Alexander Pope in the *Essay on Man* sings in a strain perhaps strictly more Leibnizian than Spinozist:

> "Of systems possible, if 'tis confess'd,
> That Wisdom infinite must form the best,
> Where all must fall, or not coherent be,
> And all that rises rise in due degree. . . .
>
> Vast chain of being! which from God began,
> Natives ethereal, human, angel, man
> Beast, bird, fish, insect, what no eye can see,
> No glass can reach; from infinite to thee,
> From thee to nothing" (I 43–6 and 1237–41)

(iv) The *Tractatus Logico-Philosophicus* of the Austrian Ludwig Wittgenstein (1889–1951) was first published, in German only, as *Logisch-Philosophische Abhandlung*. Its present title was the imaginative suggestion of G. E. Moore, made during the production of the Authorised Version, with English facing the German, in allusion to the *Tractatus Theologico-Politicus* of Spinoza. Wittgenstein as an adult held none of the theist and immortalist beliefs of his Roman Catholic upbringing. Nevertheless it was natural to say of him as of Spinoza that his temperament was profoundly religious, and many of Wittgenstein's closest associates were or became Roman Catholic converts. Though not laid out "in geometrical fashion" his *Tractatus* is divided into very short sections, most of a single often aphoristic sentence, and all numbered to indicate their logical separations and subordinations. Again, though Wittgenstein insists that all the necessary truths of logic and mathematics are tautological and uninformative, and hence must reject the possibility of any rationalist system, what he here provides nevertheless is in one aspect a system of metaphysics; an account of all that can possibly be said and, correspondingly, of all that can, ultimately, exist. Furthermore, although at the end of the *Tractatus* we are told that nothing which has been said really can be said, and although its final and conclusive proposition is "Whereof one cannot speak, thereof one must be silent"; at the beginning the author's Preface says, with no hesitation, that "the *truth* of the thoughts communicated here seems to me unassailable and definitive" (pp. 189 and 29: italics in the English translation only). No wonder that Moore was reminded of Spinoza's Letter LXXVI: "I do not presume to have discovered the best philosophy; but I know that I understand the true one" !

The *Tractatus*, like the *Ethics*, is a desperately difficult work. Wittgenstein insists on expressing a wide-ranging and original world-view in a pemmican volume of some twenty thousand often cryptic, elliptical, dogmatic, and technical words. What he is doing, in effect, is to take the new symbolic logic developed in *Principia Mathematica* as the necessary framework of all possible language; and to presume that the structure of the Universe — or, at any rate, of the knowable Universe — must ultimately correspond to the structure of that logic. In this aspect the *Tractatus* stands alongside Russell's own metaphysical manifesto, the 1918 lectures on 'The Philosophy of Logical Atomism'.

Again Wittgenstein, like the German mathematical philosopher Gottlob Frege (1848–1925), demanded that we attend to the logical as opposed to the psychological, to the semantic aspects of the employment of words and symbols as opposed to any psychological accompaniments of that employment. Hence the solemn snide acknowledgement in the Preface: "that to the great works of Frege and the writings of my friend Bertrand Russell I owe in large measure the stimulation of my thoughts" (p. 29).

Hence too Wittgenstein's own development in his second philosophical period, when he returned to settle permanently in Cambridge. In *The Blue and Brown Books* he argued with simple illustration after simple illustration — his days of "reasoning high" were over now — that the meanings of our words are, and can only be, determined by their public use, by the job they do; and therefore, ultimately, by their public usage, by the ways in which people employ them. In particular he attacked the notion that the meaning of a word could be some element of private experience, some kind of mental image. For example: the criterion for whether the pupil has understood the lesson is whether understanding is shown in public exercises, not whether in fact there occurred a 'click' of illumination private to the pupil alone. The

111

meaning of the word 'understand', therefore, is to be explained in terms not of the having of such experiences but of the becoming or being able to perform such exercises.

In the *Philosophical Investigations* Wittgenstein, while scarcely mentioning Descartes or any other predecessor, launches what is in fact a sustained onslaught upon a hidden and never previously questioned presupposition of the whole Cartesian tradition. This is the always unstated assumption that it would be possible for there to be a language, which could be understood by at least one person, and all the words in which would be definable in terms of that person's private experience. This is now known as the assumption of the possibility of a logically private language. The contrast is with a contingently private language, such as that which enabled Locke, in the lean years before the Glorious Revolution, to keep the contents of his political papers secret from inquisitive agents of Stuart oppression: there is no difficulty in principle about translating back, as in our time Locke scholars have succeeded in doing, from a contingently private language into everyday English. In so emphasising, and in educing implications of, the essentially social nature of all language Wittgenstein in his final phase became peculiarly a philosopher to the sociologists.

But these later works expressed no particular metaphysics, and drew out no consequences for a general world outlook. The *Tractatus* is different. As Wittgenstein works up towards his conclusions on "The right method of philosophy" and the necessity of silence, he has something to say about matters of life and death. (I quote always from the Authorised Version, since the retranslators of the Revised Version for small gains in accuracy sacrificed all the literary power of the original.):

". . . in death, too, the world does not change, but ceases. Death is not an event in life. Death is not lived through. If by eternity is understood not endless temporal duration but timelessness, then he lives eternally who lives in the present. Our life is endless in the way that our visual field is without limit" (pp. 187 and 185).

4. *Hume's Fork.* The principle that conclusions about what *ought* to be cannot be deduced from premises stating only what *is*, is sometimes called Hume's Law. His employment of another distinction between fundamentally different kinds of proposition is now often nicknamed Hume's Fork. It is important to realise in both cases that the point is: not that every statement

actually made expresses some proposition falling unequivocally into one or other of these contrasting categories; but rather that we need always to be aware and to take account of the distinction upon which Hume is insisting.

Much the same applies to the Law of the Excluded Middle and to the Law of Non-contradiction. The claim that there can be no middle way between that and not-that, the contention that nothing can be at one and the same time and in the same respect both this and not-this, are to be understood more as prescriptive laws for good thinking than as descriptive laws of actual thought. Certainly, if you ask whether some vague, muddled, ambiguous, or otherwise inadequate phrase describes some situation, then the only possible direct answer may be: 'It does, and yet it does not.' Certainly also, people all too often do believe and assert incompatibles. Yet it is only in so far as respect is shown for consistency that any thought at all, even bad thought, can proceed: there can indeed be no language of any kind save in so far as there are respected rules determining when its words or other elements are and are not correctly applicable. These laws of thought, therefore, are to be both understood and cherished, partly as partly defining the essential nature of thought, and partly as prescribing hypothetical imperatives for all those concerned for clarity and truth.

(i) Hume published his great *Treatise* anonymously, and before he was thirty. He later became very dissatisfied, and in the end formally disowned it. In his late thirties, when he had won a reputation with political and general essays, he produced the two *Inquiries* over his own name. His aim was to represent in an improved, more palatable form whatever materials from the *Treatise* he still considered fit for salvage. Hume's Fork was an instrument fully fashioned only in the first *Inquiry*:

"All the objects of human reason or inquiry may naturally be divided into two kinds, to wit, relations of ideas, and matters of fact. Of the first kind are the sciences of geometry, algebra and arithmetic; and, in short, every affirmation which is either intuitively or demonstratively certain. 'That the square of the hypotenuse is equal to the square of the two sides', is a proposition which expresses a relation between these figures. 'That three times five is equal to the half of thirty', expresses a relation between these numbers. Propositions of this kind are discoverable by the mere operation of thought, without dependence on what is anywhere existent in the Universe. Though there never were a circle or triangle in nature, the truths demonstrated by Euclid would for ever retain their certainty and evidence.

113

Matters of fact, which are the second objects of human reason, are not ascertained in the same manner; nor is our evidence of their truth, however great, of a like nature with the foregoing. The contrary of every matter of fact is still possible; because it can never imply a contradiction, and is conceived by the mind with the same facility and distinctness, as if ever so conformable to reality. 'That the Sun will not rise tomorrow' is no less intelligible a proposition, and implies no more contradiction, than the affirmation, 'That it will rise'" (IV (i)).

If all propositions must indeed be of one or other of these two kinds, then the rationalist hope has to be without foundation. For it follows that there can be no premises of the kind required: it is not the case "that there are self-evident and non-tautological truths from which it is possible to deduce substantial consequences about the way things have been, are, and always will be". So, wielding his absolute weapon against the foundations of rationalism, Hume incisively rejects the principle of the Ontological Argument:

"Whatever *is* may *not be*. No negation of a fact can involve a contradiction. The non-existence of any being, without exception, is as clear and distinct an idea as its existence. . . . that Caesar, or the angel Gabriel, or any being, never existed, may be a false proposition, but still is perfectly conceivable, and implies no contradiction" (XII (iii).

Hume exulted here in the promise of intellectual devastation. It was the same promise which later fired the Logical Positivists of the Vienna Circle, and that promise was for them grounded on a revised version of Hume's Fork. Their Positivism had very little to do with the Positive Philosophy of Auguste Comte (1798–1857). They were a group of scientifically-minded philosophers and philosophically minded scientists who gathered round the Austrian Moritz Schlick (1882–1936) in the twenties and the thirties – until they were dispersed into exile by the advancing forces of National Socialism. The most brilliant exposition of Logical Positivism is Sir Alfred Ayer's *Language, Truth and Logic*, and its most elaborate development is the life's work of Rudolf Carnap. The basic uniting doctrine was the Verification Principle. This was first formulated as the statement that the meaning of any statement lies in its method of verification, although many qualifications were later made in hopes of meeting objections. It was immediately added that all significant assertions, satisfying this principle, must be either contingent, synthetic, and verifiable in experience; or necessary, analytic, and verifiable, whether immediately or ultimately, by appeal to the meaning of words and symbols. The former can be known to be true, if at all, only aposteriori; the latter apriori.

The first of these two Logical Positivist categories embraces Hume's propositions stating, or purporting to state, matters of fact and real existence. ('Real' is here opposed to 'in the mind' or 'in idea'.) The second covers Hume's propositions stating, or pretending to state, the relations of ideas. The terms 'apriori' and 'aposteriori' were introduced into English by Berkeley; and they refer here to what can, and what cannot, be known without dependence on experience. (Both are usually written or printed as two words, and italicized as aliens. But I am resolved to establish a different practice: a quarter of a millenium is too long to discriminate in that way against useful immigrants.)

The terms 'analytic' and 'synthetic' were introduced into philosophy by Kant. He defined an analytic judgement (not proposition) as one in which the idea of the predicate is already contained in that of the subject; whereas in a synthetic judgement the predicate adds something to the subject. These definitions provide another interesting incidental indication of the hold upon a powerful and original mind of the assumptions of the traditional subject/predicate logic. But the present point is that they also suggest, what surely proves to be the case, that Kant's true criterion for his distinction is psychological. For him the crux was, it seems: not whether there would be a contradiction or some other kind of absurdity in denying the proposition; but whether the person actually uttering the subject words had the predicate idea in mind.

Using this criterion and this distinction, Kant argued that he had found a middle way between the prongs of Hume's Fork. All the truths of mathematics, certain fundamentals of Newtonian science, and most of the results of his own philosophical investigations, populated and adorned a third category. They are both synthetic and apriori. The Logical Positivists preferred a logical criterion, and their consequent distinction left no room for any middle way. A proposition is analytic: if it can be known apriori from a logical analysis of the meanings and implications of its terms; and if — which amounts to the same thing — it would be contradictory to deny it. So, if it is not analytic, then it must be synthetic; but never apriori. Freshly equipped with their supertuned Vienna version of Hume's Fork the Logical Positivists were ready to renew his peroratory purge. (The adjectival 'school', by the way, refers here to Scholasticism — the philosophy of the medieval schools, or universities.):

115

"When we run over libraries, persuaded of these principles, what havoc must we make? If we take in our hand any volume – of divinity or school metaphysics, for instance – let us ask, 'Does it contain any abstract reasoning concerning quantity or number?' No. 'Does it contain any experimental reasoning concerning matter of fact and existence?' No. Commit it then to the flames; for it can contain nothing but sophistry and illusion" (XII (iii)).

(ii)   The logical account of pure mathematics in the first *Inquiry* is totally different from its psychological predecessor in the *Treatise*. It also includes a seminal paragraph, with no ancestor in the earlier book, on what Hume, following Francis Bacon (1561–1626), called "mixed mathematics". What Hume wanted to show was that the operations of a calculus cannot generate any conclusions not already implicit in the premises to which that calculus is applied. Certainly the natural philosophers, the physicists, find the products of the mathematicians indispensably useful. Yet doing the mathematics never provides the physicists with any information which is not, in some form, available to them already:

"Nor is geometry, when taken into the assistance of natural philosophy, ever able to remedy this defect . . . by all that accuracy of reasoning for which it is so justly celebrated. Every part of mixed mathematics proceeds upon the supposition that certain laws are established by nature in her operations; and abstract reasonings are employed . . . to determine their influence in particular instances, where it depends upon any precise degree of distance and quantity" (IV (i)).

Had Hume been writing today he would have wanted to make his point about computers. For a computer is a device for getting calculations made mechanically or, nowadays, electronically. It is, therefore, inherently impossible to get out more or other than is put in. Notoriously it is utterly wrong, although still lamentably common, to pay to the computer a respect which would not be yielded to the mere people who write the programmes and feed in the data. This, we are told, is 'what the computer says will happen by the year 2000'. Perhaps; but only if it was fed the correct data, and programmed to make the right assumptions. As the hard men say around the HQ of IBM: 'Garbage produces only garbage.'

(a)   Two more matters need to be elucidated before we go on to the next section. The first is the difference between a proposition of pure mathematics, and any of the applications of that piece of pure mathematics. The

116

former could not be refuted — could not, that is, be not just said but shown to be wrong — by any conceivable occurrence. " 'That three times five is equal to the half of thirty' expresses a relation between these numbers." Or, to put it in a perhaps slightly better way, given the axioms and the definitions of the pure calculus of arithmetic, this follows necessarily. It can be known "by the mere operation of thought, without dependence on what is anywhere existent in the universe".

The educational psychologist might well object to this that no one could possibly learn anything of the sort unless they had something like a kindergarten training in counting out, separating, and putting together collections of beads. So the historian of science, hearing Hume's other example, might want to tell us that Egyptian land-tax assessors had after a fashion grasped the truth of the Theorem of Pythagoras long before that man of genius and legend ever thought to try to prove it. Be such things as they may. They are wholly irrelevant to the present distinction between apriori and aposteriori knowledge. For they refer to the context of discovery; to how in fact these things were, and perhaps had to be, first discovered. But the present distinction refers to the context of justification, to the meaning and implications of what is being said, and to how it could and can be known to be true.

Let us simplify the example: given the axioms and definitions of arithmetic, then to deny that $1 + 1 = 2$ is to contradict yourself. This is an egregiously elementary item of apriori knowledge, falling into Hume's first category. Now apply it, by substituting 'put together' for the plus, 'the result will be' for the equals, and construing the numerals as referring to countable and actual objects. What emerges is a proposition of Hume's second category. Is it true? Only experience can tell, and experience of the sorts of things which we have made it a proposition about. If you are now talking about drops of water, or suitably large lumps of uranium 235, then you will find that it is false.

(b) Second: whereas anything which is by the psychological criterion analytic is bound to seem empty and trivial; what is by the logical criterion analytic may be surprising, difficult, important, even exciting. In Chapter II I illustrated the distinction between logically necessary and logically contingent propositions with two examples: the first a tautological truism from Shakespeare's *Hamlet*; the second a factitious falsism from the sociologist's. That first example is analytic whichever criterion you choose to use, whichever distinction you choose to make. But this is not true of mathematics, nor of many other disputed cases. Even if all mathematics is analytic in the logical interpretation, for most of us in the psychological interpretation precious little can be. If God were, as Plato claimed, forever doing geometry then he must, presumably, suffer excruciating boredom. Yet for finite creatures it can be a fascinating activity. The proposed psychological corollaries in the *Tractatus* are not, therefore, validly drawn:

> "The propositions of logic are tautologies. The propositions of logic therefore say nothing. (They are the analytical propositons). . . . Hence there can *never* be surprises in logic. . . . In logic process and results are equivalent. (Therefore no surprises). . . . Mathematics is a logical method. The propositions of mathematics are equations, and therefore pseudo-propositions. Mathematical propositions express no thoughts" (pp. 155, 165, 167 and 169: italics in the English translation only).

5. *The nature of causal necessity.*   Having fashioned a fresh philosophical instrument Hume at once puts it to two further uses. These are to illuminate the nature, in particular of causal necessity, and in general of all argument from experience. His great negative point about causation is that we can apriori know nothing of causes: neither, quite generally, that everything which occurs must have its cause; nor, more particularly, that certain things or sorts of things either must be or cannot be causes of other things or sorts of things. These conclusions Hume enforces with the argument that there is no contradiction in suggesting, either that something might occur uncaused, or that anything might have been the cause of anything. The more basic of these two aspects of his thesis Hume makes explicit only in the *Treatise*; where he offers one of those illustrations so apt, so simple, and so compelling that it becomes itself part of the progress of philosophy. 'That every husband must have a wife' is a logically necessary truth. 'That every man or woman must be married' is not. 'That every effect must have its cause' is a logically necessary truth. 'That every event must have its cause' is not. (Another tolerably relevant case of the example which is both memorable and itself decisive was offered by Descartes to distinguish what may be conceived – thought or said significantly and without self-contradiction – from what may be imagined – that of which, in his reading, we can both form and know that we have formed a mental image. A chiliagon, a figure of a thousand sides, can be conceived; but no one could ever know that a mental image had just so many sides, and no more or fewer.)

The less basic point Hume makes in the paragraph of the first *Inquiry*

118

immediately following the second passage quoted in Subsection (i) of the previous Section 4:

"The existence, therefore, of any being can only be proved by arguments from its cause or its effect; and the arguments are founded entirely on experience. If we reason apriori anything may appear able to produce anything. The falling of a pebble may, for aught we know, extinguish the Sun; or the wish of man control the planets in their orbits. It is only experience, which teaches us the nature and bounds of cause and effect, and enables us to infer the existence of one object from that of another. Such is the foundation of . . . the greater part of human knowledge, and . . . the source of human action and behaviour" (XII (iii)).

(i)   Insisting thus that it is conceivable that anything might be the cause of anything, even that something might occur altogether without a cause, what is Hume going to say positively about causation? Above all what is he going to say about the surely familiar facts: that both professional scientists and the rest of us laymen do discover causal connections; and that sufficient physical causes always necessitate their effects while making anything else impossible? I will take some small simplifying liberties in order to package Hume's answer in handy takeaway form.

For Hume the heart of the matter was that there just are not any real connections or objective necessities in the external world. We impose these ideas on things, ideas which are nothing but projections of our feelings and our habits. This supposed discovery slotted smoothly into the whole project of *A Treatise of Human Nature*. Hume saw this work as a contribution to an emerging science of man. In the Introduction he promises that discoveries here — the booty of a "march up directly to the capital" — must lead to "changes and improvements" throughout the entire republic of learning. Our Chapter II showed Hume claiming to have discovered that value too is a projection, and compared this conception — as he did — with the then consensus among the natural scientists that ideas of secondary qualities are similarly projected out onto a world which does not actually possess such qualities. In the case of causation the projection is connected with the associations of ideas or, as Hume should say, the associations of ideas and of impressions. For Hume this makes his account of the psychology of causal thinking a big stride towards the fulfilment of an ambition — later shared by a long series of successors — to be, or at least to prepare the way for, 'the Newton of the human sciences'. The picture here was of a Cartesian categorial division between consciousness and stuff: the established principles of classical mechanics comprehensively determined all transactions between bits of stuff; the psychology to be constructed would similarly determine, through various principles of the association of ideas, all transactions between the atoms of experience.

So what Hume says is that all the external world really contains is constant conjunctions: events of this sort are regularly followed by events of that sort. We notice these constant conjunctions, and form strong habits associating the ideas of this with the ideas of that. In thinking of real connections out there, we are mistakenly projecting our own internal psychological associations; while our ideas of practical necessity and practical impossibility are nothing but projections of the felt force of these habits.

(ii) What Hume has to say here about associations and the felt force of habit may or may not constitute a considerable contribution to psychology. If, however, it is to be entertained as any kind of account of meaning, then it will have to stand: not as an analysis of the present interpretation of causal propositions; but as a revisionist proposal for the new employments which the words concerned should be given once we have allowed Hume to teach us what is what. For it is just not on at all to maintain that a claim that the cause of the trouble is sand in the magneto, could be decisively falsified by establishing that no one had or felt any particular associations of ideas, and could not be quite adequately confirmed by a mechanical demonstration.

Hume's scepticism about causation, along with his agnosticism about the external world, is of course jettisoned the moment he leaves his study. There is a famous purple passage in the *Treatise* where he compares: "that forelorn solitude, in which I am plac'd in my philosophy . . . some strange uncouth monster . . . expell'd all human commerce, and left utterly abandon'd and disconsolate"; with the return to companionable commonsense when "I dine, I play a game of back-gammon, I converse, and am merry with my friends" (I (iv) 7). Indeed Hume jettisons all his most radical scepticism even before he leaves his study. There is, for instance, no trace of the thesis that causal connections and necessities are nothing but false projections onto nature in the notorious section 'Of Miracles' in the first *Inquiry*. Hume does not scruple there to argue the difficulties, amounting in the most important case to the impossibility, of establishing upon historical evidence the occurrence of a miracle: difficulties – or an impossibility – arising because a miracle has for the purposes of natural theology to be defined as involving a violation of a law of nature; while the detritus of the past can be interpreted and assessed as historical evidence only in so far as the historian takes for granted all he knows or thinks he knows about aposteriori probabilities, about practical necessities, and about practical impossibilities. Again in his *History*, though always critical and never credulous, Hume gave no hint of scepticism about either the external world or causation. In this at least Hume may remind us of those of our own contemporaries who upon some sociological or philosophical grounds deny the possibilty of objective knowledge. They then, as I forebore to remark in Chapter I, exempt from the corrosions of universal subjectivity their own political tirades, their own rather less abundant research work, and above all their own prime revelation that there can be no objective knowledge.

In his philosophical consideration of causality, however, Hume was faithful to the Cartesian inheritance. The inquirer after causes is typically presented as an inactive, bodiless subject of experience: one extremely friendly critic describes this as 'a paralytic's eye view of causation'. Such a disembodied, pure observer contrives not to have experience of causal connection or of practical necessity and practical impossibility; which experience, surely, is familiar and shared by all of us creatures of flesh and blood engaged in effortful and mobile attempts to manipulate our environments – or, in other words, doing things and failing to do things!

(a) The outcome of this inept and purely observational approach, eschewing – as indeed an incorporeal thinking substance must – activity and experiment, has to be an account which insists that all we really find – out there – is just constant conjunctions: events of one sort just are accompanied or followed by events of another sort; and that's that. This idea of constant conjunction can be explained in terms of material implication, which is in turn one of the fundamental notions of *Principia Mathematica*. This is said materially to imply that when it is not as a matter of fact the case that you ever have this and not that. Thus $A \,]\, B \equiv\, \sim (A.\sim B)$; which reads, 'A materially implies B is equivalent to not as a matter of fact A and not B.'

It is essential to grasp the tiresome fact that if A materially implies B, this is no guarantee that in any ordinary sense A implies B, or even that there is in any ordinary sense any connection at all between A and B. The stock illustration to bring this out is 'This is true, or I'm a Dutchman'; or, in Ireland, 'This is true, or the Pope's a Jew'. These emphatic idioms can, with a little ingenious flexibility, be symbolised as material implications linking otherwise altogether unconnected truths.

Before returning to Hume's account of causality we should perhaps spend a little longer on material implication; and on the related, extremely important contrast between extension and intension. The intension of a term – and the word is 'intension' with an s not 'intention' with a t – is its meaning. This as opposed to its extension, which is everything to which in that meaning that term does as a matter of fact apply. Thus – to start with a boring, uncontentious, and philosophically trifling example – the intension of the term 'uncle' is parent's brother or brother-in-law; its extension is all the people who have been, are, or will be truly describable as uncles.

Again – but perhaps now a little more interestingly – the intension of the word 'yellow' is the colour yellow; whereas its extension might well be correctly indicated without any mention of colour at all, and by specifying whatever primary qualities of light may be as a matter of fact involved in the manifestation of that particular secondary quality. The presence and activity of such to most of us unknown physical factors may well be, both causally necessary to any perception of colour, and similarly necessary to the truth of any propositions about colour. Yet none of this makes them part of what is meant by – say – yellow; a notion which is and remains fully intelligible to many who, perhaps deplorably, have no knowledge of either physics or physiology. The investigation of intensions is thus a wholly different form of inquiry from that of extensions: the former has to be fundamentally semantic, and perhaps philosophical; the latter is essentially factual, concerned with "matters of fact and real existence", and maybe involving the truly scientific.

J. S. Mill's terms 'connotation' and 'denotation' are often employed as synonyms for, respectively, 'intension' and 'extension'; though it should be noticed that American English sometimes substitutes 'designation' for the English English 'connotation'. Frege made the same distinction in terms of sense (intension) and reference (extension), relating it to a contrast between concepts and the objects to which those concepts apply. The time-hallowed example here is the equation between the morning star and the evening star. The connotation, the sense, the intension, the designation of the two expressions is clearly different. It was no process of semantic analysis, but elementary astronomy, which revealed that their denotation, their reference, their extension, is one and the same thing – the planet Venus.

This is now the stock illustration employed by spokespersons for the Mind/Brain Identity Theory. They maintain: not that descriptions of being in certain states of consciousness mean the same as descriptions of corresponding physiological states, particularly states of the central nervous system; but that these pairs of descriptions will be found to have identical extension, reference, or denotation. The most, therefore, that as philosophers these theorists can hope to do is to explain more clearly what they have in mind, and to dispose of purely philosophical objections. For it is only through the progress of physiological research that their theory can be either established or falsified.

The notion of material implication is extensional rather than intensional; and it is because this notion is fundamental in *Principia Mathematica* that that work is correctly said to expound a system of extensional logic. If A materially implies B then you can, in a perfectly good but weak sense of 'infer', infer B from A. Your premise precisely is: not that there is anything which you might uninstructedly call a connexion between A and B; but that A will nevertheless not in fact occur without B. It is nevertheless equally clear that you cannot in the strict sense deduce B from A. For your premise emphatically does not say that B is part of the meaning of A, that it would be self-contradictory to assert A while denying B.

We return now to Hume. Towards the end of a section 'Of the idea of necessary connexion' Hume provides his own summary of his account of the nature of causality. This account, as we are beginning to see, maintains that really there are in the universe around us no connections. What is found is just constant conjunctions; which, now that we have learnt the meaning of that expression, we can represent as material implications.

For, as we have already seen, in a statement of a material implication between A and B there is no claim "that there is anything which you might uninstructedly call a connexion between A and B". Thus Hume concludes: "Suitably to this experience, therefore, we may define a cause to be an object, followed by another, and where all the objects similar to the first are followed by objects similar to the second. Or, *in other words*, where, if the first object had not been, the second never had existed." (VII (ii): italics mine).

This is totally, even diametrically, wrong. It can, therefore, be made extremely instructive. First, notice that from any causal proposition, as from any proposition stating what is presumed to be a law of nature, some propositions of the second, hypothetical sort must follow. Propositions of the former of these last two kinds are called nomologicals; and those of the latter, straightforwardly, subjunctive conditionals. For example: from that claim that the cause of the trouble was sand in the magneto, everyone is entitled to infer that – all other things being equal – if there had been no sand there then there would have been no trouble. The important corollary of this is that from any adequate analysis of causation, from any adequate definition of the word 'cause', it must be possible to deduce some subjunctive conditional.

Second, the subjunctive conditional in Hume's summary is not equivalent to, and does not even follow from, what comes before. For that is, as in consistency it should be, a matter only of constant successive conjunction. When this second point has been shown to be correct we shall have demonstrated that a Humian analysis of causation cannot be adequate. For we shall have shown that such an analysis cannot carry one particular sort of logical implication which the previous paragraph proved to be necessary.

I will now illuminate and enforce this second point by adapting a famous illustration from an otherwise unmemorable Flemish philosopher, who rejoiced in the unpronounceable name of Geulincx. (Two expatriate compatriots of his were once so kind as to pronounce it for me several times in Washington D.C.; but I still failed to achieve a tolerable imitation.) The special interest of this illustration, which must have been familiar to the well-read Hume, is that it was presented precisely in order to show that mere constant conjunction, however perfect the correlation, cannot yield the idea of causal connection. For Geulincx was a spokesman for the Occasionalist answer to the Cartesian question of Mind and Matter. This was presented by Descartes as the problem of the relations or lack of relations between consciousness and stuff. Notwithstanding that he was very much inclined to believe that causal transactions between two such categorically different parties must be inconceivable, his own official story was that they do in fact constantly occur in the pineal gland; where mechanical impulses produce forms of consciousness, and the other way about. In all its various forms this view is known as Two-way Interactionism. Another view is Epiphenomenalism, holding that consciousness is a causally idle accompaniment to real transactions which are exclusively material: favourite analogies are phosphorescence on water or − in the words of the American philosopher C. J. Ducasse (1881−1974) − "the halo on the saint". Since World War II there have been powerful advocates − most prominent first in Australia − for an Identity Theory: in its most sophisticated form this maintains that being in a certain state of consciousness just is being in a certain state of body, and particularly of central nervous system.

The Occasionalists, who were one variety of Psycho-physical Parallelist, held that in fact there are no causal transactions between consciousness and stuff, although the occurrences of all the various kinds of consciousness are in fact constantly conjoined with the occurrences of corresponding physical events. Each is the occasion of the occurrence of the other, not the cause; and the Occasionalists of course went on to attribute the "preestablished harmony" of these perfect correspondences to ultimate Divine causation. Geulincx hypothesised two everlasting clocks, perfectly regular in their mechanism. Suppose now, and here I am slightly adapting Geulincx, that these two clocks are touching and that one is always a split second fast on the other. Finally suppose an ideal Humian observer, who is committed never to interfere by making any experimental tests. The imagined case will clearly satisfy all Hume's requirements, both psychological and physical. Yet, equally certainly, no one would be willing to allow that when the fast clock tells a particular time it is causing the slow clock to tell the same time a split second later.

Why not? Surely because we all believe – rightly – that there is no direct connection between the first event and the second? The reason why we believe this is that we also believe – rightly again – that if the ideal Humian observer were to deviate into participant observation, then he would find that he could damage or destroy the first clock without thereby affecting the timekeeping of the second. The moral is, I suggest, that causal connection is what warrants – or perhaps just is the truth of – the appropriate subjunctive conditionals. When we assert that this is the cause of that we are asserting something stronger than and quite different from the proposition that occurrences of the one kind are as a matter of fact always followed by occurrences of the other kind. The crux is the claim that if this, or a this, had not occurred that, or a that, would not have happened.

(b) The complementary ideas of causal necessity and causal impossibility are themselves necessarily connected with that of causal connexion; and it surely is, as has been suggested already, as physical agents among other physical things that we become acquainted with necessities and impossibilities of this kind. Hume's first concern in this discussion was to establish that nothing about what in fact causes what can be known apriori. This prime concern, together with his secondary concern to develop an account of causal thinking in terms of an associationist psychology, distracted him from ever recognising that there are senses of 'necessity' and 'impossibility' other than those of logical necessity and logical impossibility.

To grasp these distinctions, look back at two arguments from Leibniz mentioned in Subsection (ii) of Section 3 in the present Chapter IV. Leibniz dismissed the notion of atoms of matter as incoherent, on the grounds that anything with any size at all must be further divisible. He and the atomists are here at cross-purposes. He insists, quite correctly, that there is no self-contradiction or other incoherence in suggesting that anything which has size might be further divided: further division is, in that sense, logically possible. The atomist need not and should not deny this. His thesis is, or should be, only that there are some tiny bits of stuff which it is as a matter of fact impossible further to subdivide. Much the same applies to the proof given by Leibniz that there can be no fastest possible motion. Leibniz wanted to prove, and did prove, that the idea of a fastest possible motion, though it might look alright, really is incoherent. (His ulterior object was to bring out that any protagonist of the Ontological Argument has to demonstrate, as Leibniz thought that he could, that the crucial notion of God as a logically necessary Being is not afflicted with a similar deep incoherence.) But the proof which Leibniz has just given, that the idea of a fastest thinkable motion is at bottom self-contradictory, has no tendency to show that our scientists are mistaken when they assert that it is, in the actual Universe, impossible as a matter of fact for anything to go faster than the speed of light.

Back in Section 1 of the present Chapter IV we had occasion to distinguish two applications of the concepts of logical necessity and logical impossibility: that to inferences between propositions; and that to the propositions themselves. Let us now conclude Section 5 by deploying both this distinction, and the distinction between the two kinds of necessity and impossibility, to deal with an ancient paralogism. (A paralogism purports to be a proof, yet is in truth fallacious.)

This one appears first in Chapter IX of Aristotle's *Interpretation*, and in this form it is called the Problem of the Sea-Fight. The issues raised were much discussed in the Middle Ages: for instance, in a treatise on *Predestination, God's Foreknowledge, and Future Contingents* by William of Ockham (About 1290–1349). In the modern period the argument was presented in a pamphlet *Of Liberty and Necessity* by the always intellectually audacious Thomas Hobbes (1598–1679). He thought that it provided knock-down proof of an absolutely general conclusion "that all events have necessary causes"; that is, that universal causal determinism must be true. It was known to Leibniz, in a form which drew and stressed an unequivocally fatalist human conclusion, as the Lazy Sophism. That form will itself be familiar to an older generation of filmgoers from a work in which Miss Doris Day sang a theme song: beginning "Che sarà, sarà. Whatever will be, will be"; and concluding that there is nothing which anyone can do to stop anything. Hobbes being – for all his intellectual audacity – a physically timorous Englishman, prefers to talk not about a Sea-Fight but the weather:

"It is necessary that tomorrow it shall rain or not rain. If, therefore, it be not necessary that it shall rain, it is necessary that it shall not rain; otherwise there is no necessity that the proposition 'It shall rain or not rain' should be true. I know there be some that say it may necessarily be true that one of the two shall come to pass, but not, singly, 'That it shall rain', or 'That it shall not rain'. Which is as much as to say that one of them is necessary, yet neither of them is necessary" (p. 277).

It should by now be obvious that all such arguments derive their plausibility from the misplacing and consequent misinterpretation of the term 'necessary'; and of such other apodeictic associates as 'possible', 'impossible', 'must' and 'cannot'. (The word 'apodeictic', which means pertaining to demonstration, is one to know, if only because it was such a favourite with Kant.) But I will leave the Hobbes passage as a practice exercise for you to tackle on your own, and instead treat a version which introduces more explicitly the further complication of the two senses of 'possibility' and 'impossibility'.

If the premise 'Whatever will be, will be' is to provide a basis for a proof of a fatalist conclusion, then it must not be construed as a question-begging statement of precisely that conclusion. The alternative is to read it as a tautological statement like the original 'Either there will be a sea-fight tomorrow or there will not'. So it must amount to saying that, for all values of X, from 'X will be' it follows necessarily that 'X will be'. Given this reformulation, it becomes immediately obvious: first, that no such tautological premise could by itself entail any such substantial conclusion as is here proposed; and, second, that the fallacy is to mistake it that the logical necessity, which does indeed qualify the crashingly inevitable inference from 'X will be' to 'X will be', must by the same token also qualify that proposition itself. The first mistake is like arguing: from the tautology that 'All husbands have to be married' (by definition); to the falsehood that 'All who are husbands have been irresistibly forced into marriage' (in fact). The second mistake is that of arguing that: because from 'Joe will in fact win' it follows necessarily that 'Joe will in fact win'; therefore it also follows from the same premise that 'Joe will win: and nothing can stop him; nor can he help himself'. In every version of the Lazy Sophism we thus move fallaciously: from some empty and logically necessary truism; to the formidably substantial falsism that everying, including all human action, is either in fact necessary or in fact impossible.

6. *Argument from experience*. Having applied his new philosophical instrument to the concept of causation in particular, Hume turns next in the first *Inquiry* to argument from experience in general:

"When it is asked 'What is the nature of all our reasonings concerning matter of fact?' the proper answer seems to be, that they are founded on the relation of cause and effect. When again it is asked, 'What is the foundation of all our reasonings and conclusions concerning that relation?' it may be replied in one word, 'Experience.' But if we still carry on our sifting humour, and ask 'What is the foundation of all conclusions from experience?' this implies a new question which may be of more difficult solution and explication" (IV (ii)).

In giving his answer to this new question raised by his "sifting humour" Hume set what has come to be called, using a term which was not his, the Problem of Induction:

"As to past experience, it can be allowed to give direct and certain information of those precise objects only, and that precise period of time, which fell under its cognizance. But why this experience should be extended to future times, and to other objects . . . is the main question on which I would insist. The bread which I formerly ate nourished me. . . . But does it follow that other bread must also nourish me at another time? The consequence seems no wise necessary. At least, it must be acknowledged that there is here a consequence drawn by the mind, that there is a certain step taken, a process of thought, and an inference which wants to be explained. These two propositions are far from being the same: 'I have found that such an object has always been attended with such an effect'; and 'I foresee that other objects which are in appearance similar will be attended with such effects'. . . . The connection between these propositions is not intuitive. There is required a medium which may enable the mind to draw such an inference, if indeed it is drawn by reasoning and argument. What that medium is passes my comprehension . . ." (IV (ii)).

This manifesto provides an excellent illustration of the Russellian claim that logic is the essence of philosophy. For the challenge, as Hume presents it, is to find a suitable minor premise to complete a valid syllogism; and the word 'syllogism', like 'medium' or 'middle term', is a semi-technicality of traditional Aristotelian formal logic. The problem thus set will be appreciated best if we introduce a modicum of self-explanatory symbolism. How do we get: from the major premise 'All observed X's are or have been φ' (read phi); to the desired conclusion 'All X's have been, are and will be φ'? These are simpler than Hume's own two representative propositions. By covering moves not only from present and past to future but also from present or past to present or past, they make this logical question properly indifferent to time. And of course Hume the future historian must himself have wanted to include all attempts to reconstruct, on the basis of evidence presently available, 'what actually happened'.

(i)   If we accept the framework provided, then the possible kinds of response are few, and all seem to collapse almost at once. Two such moves have simply to be disqualified, on the ground that they would leave us with something other than argument from experience. One of these moves off the board stipulates that the first premise is to be construed as logically necessary; from which the conclusion, itself also now to be similarly construed, must follow immediately – but to no present purpose. Again, one minor premise which would yield a valid syllogism is 'All X's have been observed'. But this suggestion has to be disqualified, since where it applies we have: not an argument from experience; but an analysis of it. Any argument from experience must, whereas an analysis of experience cannot, employ observed cases as a guide to expectations about those which have not been observed.

The only alternative kind of minor premise, which is the one considered by Hume, is some statement about the uniformity of nature. It has often been asserted, usually with very audible initial capitals, that all inductive science presupposes a huge commitment of faith – Faith in the Uniformity of Nature. The first objection to this move, as a response to the Humian Problem of Induction, was first made by Hume himself. It is that the move is question-begging, since such a minor premise could be known to be true, if at all, only on the assumption that argument from experience is a valid form of argument: precisely what is in dispute.

A second and still more devastating objection emerges as soon as we have found a formulation for our minor premise adequate to yield a demonstration. This premise needs to be something like: 'For all values of X, the subclass of the observed is in all respects a perfectly representative sample of the class of all X's'. The trouble now is: not that this could be known to be true, if at all, only by employing argument from experience; but that it can be, and is, known to be false by direct appeal to familiar counter-examples. There are innumerable cases where all the instances observed up to a certain time, or within a certain area, have shared some characteristic not common to all instances observed later, or elsewhere. What the Signers of the American Declaration of Independence called "a decent respect" dictates some re-employment here of an example hallowed by tradition: until – was it? – Abel Tasman and his crew discovered the blacks of Western Australia all swans observed by Europeans had been white.

(ii)   The moral which Hume drew is that argument from experience is without rational foundation. He seems nevertheless to have felt little scruple over the apparent inconsistency of then proceeding to insist: first, that such argument is grounded in the deepest instincts and the most unshakable habits, instincts and habits which are part of the animal nature which humans share with the brutes; and, second, that the rational man everywhere proportions his belief to the evidence, evidence which crucially includes the outcome of ongoings earlier alleged to be without rational foundation.

Two other kinds of response to what has been stigmatised as this scandal of induction make no challenge to the assumption that Hume's representation of the nerve of argument from experience is correct. One of these appeals in one way or another to all the successes we seem to have had – so far! – in thus arguing from experience: surely induction is sufficiently justified by this record of success? To the objection that this is itself an argument from experience and hence in the present context question-begging, the response is: 'You too!' For any parallel attempt to justify deduction as a fundamental form of argument would have to be deductive, and hence equally question-begging.

Another such response is that of Sir Karl Popper. He started by finding "Hume's refutation of inductive inference clear and conclusive" (1963, p. 42). The method of science, however, is not, Popper maintains, inductive but hypothetico-deductive. It is not a matter of noticing that all X's so far observed seem to have been φ; and then jumping to the conclusion that all X's have been, are, and will be φ. Instead the creative scientist forms some bold conjecture, deduces the consequences which must obtain if this conjectured hypothesis is true, and then seeks for falsifications which will force him either to amend or to replace the original conjecture. All the reasons for stressing falsification here, not verification, ultimately rest upon one simple yet vastly important point of logic. It is a point about open, universal generalisations – those covering any possible instances, past, present and to come, not just some finite list. Such a generalisation can not be decisively verified by any number of confirming instances. But it can be decisively falsified by even one authentic counter-example. Therefore, Popper argues, the paradoxical fact is that every firm step towards the scientific truth must be through the decisive refutation of previous false conjectures.

As a response to "Hume's refutation" Popper's philosophy of science, despite its other enormous merits, had one defect. It cannot provide any consistent rationale for the Popperian scientist's suitably tentative and undogmatic acceptance and employment of his own not yet falisified theories. "In such an acceptance", Popper says, ". . . there is nothing irrational. There is not even anything irrational in relying, for practical purposes, upon well-tested theories, for no more rational course of action is open to us" (*Ibid.*, p. 178). Well, maybe nothing irrational; but, surely, nothing rational either? For here, after all, we have again just that old familiar use of experience as a guide which Hume was in his "sifting humour" probing; albeit with now the judicious and important modification of that tentativeness which he wanted to teach us.

(iii)   The last possibility, and the last to be recognised by philosophers, is to question the whole framework within which the discussion has been conducted. It is as if someone were to respond to that bad old question, 'When did you stop beating your wife?' by asking 'But has any spouse-battering in fact occurred?'. That it is sometimes both possible and necessary to question the framework is indeed one of the most generally useful lessons which you can learn from doing some philosophy. In the present particular case: was Hume right to represent argument from experience as always and inherently an attempt to deduce conclusions necessarily wider than the available premises can possibly contain?

If so, then indeed it must be irreparably fallacious. But surely Hume was in this wrong? The great rebel against philosophical rationalism was, as is so often the case, still to some extent the unconscious client of those very assumptions which consciously he rejected. As an empiricist Hume is committed to maintaining that "matters of fact and real existence" can be known, ultimately, only by reference to experience. Yet he still represents argument from experience, not as a genuinely different form, but as simply — to borrow an idiom from the Indian sub-continent — failed deduction.

The alternative is to represent the nerve of argument from experience, and hence the much talked of yet much more rarely formulated Principle of Induction, as a rule of procedure to guide us in shaping always fallible expectations in which to approach the unknown. This rule in its most elementary and fundamental form would be something like: 'Where and so long as all known X's are and have been φ, there to presume that all X's have been, are, and will be φ; until and unless some positive reason is found to amend this presumption about these particular X's.'

Certainly this fits well to the way in which sensible people actually do argue from experience: we do not in fact assert – as we should if we believed that Hume's broken-backed syllogism was, or could be made, valid – that to affirm the conclusion of our argument while denying its premises would be self-contradictory. Since what is being offered is a rule, there can be no question either of its truth as a proposition or of its validity as an argument.

About a rule as a rule the only questions concern its reasonableness, and the results of its adoption and observation. But, in so far as this particular rule is the principle of all argument from experience, to follow it must be as paradigmatically reasonable as to try to learn from experience. To challenge its reasonableness is to challenge the paradigm established.

Such a challenge might of course be mounted by a suitably radical philosopher. But he would run at once into Popper's counter-challenge: What "more rational course of action is open to us"? Next, if and when he was able to think up some alternative concrete proposal, he would surely be bogged down and overwhelmed by Humian defences in depth. For, in so far as it was a proposal for some systematic counter-inductive strategy, that strategy would, as Hume indicated, go against the grain of the most fundamental habits and instincts of our human nature.

The conservative alternative suggested in the last paragraph but one through its defeasibility accommodates another of Hume's chief concerns. To say that a principle is defeasible means that it provides for its own defeat in certain specified circumstances. The English Common Law, for instance, insists not, crazily, on an assumption but, splendidly, on a presumption of innocence. This is in fact defeated whenever, on some particular charge, the prosecution makes out and wins its case. So, in the present instance, the conservative rule tells us: not, as a rationalist might, to assume that the conclusion drawn necessarily must hold true; but instead, as an empiricist should, simply, and until and unless we find particular reason to change our minds, to presume that it does. If this rule is accepted, then its built-in defeasibility can be most properly paraded as a trophy of Hume's philosophical investigations. "They may even prove useful", as he reflected in the first *Inquiry*, "by exciting curiosity and destroying that implicit faith and security which is the bane of all reasoning and free inquiry" (IV (i)).

CHAPTER V

God and the limits of Explanation

'Why is there anything at all?' That, surely, is the most general and fundamental question? For a century or more it has typically been contrasted with all the particular and humdrum questions of science. Thus in that late Victorian epitome *The Grammar of Science* Karl Pearson (1857–1936) reviews all studies of change in the Universe: "But in no single case have we discovered *why* it is that these motions are taking place; science describes how they take place, but the *why* remains a mystery" (p. 120: italics original). More recently Malcolm Muggeridge, a leading British television pundit, introduced a new series in the BBC journal *Radio Times*: "There are always two questions, 'How?' and 'Why?'. . . . There is not situation to which the question 'Why?' does not apply, and none in which an attempt to answer it is other than beneficial" (4/VII/68).

It was this most fundamental question 'Why is there anything at all?' which Schopenhauer, sometimes called the philosopher of pessimism, identified as an expression of the primal metaphysical urge. In the chapter on 'Man's Need for Metaphysics' in his *The World as Will and Idea* Schopenhauer wrote:

"In fact, the pendulum which keeps in motion the clock of metaphysics, that never runs down, is the consciousness that the non-existence of this world is just as possible as its existence . . . what is more, we very soon apprehend the world as something the non-existence of which is not only conceivable, but indeed preferable to its existence. . . . Not merely that the world exists, but still more that it is such a wretched world, is the . . . problem which awakens in mankind an unrest that cannot be quieted by scepticism nor yet by criticism" (II, pp. 374–5).

1. *Three explanatory preliminaries.* It is perhaps the psychological fact that

this unrest will in the end never be quieted. Philosophical scepticism and criticism must nevertheless begin to have their say.

(i) To get clearer about this most fundamental 'Why?' we have to notice, as Pearson himself did not, that the usage followed in making the present distinction between how and why is not that of ordinary, unphilosophical scientific discourse. For, when they are not rather self-consciously wearing their metaphysical Sunday best, scientists do speak perfectly naturally and correctly of their own achievements in explaining why certain things happen, or why certain laws obtain. The contrast for them is: between discovering what in fact happens, or how things actually are; and providing an adequate theoretical explanation why what in fact happens does happen, or why things are how they actually are.

But of course this is not at all what Pearson and others have in mind when they tell us that science never answers the question 'Why?'. For that has here to be construed as asking for the purpose, the intention, and perhaps also some justification, of whatever it is asked about. And certainly nothing of this sort is ever attempted, much less achieved; except by some of the human sciences, the scientific status of which is — partly on these grounds — disputatious, or at any rate disputed.

(ii) Once we have got clearer about its present meaning it is no longer obvious that "There is no situation to which the question 'Why?' does not apply, and none in which an attempt to answer it is other than beneficial." On the contrary: to press this question everywhere, without discrimination, is like asking all your acquaintance, old and young, male and female, married and unmarried, 'When did you stop beating your wife?' The truth is that the question 'Why?', in the relevant sense, applies, and it is beneficial to ask it, where, but only where, we are in fact confronted by a product of purpose or intention. Both presuppose a purposer and an intender. Since none is to be found within their fields the natural scientists are absolutely right to have no truck with Muggeridge. It may be that there is indeed behind the whole Universe a single supreme Purposer and Intender. Nevertheless, until we have reason to believe that this is so, it is prejudicial to press the question: 'Why is there anything at all?' That, and the answer 'God', were too much made for each other.

Having seen that it is not apriori guaranteed that there always is a true answer to the question 'Why?', in the present sense, we should also recall that it is not so guaranteed in any other and weaker sense either. For, if Hume was right to urge that we cannot know apriori that every event must have a cause, then, by the same token, we cannot know apriori that anything has any other desired kind of explanation. In particular, although scientists have in fact been enormously successful in discovering those unshakable general regularities which we have learnt to call laws of nature, and although they have been similarly successful in finding theoretical explanations why those laws which obtain do obtain, that the Universe is such that these achievements are possible, and the extent of this possibility, are both entirely contingent matters. Certainly it is reasonable to seek explanations. For unless we look we are not likely to find whatever may be there to be found. But it would be a mistake, a mistake quite often made, to confuse this methodological dictate with a metaphysical assurance that it is a logically necessary truth, a truth of a reason rather than a truth of fact, that whatever it may be reasonable to seek must be there to be found. It is enough that you want to find it if it is there, and have no good reason to think that it is not.

(iii)   The third preliminary can be most strikingly put by saying that the Principle of Sufficient Reason is necessarily false. In 'The Principles of Nature and of Grace founded on Reason', written in 1714 in French, Leibniz argued:

> "Now we must raise ourselves up to metaphysics, and make use of the great principle — generally not much employed — that 'Nothing happens without sufficient reason'; in other words that nothing occurs without its being possible for someone who had a sufficient knowledge of things to provide a reason sufficient to determine why it is thus, and not otherwise" (§ 7).

This cannot be right. For every explanation starts with something which is allowed to require explanation (the *explicandum*), and proceeds to explain this in terms of something else which is taken to be, at least at this stage, sufficiently understood (the *explicans*). Thus the particular event may be explained by subsumption under some law of nature, or some other generalisation of which it constitutes an instance. Later, that law may be in turn itself explained by being deduced from a wider theory. Later still that theory itself may be derived from still wider theory. Or a piece of conduct may be explained by reference to the beliefs and purposes of the agent; and then later perhaps his desires too might be brought under some more general account of human nature. But in every explanation, and however far any series of explanations may be carried, there must always be something to be explained and something taken as understood. The suggestion that there must always and everywhere be a sufficient reason for everything, that everything could be simultaneously and sufficiently explained, therefore contradicts the very concept of explanation. It is illuminating to compare this fundamental truth about explanation with a parallel point about proof. For to prove everything at one and the same time is equally impossible: if anything at all is to be proved, then some premises have to be accepted without proof.

The immediate relevant consequence is that, while there is room for controversy and choice about what we ourselves are going to accept as our own, there is no escape anywhere from the need to recognise some unexplained ultimates. Some people, like the Classical Greek atomists Leucippus of Miletus and Democritus of Abdera in the 400's BC, will take as theirs the existence of the Universe, and whatever science finds to be its most fundamental laws. They may of course be wrong, even ruinously wrong, to refuse to return the usual answer so trimly tailored to the question 'Why is there anything at all?' But one thing upon which their opponents are not entitled to preen themselves is having in their own theism reached a position with no similar untidy and unexplained loose ends. For to give the answer 'God' just is to undertake the alternative commitment of accepting the existence and the basic characteristics of that Being as the last word, beyond further explanation.

2. *Cosmological Arguments*.   In the *Critique of Pure Reason* Kant expounds a magisterial trichotomy:

> "There are only three ways of proving the existence of a Deity on the grounds of speculative reason. All the paths leading to this end either begin with determinate experience and the special constitution of the world of sense-experience and rise, in accordance with the laws of causalty, from it to the highest Cause existing apart from the Universe; or they begin with a purely indeterminate experience, i.e. some empirical existent; or abstraction is made from all experience and the existence of a supreme Cause is inferred from apriori concepts alone. The first is the Physico-theological Argument, the second is the Cosmological Argument, and the third is the Ontological Argument. There are no more, and more there cannot be" (A590–1, B618–9).

We have already in Chapter IV examined the attempt to deduce a tremendous conclusion about "matter of fact and real existence" from a contention about "the relations of ideas" – from the mere concept of God as a logically necessary Being. Let us here look in turn at the other two ways. You should be warned that usage of the expression 'Cosmological Argument' is not everywhere clear, strict and consistent: confusion has even crept into some standard works of reference (Flew 1976b, Ch. 4). Since Kant was responsible, if not for introducing, then at any rate for popularising it, and since he has proposed a clear principle for distinguishing three sorts of argument, it is best to follow him. A Cosmological Argument, therefore, is one which tries to prove the existence of God from the most indeterminate and general contingent premise. The starting point is in fact the undisputatious presupposition of the question with which the present chapter opened.

(i) The dull and common response is to press the prejudicial 'Why?' to the ready-made answer 'God'; usually insisting by the way that there has to be an initiating or sustaining outside cause, which is nevertheless itself uncaused. In addition to the Humian point that a cause is not always necessary, much less another cause external to whatever is to be found within the Universe, every version of this argument should be met with a challenge: 'Why, if it is compulsory to go so far, is it at once forbidden to go further?' This second point has never been better put than by Schopenhauer, in *The Fourfold Root of the Principle of Sufficient Reason*: "We cannot use the causal law as if it were a sort of cab, to be dismissed when we have reached our destination" (§ 20).

(ii) The interesting but more difficult move is made by Leibniz, and made best immediately after the passage quoted in the previous Section 1:

"This principle given, the first question which we have a right to put will be 'Why is there something rather than nothing?' For nothing is simpler and easier than something. Next, given that things must exist, it must be possible to provide a reason, 'Why should they exist thus, and not otherwise?'

Now this sufficient reason for the existence of the Universe cannot be found in the procession of contingent things. . . . So the sufficient reason, which needs no further reason, must be outside this procession of contingent things, and is found in a substance which is the cause of that procession and which is a necessary Being containing the reason for His existence in Himself; otherwise we should not have a sufficient reason at which we could stop. And this final reason for things is called "God" (§§ 7–8).

Pause a moment to relish this elegance and mastery. The Principle of Sufficient Reason strikes Leibniz as a luminous and inexpugnable revelation. This granted there must indeed be some sufficient reason, both why there is anything at all, and why everything which there is, is "thus, and not otherwise". But any series of explanations of contingent facts — any "procession of contingent things" — must end, as it began, in facts which are themselves contingent. These ultimate contingencies, and no doubt all other contingencies too, can be explained sufficiently only in so far as they really are, or can be deduced from, logically necessary truths; these alone and as such contain within themselves sufficient reason for their own truth.

This swinging rationalist movement, like all valid deductive arguments, may be reversed. When the conclusion is false any such argument becomes a disproof of at least one of its premises. (This is the principle which scientists, detectives, and intelligent plain men employ when they take the falsification of some of the consequences deduced as a disproof of a theory). So, granting that the concept of God employed in the Ontological Argument is incoherent, and granting that every explanation of contingent facts must always end in further contingent facts not themselves explained, then we must interpret this most powerful form of Cosmological Argument: not as a proof of the existence of the God of the rationalists; but as a disproof of the Principle of Sufficient Reason.

(iii)   Notice too, before we proceed to Kant's first way, the assumption that "nothing is simpler and easier than something". This is one member of a large class or, as philosophers sometimes say, one token of a large type. The class or type is that of assumptions that we can apriori know what are the fundamental natural conditions, all departures from which demand explanation. Thus to Leibniz it appears obvious, even a logically necessary truth, that the base line must be total non-existence: the contingent existence of anything at all, a Universe of conceivably might-not-have-beens, is an intrusion or deviation which as such demands to be explained. An application of Hume's Fork, however, quickly shows that Leibniz — like in his own way all those who insist upon an answer to the question 'Why is there anything at all? — is here helping himself to an assumption for which he can have no warrant.

For another example of the same sort of assumption, consider the conflict between the old Aristotelian and the new Galilean physics. The old system accepted that the natural condition of bodies is rest, and required that not only all changes of motion but also all continuation of motion be explained. The new system introduced an alternative base line, that embodied in the First Law of Motion which we all learnt, or should have learnt, at school: "Every body continues in its state of rest, or of uniform motion in a right [straight] line, unless it is compelled to change that state by forces impressed upon it." To accept this alternative base line is to accept that only changes of motion, not its mere continuation, need to be explained. Those Aristotelian critics who importuned Galileo to specify a cause of such mere continuation – a cause, that is, of inertial motion – were, like Leibniz here, taking their own preferred base condition as uniquely necessary and apriori given.

This fundamental feature of the physics of Aristotle has been of historical significance for natural theology. (Natural theology is the attempt to prove the existence of God, and sometimes human immortality, from premises provided by observation of the ordinary course of nature. The contrast here is between natural and revealed, – with the latter term referring to any further and special steps which the Deity may have taken to reveal Himself.) Aristotle, who believed that the Universe is eternal, argued that not the beginning but the continuation of motion therein required as its sustaining cause an Unmoved Mover. Similar arguments were developed in the Scholasticism of all the three great Mosaic traditions, in Islam and Judaism as well as in Christianity. They are found, for instance, in Ibn Rushd (1126–1198) known in the West as Averroes, in Moses ben Maimon (1135–1204) called by the Greeks Maimonides, as well as in Aquinas. For Aquinas this argument to a First Mover or Prime Changer provided "the first and most manifest" of the Five Ways.

That implications of this sort could and perhaps had to be drawn was well appreciated by both the defenders and the attackers of Aristotelian physics. For instance: in the 1300's Jean Buridan – he of Buridan's Ass, that could not decide what to eat first of two equidistant equal carrots – pointed out that his own suggestions would eliminate the need for Aristotle's Intelligences to turn the celestial spheres. Conveniently Buridan could find no Scriptural warrant for these Intelligences; whereas Maimonides – the Jewish Aquinas – who did not question Aristotle's physics, equally conveniently, could. The difference between the world-picture erected upon Aristotle's assumption about what the natural condition is, and that developed from the new alternative base line of modern physics, is excellently summarised by Herbert Butterfield in *The Origins of Modern Science: 1300–1800*. In the former:

"the things that were in motion had to be accompanied by a mover all the time. A Universe constructed on the mechanics of Aristotle had the door half-way open for spirits already; it was a Universe in which unseen hands had to be in constant operation, and sublime Intelligences had to roll the planetary spheres around. . . . The modern law of inertia, the modern theory of motion, is the great factor which in the seventeenth century helped to drive the spirits out of the world and opened the way to a Universe which ran like clockwork" (p. 7).

3. *Miscellaneous 'Physico-theological Argument'*.   Kant's first class of arguments includes all those which start from premises more particular than the indeterminate assertion that something does exist. The formidable expression 'Physico-theological Argument' ought, therefore, to be construed as more than a superfluous synonym for the label 'Argument to Design'; which refers to what Kant himself seems to have mistaken to be the only token of this type.

(i)   One subclass is represented by two arguments employed by Descartes in *Meditation III*. He is attempting to prove the desired conclusion "without going out of myself". Both appeal to substantial principles of causality which he believed were known apriori by "the natural light of human reason"; a light which Humian critics would suggest was in fact artificially switched on by shrewd Jesuit teachers. The one sometimes called the Trademark Argument is often confused with the Ontological. But, whereas the premise of that is a logical point about the supposed coherence of a concept, this starts from the psychological fact that Descartes is equipped with a notion of a Perfect Being. Since Descartes knows that he is himself very imperfect, and since he also believes that he knows that everything must of necessity have not only a cause but also a worthy and adequate and proportionate cause, he deduces that that notion must have been impressed on his mind by an actual Perfect Being: serving, "as it were, for the mark of the workman impressed on his work." The other similar argument again starts from his own awareness of his imperfections: "But if I were myself the author of my being, I should doubt of nothing . . . no perfection would be wanting to me." Apart from the appeal here too to that substantial kind of apriori knowledge of causality which Hume was later to show we cannot have, the interest of this second argument lies in the fact that its conclusion is not an initiating but a sustaining cause.

(ii)   The same applies to all the Five Ways of Aquinas: these were designed to prove, not that there was a First Mover or First Cause "in the beginning", but that the entire Universe is a creation now and always absolutely dependent upon its Creator. Although he does little here to make this clear Aquinas believed that it cannot be proved by natural reason, without benefit of revelation, that the Universe ever had a beginning. He even wrote a pamphlet *Concerning the Eternity of the Universe: against Murmurers*

– the "murmurers" being contemporaries who, having no means of knowing his future status, were accusing him of heresy.

We have already noticed, in Section 2 of Chapter III, that these Thomist arguments, unlike the Cartesian on the one side and the Cosmological on the other, start from what are supposed to be very general features of (what Aquinas would not himself think of as) the external world; and now I must simply remark in passing that it is wrong to read the peculiar Aristotelian technicalities of the third way as expressing a token of the Cosmological type. Another significant point about all the Five Ways, often overlooked, is that they are presented as an attempt to meet and defeat a presumption of atheist naturalism. Following Hume and the sceptical Huguenot Pierre Bayle (1647–1706), and in deference to Strato of Lampsacus who was next but one in succession to Aristotle himself as Director of Aristotle's own Institute the Lyceum, this is sometimes known as the Stratonician Presumption. The nub is to insist that the burden of proof must rest on anyone who proposes to go beyond the existence and basic characteristics of the Universe, and to contend that all this is somehow the derivative product of Something Else. The Thomist formulation constitutes the second of the two Objections to which the Five Ways are the Response. This accords with the pattern observed throughout the *Summa Theologica*. Those who have had in all spheres more than their fill of official spokespersons should in fairness remember that Aquinas was the author of every element in every Article: his thought here is in a very literal sense conducted as a dialogue with himself. So he puts the case that the burden of proof rests on him as the theist:

". . . what can be accounted for by fewer principles is not the product of more. But it seems that everything which can be observed in the Universe can be accounted for by other principles, on the assumption of the non-existence of God. Thus natural effects are explained by natural causes, while contrived effects are referred to human reason and will. So there is no need to postulate the existence of God" (I, Q2 A3).

I shall say no more here about the Five Ways. If you want to study the several arguments in the original words, along with a detailed and in the end devastating examination, you should go to a book by the ex-priest who was recently elected Master of Balliol College, Oxford (Kenny). The necessary demolition charges were laid out in Section 5 of Chapter IV, and earlier in the present Chapter V.

(iii)   Another argument which must fall in Kant's first category is the characteristically Protestant appeal to immediate personal experience. What need is there of elaborate or indirect inferences for persons who are directly acquainted with God, or His son, in their own lives? You require no build up of evidence that the Ruritanian tanks are crewed by Cubans if you have yourself met them on the job, and perhaps even been into action with them. And anyone who challenges your assurances must, surely, be calling you a liar.

Yet the two cases are in crucial respects not alike. I was not in Ruritania with you; and, had I been, I too should have met the Cubans. But we are all of us in the same places where some claim to be meeting God; and, to all appearance, there is nothing there beyond what both we and they agree is perceived by everybody. Against this it will of course be protested that God, being by definition incorporeal as well as omnipresent, may be present, indeed if present could not but be, unperceived. Just so: precisely this is one reason why the desired analogy breaks down. God is so defined as to preclude all possibility of any perception of or, generally, in the public and objective sense, of having experience of God. What people are entitled to feel certain about, and what they may reasonably require us to accept their assurances on, is their own experience in the purely private and subjective sense. But here the warranted certainty is only that it seemed as if God was speaking to or working in you; and a reason is still wanting why anyone — including you — should believe that He really was.

Two more particular points before Hobbes has the last word on this seductive yet spineless argument. First, it is curiously common in at least one case to confound the effects of his believing something about someone with the direct effects of the activities of that someone. Contemplate as an instructive contrast another case in which no one would make this mistake: "Lenin's thoughts and Lenin's ideas live", the posters were screaming when I visited the Russian Empire, "he is an inspiration to millions." Second, there is an obscurantist usage, sponsored by the Swiss psychotherapist C. G. Jung (1875–1961), in which beliefs are spoken of as 'psychologically true' or 'true for them' in so far as these are supposed to satisfy some deep craving in the believers. This deplorable usage encourages, and it is hard not to judge that it was always intended to encourage, a flagrantly fallacious move: from the exhibition of such a need to believe; to the conclusion that the belief itself has been thereby shown to be true. I have, sadly, to abbreviate the Hobbes passage from Chapter XXXII of *Leviathan* and, less sadly, to suppress some gratuitous offensiveness:

". . . if a man pretend to me that God hath spoken to him supernaturally and immediately, and I make doubt of it, I cannot easily perceive what argument he can produce to oblige me to believe it. . . . For to say that God hath spoken to him . . . in a dream, is no more than to say that he dreamed that God spoke to him. . . . So that though God almighty can speak to a man by dreams, visions, voice, and inspiration; yet He obliges no man to believe that He hath done so to him that pretends it; who (being a man) may err. . .".

4. *Arguments to Design*. The most important subdivision of the first Kantian category covers Arguments to Design. I write Arguments *to* Design rather than, traditionally, Arguments *from* Design because their nerve is inductive rather than deductive: the move is not, from what is admitted in the beginning as design, to a Designer; but from various sorts of order, by way of an appeal to experience, to an Orderer.

The next thing to recognise is the difference between applying such a contention to some recalcitrant phenomenon within the Universe, and applying it to the Universe as a whole. Confronted by any unsolved problem of naturalistic explanation, it may be tempting to make a move of the former sort: 'How', someone might have asked, 'could non-living, non-conscious, non-intelligent matter have given rise to living, conscious, and intelligent beings?' Yet such moves are forever liable to be discredited by the latest news of successes on the science front; which is one reason why sophisticated theists are nowadays apt to speak disrespectfully of 'a God of the gaps'. A thesis of the latter kind, which some discover in the last of the Five Ways, is not similarly exposed. On the contrary: it can afford to hail all the triumphs of science as further enriching its premises. So, whereas Darwin's theory of the origin of species by natural selection might be immensely upsetting to the protagonist of the first sort of design argument, it could be welcome to anyone committed solely to the second.

This is the one putative proof of natural theology to which Hume attended at some length and with respect. His first reason was that it is the argument with by far and away the widest and deepest popular appeal. His second was that, unlike almost all the others, it tries to establish what is supposed to be a "matter of fact and real existence" in the only appropriate way: by appealing to our actual experience, and not to our non-existent substantial apriori knowledge of causality. Nevertheless, these two things granted, there are decisive objections to what Hume enjoyed calling "the religious hypothesis". These objections he put first in the first *Inquiry*; and they reappear, in an extended and enriched form, in his cherished posthumous masterpiece the *Dialogues concerning Natural Religion*. The message is wrapped discreetly. For Hume was undermining what had been, was, and would long remain, ground common to the Christian establishment and its deist or – as we should perhaps prefer to say – unitarian critics. But to any reader as careful as Kant it is clear.

The hard question for any opponent of Arguments to Design is this: 'If on a building site, for instance, it is right to argue from the signs of work in progress to the conclusion that there are building workers who are not at the moment visible; then why is it not right, by parity of reasoning, to argue from all the indications of order in the Universe as a whole to an unseen Orderer?' Hume's reply is that the parity collapses, since the two cases are dissimilar in two crucial respects: in the Argument to Design both the putative cause and the putative effect are essentially such as to rule out this sort of reasoning.

(i)   In the first place the putative cause in this case is defined as infinite, incomprehensible, a member of no (created) species or genus, and so on. All this carries the necessary consequence that it must be impossible to infer, by natural reason and without benefit of revelation, any practical implications of the truth of the hypothesis proposed. The hypothetico-deductive method of science and commonsense, therefore, cannot accommodate "the religious hypothesis". To underline this point it helps to contrast finite and plebeian gods with the infinite and incomparable God of theism. Hume's objection does not bear against the former, and he could scarcely have faulted on grounds of method those characteristically practical Chinese peasants who faced the alleged "Spirit controlling wild life" with robust address: "Does the Spirit realise that each time a villager is eaten the Spirit loses a worshipper and diminishes the number of sacrifices that are made to him, and on which he depends for sustenance? If the trouble continues we shall begin to doubt . . ." (Waley, p. 148).

One way of meeting, or avoiding, this first Humian point is to take up his own suggestion that any Argument to Design could at best prove a powerful but still finite Designer, endowed with sufficient powers to produce the actual Universe, but no more: after all the very idea of design appears to involve being subject to, while with skill circumventing, limitations. This avenue was indeed tentatively explored by J. S. Mill in the last and longest of *Three Essays on Religion*. Any such move must be totally unacceptable to the traditional Mosaic theist, who would presumably execrate the worship of any finite being as idolatrous.

(ii)   In the second place the putative effect is also in its own way by definition unique. For in the relevant sense of the word 'Universe' – the one which I have systematically distinguished by an initial capital – the Universe is everything there is; with the exception of God, if God there be. Not merely do we not have, we could not have, experience of other Universes. There are not, there could not be, other like cases from which to learn. So, Hume argued, we cannot have any experiential basis for saying that either the existence or the basic characteristics of the Universe either must have been, or very probably would have been, produced by Design. On the Universe as a whole there simply is no purchase for any notions of either empirical impossibility or empirical probability. To underline this second point it will again help to contrast cases to which it will not apply. Popular writers on astronomy, if not the astronomers themselves in their working hours, do favour a second sense in which it is correct to speak of more than one actual universe: the Andromeda nebula may thus be said to be one of innumerable 'island universes'. In this second, lower case, sense of 'universe' there is of course no parallel difficulty in principle about acquiring relevant experience on possibilities and probabilities.

(iii)   In the *Dialogues* Hume went on to recommend, albeit and with good reason somewhat equivocally and furtively, "the Stratonician athe-. ism". This is the actual phrase which Hume borrowed from Bayle's *Historical and Critical Dictionary*, the work which is truly said to have 'stocked the Arsenal of the Enlightenment'. This is the open and undogmatic position from which the Stratonician presumption starts, and Hume's final sugges-tion is that this is where the rational man, "who proportions his belief to the evidence", should end. For the Argument to Design has no strength to defeat that presumption. And simply to postulate a hypothetical Being as a made-to-measure explanation of the existence and fundamental regularities of the Universe, perhaps adding that no similar questions are to be pressed about that Being in its turn, is a wanton violation of the economical principle of Ockham's Razor. Whyever should the orderliness be construed as exter-nally imposed upon rather than, as it surely seems to be, intrinsic to the Universe itself? ('Ockham's Razor' is the accepted nickname for the principle usually formulated as 'Entities should not be multiplied unnecessarily'. These precise words are not to be found in the extant works of William of Ockham, though the idea is.)

5.   *Pascal's Wager*.   This last argument is so totally different from all the

others that it has to have a short section to itself. They labour to show evidencing reasons, reasons which would demonstrate that the possible belief embodied in the recommended conclusion is true. This is trying to provide a prudential reason, a motivating reason, for persuading ourselves to believe whether or not the belief is true. It is as if someone were to tell us that this lot are in power, and are likely to remain; and so, if we want to get our hands on some of the sweets of office, and perhaps to avoid relegation to any local equivalent of *The Gulag Archipelago*, we would be well-advised to persuade ourselves into their ideology. Reasons of this kind can possess tremendous force. But they are precisely not evidencing reasons.

Pascal, a considerable French mathematician who made some contribution to probability theory, put this argument in his *Pensées*. It had certainly been used before, and probably entered France from the Moslem world through Spain. Pascal starts by presenting our human predicament as a betting situation, in which each one of us cannot but stake our destiny upon some world-outlook. He then concedes to his opponent, what perhaps he did not himself believe, that we are and must remain in these vital matters ignorant. There is no positive natural theology, and we cannot rationally identify any putative system of religious revelation as the genuine article: "Reason can decide nothing here."

It is upon this agnostic assumption that Pascal proceeds to argue that sane and prudent persons must bet their lives on Roman Catholicism, labouring to persuade themselves of the truth of that system. If they do, and it turns out to be true, then they have won an eternity of bliss. If it turns out to be false, and death is after all annihilation, still what has been lost? If instead they choose to make the best of what this world has to offer, then at best that is what they win, while at worst they suffer an eternity of torment. "And so", Pascal insists, "our contention is of infinite force, when there is the finite to stake in a game in which the chances of winning and of losing are equal and there is the infinite to gain" (Brunschvicg arrangement, § 233).

The main but not the only fault in this argument is that Pascal assumes that there are only two alternative bets: become a Roman Catholic; or not. But on his own basic premise of total ignorance the set of conceivable alternative cosmic systems, all by the hypothesis equally probable, must be infinite; as must be the subset of those promising eternal bliss, and threatening eternal torment, respectively, to reward, and to punish an infinite range of different favoured or disfavoured ways of life (Flew 1976b, Ch. 5).

This refutation is on Pascal's own assumptions decisive. But if the options can in some way be limited to two, or even few, then the argument can still have great force. In a famous essay on 'The Will to Believe' William James, employing an electrical image which has since become part of common idiom, noticed that for no one are more than a few such options "psychologically live". We should notice too that, however inept motivating reasons may be to issues of truth or falsehood, they are relevant to questions of policy. It is, for instance, rational to require the presumption of innocence if but only if you are more keen to ensure that no innocent person is convicted than to ensure that no guilty ones are not. The Stratonician presumption, similarly, is in the same sense the rational policy if but only if your overriding concern is to proportion your belief to the evidence; and not to believe, much less to claim to know, what you do not in fact know, or even, what is actually false.

CHAPTER VI

Freewill and determinism

Towards the end of Section 5 of Chapter IV I quoted from a pamphlet *Of Liberty and Necessity*. Its subtitle could have been written by the never noticeably modest Hobbes, although this puff to end all puffs appears in fact to have been supplied by a piratical publisher: "A treatise wherein all controversy concerning predestination, election, freewill, grace, merits, reprobation, etc. is fully decided and cleared." The present chapter, like its predecessors, promises no such exhaustive finality. Here as always the aim is, while forswearing unrealistic ambitions, to secure some solid progress. It is not the last word which you will be getting, but some considerations of which any informed judgement must take account, and some insights which any future ideal comprehensive treatment will have to incorporate.

The first of these came back in Section 2 of Chapter I. I described there the different contexts in which the overlapping philosophical problems arise: both the secular problems of freewill and determinism; and the religious problems of freewill and predestinationism. I also insisted that these ranges of problems must not be misrepresented, as they so often are, in ways which prejudice all the philosophical issues in the Incompatibilist direction; and leave open only the non-philosophical questions of which of the putative incompatibles is to be abandoned.

Again, in the final section of the same Chapter I, it was with special reference to this present area that I gave the general advice that progress in philosophy is best made by taking short, firm steps and by sticking close to the solid ground of the concrete. The devils in Pandemonium, I suggested, "found no end, in wand'ring mazes lost" precisely because they "reason'd high". They refused, that is to say, to put high, wide and abstract generalisations to the test of concrete particular instances. No doubt they also misused and misunderstood the rich and subtle vocabulary of extenuation and excuse available in every sophisticated vernacular, confusing it with their own in all probability inadequately distinguished and insufficiently explained technicalities. The previous paragraph provides one salutary example of such confusion between an ordinary meaning and various not very valuable technical usages not recognised as such. For a witty and masterful display of the wealth and subtlety available even before any new terms are introduced I refer to the classic article 'A Plea for Excuses' by the Oxford philosopher J. L. Austin (1911–1960).

The third previous contribution came once more in Section 5 of Chapter IV. All three show the impossibility of subdividing philosophy into walled off compartments. But this one also illustrates the way in which great intellectual issues may be raised by what looks like a frivolous and trivial brain-teaser. There the Problem of the Sea-Fight was exploited in order to bring out the difference between logical and contingent impossibility, and the importance of not confusing the necessity which qualifies valid inferences between propositions with any kind of necessity or impossibility referred to in these propositions themselves. The whole exercise, again vitally relevant to the topic of the present chapter, constitutes a diagrammatic treatment of the ways in which fatalist and false conclusions are invalidly derived from premises which warrant nothing of the kind. Thus historical or psychological or sociological material, which may in fact only and at most show that the agents had or would have excellent reasons for acting in some particular way, and might have been or might be expected so to act, is through these various paralogisms mistaken to prove that any alternative course of conduct must have been, or must be, contingently impossible.

The same point about big issues arising from what might seem only trivial brain-teasers applies, incidentally, to the perennially fascinating paradoxes of Zeno: the putative proof that that archetypal Olympic gold medallist Achilles could not in a handicap race catch even a tortoise; and so on. These paradoxes originated in the genius of Zeno of Elea, a younger follower and associate of the metaphysician Parmenides of Elea, in the middle 400's BC. They were intended to defend the monistic Parmenidean Way of Truth against the commonsense, pluralistic Way of Seeming, and to do this by showing that all notions of time, motion, and plurality are ultimately incoherent. One trophy to be won by discovering precisely what is wrong with these arguments is insight into the nature and limits of the application of mathematics. Zeno persuades himself and us to look at the race through the framework of a mathematical series which approaches a limit asymptotically. That limit is the point or side of overtaking the tortoise. And an asymptotic approach is defined as one which gets ever closer yet never arrives.

(See Kirk and Raven, Ch. 10 and 11; Black, Part II; and Ryle 1954, Ch. 3.)

1. *Human powers*. The first fresh contribution is to distinguish two fundamentally different concepts of power, and to demonstrate that there can be no question but that both find abundant application. In the first sense of 'power', the only sense in which the word can be applied to inanimate objects and to most of animate nature, a power simply is a disposition to behave in such and such a way, given that such and such preconditions are satisfied: their satisfaction is both the necessary and the sufficient condition guaranteeing its manifestation. It is in this sense that we speak of the horsepower of an automobile, and of its capacity to achieve certain levels of performance. Let us label this 'power (physical)'.

In another sense, that in which the word is typically applied to people, and perhaps to people only, a power is an ability at will either to do or to abstain from doing whatever it may be. To say that someone possesses a power, in this sense, is not to say that, granted certain conditions, that person will in fact exercise that power. Let us label this one 'power (personal)'. In order better to appreciate both what is meant and that we all do possess such powers, ponder some words in Locke's *Essay*:

"Everyone, I think, finds in himself a power to begin or forbear, continue or put an end to several actions. . . . From the consideration of the extent of this power . . . which everyone finds in himself, arise the ideas of liberty and necessity. . . . So that the idea of liberty is, the idea of a power in any agent to do or forbear any action . . . : where either of them is not in the power of the agent to be produced by him according to his volition, there . . . that agent is under necessity. . . . We have instances enough, and often more than enough, in our own bodies. A man's heart beats, and the blood circulates, which it is not in his power by any thought or volition to stop. . . . Convulsive motions agitate his legs, so that though he wills it ever so much, he cannot by any power . . . stop their motion, (as in that odd disease called *chorea Sancti Viti*) but is perpetually dancing . . ." (II (xxi) 7, 8 and 11: the Latin, of course, translates 'St. Vitus' dance').

It is beyond dispute that Locke here is indicating an authentic, absolutely fundamental, and utterly familiar difference. Of course different people may have different powers (personal), and the same people too at different times — less in sickness or senility, and more perhaps after a stint of Yoga training. Of course too, and as usual, there may be marginal and disputations instances where it is hard or impossible to say whether someone does have the power to do or to refrain at will. But it is simply not on to maintain that there is not an abundance of clear cases of both sorts: both those in which I cannot move, or cannot stop moving, however hard I try; and those in which I can act or not act at will. And furthermore, as Locke suggests, it is scarcely possible to explain, if it is not by reference to this difference familiar in every moment of our waking lives, either how we in fact come to have, or how we can now understand, the antithesis between what is and is not contingently necessary.

Certainly, what has been said so far in Section 1 is a most important part of the heart of the matter. But equally certainly, it is not even the beginning of the end of the affair. We need to be meticulous not to draw any unwarranted conclusions, and not to misdescribe the phenomena in terms which carry illegitimate implications. Suppose that it is granted that the power to do or to refrain at will can be ostensively defined in terms of the contrast just pointed; and that, in consequence, the reality of such powers is beyond dispute. It has not thereby been shown: either that the conduct of the agents exercising them is not fully predictable and completely determined by reasons; or even that we are not at all times creatures of a Creator arranging that we will choose in whatever sense we do choose. (Ostensive definitions are effected by some sort of pointing or showing, rather than by saying; the opposite of 'ostensive' is, therefore, 'verbal'.)

Philosophers impressed, and rightly impressed, by the familiar realities in terms of which we have just defined the idea of (personal) power are apt to conclude that these show, indeed are, the fact of human freewill. The danger is that they may then come to believe that they have done more than they have done; and, in particular, that they have already proved some point about what the facts indicated imply. The temptation is the greater if they fail to recognise that any application of the word 'freewill' here must be to some extent technical, requiring stipulative explanation. For in the ordinary, non-technical, everyday sense to act of one's own freewill is contrasted with, and excludes, to act under compulsion. But in these interpretations both freewill and its opposite presuppose the basic (personal) power to act or to refrain from acting. To act of one's own freewill and to act under compulsion are both equally to act. The person who is by threats forced – say – to join a labour union is just as much an agent as the voluntary recruit; although, where the volunteer acts of his own freewill, the conscript acts only under coercion. Both still have the (personal) power to say 'No';

however monstrous the price the union bosses and their creatures may exact for so doing. So the cases of both are altogether other than that of the person overpowered by main force and projected bodily: that person is in that moment no agent but a missile victim.

At the present most fundamental level it can also be misleading to follow Locke in speaking of liberty. For that word too is most usually employed to indicate the absence of any (external) constraint upon our actions. Someone may be thus at liberty, and not under (external) constraint, when he has no desire to act, or is internally inhibited from acting, or even when he is by paralysis deprived of all power of action. So questions of whether someone is or is not at liberty typically arise only when it can already be taken for granted that they are endowed with (personal) powers.

2. *Two peculiarities of the human sciences.*   The first purpose of Section 1 was to make a fundamental distinction between two senses of the word 'power'. Personal powers are a prerogative of human beings, although the notion might perhaps be extended to apply to some of the higher brutes. To inanimate objects, and even to people in our purely physical aspects, it is possible to attribute only physical powers. From this and other associated differences between their subject materials there arise two crucially relevant conceptual differences between the physical and the human sciences; differences which are, of course, also paralleled in untechnical commonsense explanations of ongoings in the two areas.

(i)   The first of these is revealed in applications of the key word 'cause'. The causes of an explosion necessitate that explosion: given whatever happens in fact to be the sufficient cause, then it is a contingent truth that it is impossible for the consequent explosion not to occur. But if we are talking of the causes of human conduct, as opposed to the causes of the things which people find happening to them willy-nilly, then there is no parallel implication of contingent inevitability. If, to develop illustrations sketched at the end of the previous section, my straining arms and legs are pinioned, and I am forcibly projected from the window above your treasured flowerbed, then it becomes as a matter of fact inevitable that some of your prize tulips will be crushed by my fall. In the heat of the moment both you and I might lapse from the strictest linguistic propriety. But certainly you ought not to reproach me for misconduct, and I ought not to protest that I acted under duress. For I did not act at all, though my assailants did. Those agents, to whom your reproaches should be directed, caused both my fall and the consequent ruin of your tulips. Their causing, though the work of people, was, in as much as it necessitated its effects, physical or necessitating.

The contrast here is with another kind of causing, causing in another sense of 'cause'. If someone gives me cause to celebrate, perhaps by telling me a piece of splendid news, then he provides me with a motive for celebration. But to perform this grateful task is not to necessitate a celebration; to ensure, that is, that a celebration occurs regardless of whether I or anyone else in fact choose to celebrate. It is this same second kind of causing which is involved when someone is given much less grateful motivating reasons for acting, yet still acting, under duress. Thus the shop steward who orders you to join a labour union, and to pay the political levy to support its favoured party, on pain of exclusion from your present and any similar future employment, does not thereby physically necessitate your adhesion to the organisation. You remain for all he can do an agent, with the power to say 'No'; as some, braver and more principled perhaps than you or me, in fact have done and will do.

(ii) This distinction between causing (motivating) a person to act and causing (necessitating) a physical event to occur, requires a further discrimination between two associated doctrines of determinism. First: suppose that someone proposes a universal causal determinism, to be defined in terms of physical causes but extended to cover not only impersonal physical events but also what may be distinguished as human action. Then it is very hard to see how this proposal can leave room for human agency, and for the personal powers which all such agency presupposes. But if that is so, then the very incompatibility constitutes a decisive reason for drastically qualifying a universal determination of this first kind. For, as we saw in Section 1, personal powers just simply are an inexpugnable reality.

Second: suppose that someone proposes a more modest determinism, confined to human conduct, and defined in terms not of physical causes but of motivating reasons; the claim being, not that every event has a physical cause, but that every human action can be referred to the desires and purposes of the agent. Then, since only the second and non-necessitating sort of cause is involved, there is no question of any challenge to the reality of human agency. If the work of any of the human sciences either presupposes or implies any kind of determinism, then surely it is this. But such motivational determinism is certainly not, what it is often assumed to be, the local special case in the human area of a universal determinism of physical causes. Whereas the latter implies contingent necessities and contingent impossibilities everywhere, the former presupposes that within its limited territory there is a vital measure of choice, that there are some real alternatives

153

When, for instance, historians explain the conduct of some agent or class of agents, they reconstruct the agents' motivating reasons for acting as they did. By thus explaining they may at the same time show: both that anyone who knew those historical characters, and knew what they believed their situation to be, could have predicted that they would act as they did; and even that, given our full understanding of their nature and beliefs, their actual conduct was at least excusable. But none of this is to begin to show that and why what happened was inevitable, even by them. On the contrary: for, precisely yet only in so far as "what happened" was their conduct, there must have been alternatives. This must be so; although their actions cannot but have included necessitating as well as motivating causings; and although – like all other human actions – they will have been performed within some framework both of beliefs about contingent necessities and contingent impossibilities and of actual contingent necessities and actual contingent impossibilities.

(a)   It is also perhaps before moving on worth pointing out that these actualities are none the less actual and objective for being all, like motion, essentially relative. What is impossible to man may at the same time be possible to God. What I and my friends cannot now prevent we ourselves might have prevented if only we had taken the right course earlier, and it could perhaps still be prevented by you and yours. So some people like to speak of the essential relativity of all contingent necessity, and to contrast this with the absolute universality of logical necessity and logical impossibility. But this last intrusive touch of pretentiousness is optional.

(b)   Sigmund Freud – rightly hailed as "psychology's one man of genius" (Ryle 1948, p. 324) – insisted that psychoanalysis must both presuppose and progressively prove the truth of what he called psychic determinism. This he always took to be the psychological special case of that universal determinism of necessitating physical causes which he had imbibed as a medical student and a young research worker in the physiological sciences. Freudian psychic determinism is nevertheless very like the motivational determinsim which I have just been distinguishing. To that extent it is, for reasons already given, wrong to assimilate it as a special case of a universal determinism of the other and more formidable kind. Yet we do need to notice that Freud's doctrine was applied not only to ordinary everyday human conduct but also both to certain paralyses and to those symptomatic movements which his patients could not initiate or stop at will. This extension, and the further fact that he attributed such immediately uncontrollable phenomena to unconscious motives, are both complicating factors. For discussion of their nature and significance I have, however, to refer the reader elsewhere (Flew 1978, Ch. 8 and 9).

(c)   It is common to follow William James in distinguishing hard from soft determinism. This was nevertheless not a happy innovation, and it has been rendered obsolete by the introduction of the terms 'Compatibilism' and 'Incompatibilism'. It was unhappy, because what was being distinguished was: not different kinds of determinism; but opposite philosophical contentions associated with the would be factual belief that the world is in some sense deterministic. Hard determinists combine what is typically a universal determinism of necessitating physical causes with some kind of Incompatibilism. Their softer siblings mix some sort of determinism with a Compatibilism.

3.   *"Here I stand. I can no other. So help me God."*   Consider next a statement by Ernest Jones, a founder member of Freud's Fellowship of the Ring. He is writing the official biography: ". . . man's belief in free will seems to be stronger in proportion to the unimportance of the decision. Everyone is convinced that he is free to choose whether to stand or to sit at a given moment, to cross his right leg over his left or vice versa 'as he wishes'. With vital decisions, on the other hand, it is characteristic that he feels irresistibly impelled towards one and one only, and that he really has no choice in the matter nor desires to have any. Luther's famous '*Hier stehe ich. Ich kann nicht anders*' . . . is a classical example" (Jones, Vol. II pp. 181–2).

Do not be distracted by the curious and questionable psychological claim that vital decisions are, characteristically, easy to make. Concentrate upon the classical example; which is, it seems, being classically misunderstood. Yet note in passing that Freud himself once employed it, and erred in the same way (Freud, pp. 253–4). Certainly Luther's words were as truly spoken as they are magnificent. But it is quite wrong to read them as implying that he was somehow paralysed, literally unable to retreat from his defiance. It is not as the patient victim of a sudden paralysis that anyone admires Luther; but rather as the steady, active, dedicated incarnation of the protestant conscience.

The moral for us is that such phrases as 'he had no choice' and 'I can no other' are not to be taken – as the French would say if only they spoke English – at the foot of the letter. On the contrary: they are in their ordinary interpretations applicable, as on that extraordinary occasion before the Diet of Worms, only when and in so far as an agent is in truth an agent: and hence has or had personal power, power to do otherwise. If we say, idiomatically, that Luther had no choice; then we are precisely not saying that he had literally no choice, that he was in truth not an agent but a passive victim. We are instead maintaining, through an idiom which clearly is sometimes misleading, that there was no tolerable alternative to his own chosen option. When Luther himself said, "Here I stand. I can no other. So help me God.", he too meant exactly the same. Of course there were alternatives, in the sense indicated in Section 1. But all these were for him just not on.

Both the two phrases under consideration are employed both in explaining and in excusing conduct. These are two entirely different operations; notwithstanding that they are often performed simultaneously, and that they both assume that what is in question is the conduct of an agent rather than the passivities of a patient. Take now another and less elevated example. Associates of *The Godfather* – as the catchwords have it – make someone an offer which he cannot refuse: "After thirty seconds I shall have either your signature or your brains on this paper."

The recipient of such an offer may indeed, and very reasonably, both explain and at the same time excuse his acceptance by pleading that he had had no choice. There was no alternative. Yet of course he had. And there was. There was that sole alternative so brutally indicated by the threatening mafioso. That there was at least one alternative is the essential assumption common to both the two quite different questions which may be answered by these two phrases, differently interpreted.

One concerns explanation, and perhaps predication. Thus it may be asked, 'What would you have expected?'; where the word 'expected' is to be construed in its descriptive sense. What, that is to say, would you have believed that they would in fact do? Here the answer that 'They could not have done otherwise than they in fact did' expresses the conclusion of an argument inferring the certain or most likely consequences of people such as they were finding themselves in that situation as they saw it.

The other question concerns justification, extenuation and excuse. Here again it may be asked, 'What would you have expected?'; but this time the word 'expected' has to be heard in its prescriptive sense. What, that is to say, would you have required – or would you require – that they ought to have done? Here your answer that 'They could not have done otherwise than they in fact did' expresses your commitment: recognising the actual alternatives with which they were confronted, you are not prepared to reproach them for acting as in fact they acted.

The distinction just made in the previous paragraph between prescriptive and descriptive senses of the word 'expect' is a useful addition to the store of thinking equipment. For it is lamentably common, especially perhaps in academic circles, to sidestep uncomfortable moral questions, about what we ought to expect (prescriptive), by slipping into personally undemanding inquiries into what we in fact did or should expect (descriptive). It is also well to realise that many wise encouragers of the young and of the not so young exploit this ambiguity for worthwhile purposes. The most famous example here is Nelson's signal before Trafalgar: "England expects every man to do his duty."

Before proceeding to Section 4, there are two further points to be made about the often misleading idioms from which we started. The first is that it is only because, as I have been insisting since Section 1, for any agent there always must in the most fundamental sense be some alternative, that we properly can, as we regularly do, require that the unacceptability of any alternative which is to be admitted as constituting excusing compulsion should be proportionate to the heinousness of the offence to be excused. It might – to descend from the thin air of the abstract – be acceptable for me to claim that I was forced into some fairly venial offence by someone's threat to spoil my one halfway presentable sabbath suit. Yet the same plea in mitigation of a grosser fault would not be well seen at all. Aristotle in the *Nicomachean Ethics*, in his Classical investigation of the grounds upon which an agent may be held to be either not or not fully responsible, did not hesitate to maintain that there are some actions – he instanced matricide – which nothing could excuse; and which could never in any circmstances, therefore, be said to have been done under compulsion (1110 A 26–9). If threats and bribes did indeed necessitate, then such a stance would be scandalously unjust; rather than – as perhaps it may be thought – heroic and austere.

The second appendix point is that it is one of the characteristic insights of those who are called Existentialists – such as the forever fellow-travelling French dramatist Jean-Paul Sartre (1905–   ) – to emphasise the extent to which we are all inclined to self-deception and, in their terms, Bad Faith in pretending that we do not decide nearly as much as we do (Flew 1978, Ch. 4). Both the common employments of the phrases 'I had no choice' and 'I could do no other', and their common misinterpretations provide, once they are understood, striking illustrations of this ignoble inclination. A further illustration is the practice of protesting that we ourselves have not the time to engage in activities which others manage to pursue. Since we all have exactly the same twenty-four hours in all our days, this turn of phrase is a decently polite or sometimes merely self-deceiving device for not uttering the truth;

which is that we, in our circumstances, choose to spend all that same time in other ways.

4. *The Oedipus Effect*. Continuing to review some of the main insights and distinctions with which inquirers in the present area have to come to terms, we must consider next what Sir Karl Popper so aptly and usefully christened the Oedipus Effect (Popper 1957, pp. 13 ff.). This is in general the impact of the actual making of a statement, and especially a predictive statement, upon the human situation to which that statement refers. But the label was chosen in order to underline the more particular point that the publication of predictions about human affairs may have a tendency to bring about either their verification of their falsification. Indeed it may possess both causal tendencies at the same time, notwithstanding that these cannot of course achieve simultaneous and complete fruition.

This ambivalence is clearly seen in the legendary paradigm case of *Oedipus the King*. For in that tragedy Sophocles makes the parents of Oedipus respond to a prophecy, that their son will kill his father and marry his mother, by trying to do away with the baby. Their mistaken confidence that they are in fact successful becomes itself a necessary condition making possible the fulfilment of those prophecies. Further textbook examples have been provided in our century by the publication of demonstrably reliable surveys of voting intentions. For instance: late in 1947 the trusted Czechoslavak Institute of Public Opinion found that, if another free election were to be held, as was constitutionally required the next year, then the Communist Party and its allies must expect to lose heavily; and this discovery was surely a main factor in persuading the professing proto-Eurocommunists of the Central Committee to prepare the coup of February 1948 (Zinner, p. 198). Again: there have by now been several bye-elections in Britain – most famously that at Orpington in 1962 – in which after the publication of a poll showing that some third party candidate was in with a chance to win, and that a vote there would not be wasted, that candidate has on the day massively bettered the original expectations of the pollsters (Cook and Ramsden, pp. 198 ff.).

Although the Oedipus Effect only acquired this memorable title very recently, its relevance to questions about the possibilities of foreknowing human conduct has been grasped since at latest the middle 1400's. In a luminous and elegant dialogue 'On Free Will' the Italian Renaissance humanist Lorenzo Valla (1405–57) makes his Antonio say: "Predict which foot I will move first, and, whichever you have said, you will lie, since I shall move the other" (Valla, p. 165: but compare Boethius, V (vi)). However, as other characters proceed to show, this vigorous possibility of falsifying a communicated prediction does not preclude all knowing what someone else will do. It shows only that if such foreknowledge is to be possible – as it manifestly is – then the would be foreknower has got to make sure: either that the subject of this knowledge never hears of the predictions made; or that, if these do get out, they do not in fact stimulate a falsificatory response. Hume too in the first *Inquiry* deploys a similar example, and draws a similar conclusion (VIII (i)).

There is more to be learnt here. For the Oedipus Effect itself is an important and interesting special case of a general phenomenon. This phenomenon is the impact of investigators on the subjects of investigations. It has in our century in the Principle of Indeterminacy, also called the Uncertainty Principle, been recognised by the theoretical physicists – the acknowledged keepers of the intellectual conscience of the whole scientific community. But it is, of course, primarily in the human disciplines that such interactions give rise to perennial and pervasive methodological problems. They do say, for instance, that psychoanalytic patients tend to report the types of dreams which their analysts might be expected to wish to hear; dreams, that is, supporting their own most cherished theories. Certainly we have abundant evidence of the reality of the Hawthorne Effect, a raising of morale simply through being the cossetted subjects of investigation. This effect must surely be part, though only one part, of the reason why even those few educational innovations which have been researched before being widely adopted, seem never to live up to expectations based upon the supposed findings of that research. (Hawthorne was the name of the plant of the Western Electric Company where the Hawthorne Experiments were carried out.) Further examples do not need to, but could, be added indefinitely.

One strictly philosophical application of the particular idea of the Oedipus Effect is to the putative hypothesis of paranormal precognition. For it is often suggested that, if this is a real phenomenon, then it may, or must, be a close analogue of memory; though operating not backwards but forwards. Yet this cannot be right. Our memories embrace a lot of disagreeable happenings, which we could and would have prevented had we realised the dangers in time. But our possible precognitive powers, unless there were other drastic changes in the fundamentals of human nature, could not have a corresponding scope and reliability. For we should be forever taking steps to preclude the fulfilment of all the most disagreeable of these putative precognitions. If

159

these steps proved normally effective; then either the scope or the reliability of this new faculty, or both, would be much less than that of memory. If instead they turned out to be mysteriously ineffective; then this would reveal a sinister and drastic alteration, not in our own natures, but in the structure of the surrounding world. It would have become in reality, not on the stage alone, that of Oedipus. There, characteristically, nothing can ever be avoided (Flew 1959, pp. 433–5). However, in the words of the much loved Danish physicist Niels Bohr, in our actual world, "It must never be forgotten that we . . . are both agents and spectators in the drama of existence" (Bohr, p. 318).

5. *The forces of desire.* James Boswell once confessed, of one book he had read, that it "puzzled me so much as to the freedom of the human will, by stating with wonderful acute ingenuity, our being actuated by a series of motives which we cannot resist, that the only relief I had was to forget it . . .". To this Dr Johnson responded: "It is certain I am either to go home tonight or not; that does not prevent my freedom". Boswell made so bold as to object: "That it is certain you are *either* to go home *or* not, does not prevent your freedom. . . . But if one of these events be certain *now*, you have no *future* power of volition. If it be certain you are to go home tonight, you *must* go home." Anyone who has managed to keep up so far, mastering the treatment of the Problem of the Sea-Fight earlier, should find no difficulty in disposing of such an objection: if I know what you are doing, then it follows necessarily that you are indeed doing whatever it may be; but this has no tendency to show that you cannot do otherwise – only that you are not in fact so doing. There may even be a temptation to conclude, much too quickly, with a magnificently swinging Johnsonian finality: "We know our will is free, and there's an end on't" (Boswell, for 10.X.1769).

But all this leaves the puzzlement about "motives which we cannot resist" untouched. The perennially seductive suggestion is that our desires are independent and irresistible forces, acting upon us as it were from outside. In our day this frequently adopts a psychoanalytic garb; although it has been, and often still is, dressed in the clothes of classical mechanics. For instance: in a now thirty year old article, but one reprinted in at least two widely circulating textbooks, a philosophical spokesperson for psychoanalysis maintains that "the unconscious is the master of every fate and the captain of every soul"; on the ground that "unconscious forces drive . . . into the wanting or not wanting" (Hospers, pp. 82 and 80).

The argument proceeds: ". . . we are not free with respect to the emotions that we feel — whom we love or hate, what types we admire, and the like" (*Ibid.*, p. 77). This is, of course, perfectly true. But it is neither a discovery of psychoanalysis nor an occasion for lamentation. For, in general and in the short run, what it is open to us to choose is what we do, rather than what we feel: ". . . we say, for example, that a person is free to do so-and-so if he can do so if he wants to — and forget that his wanting is itself caught up in the stream of determinism, that unconscious forces drive him into wanting or not wanting to do the thing in question." From this it is concluded that "the analogy of the puppet whose actions are manipulated from behind, by invisible wires, is a telling one at almost every point" (*Ibid.*, p. 80).

It is not. In the first place the supposed cause of our having the desires which we do have is not itself a person, whereas the puppetmaster is. So even if those desires were to result in performances occurring either without or against the performer's will, there could be no question of referring to that puppetmaster rather than to the performer as the truly responsible agent. Here lies the crucial difference between Godless determinism and theist predestinationism. In the former, if the human performer is not responsible, then no one is. In the latter, God must always be at least an accessory in everything.

Second, and more immediately to the present point, it seems to be being assumed that no one can make a choice, and be in this making the ultimate chooser, unless that same person originally chose to have the various desires involved. Certainly any agent may decide to try either to get or to lose any possible taste: we may set about either acquiring a liking for beer or even extinguishing a craving for tobacco; and, if we persist intelligently in our enterprise, succeed. Yet the notion of thus selecting and nurturing all your initial desires is incoherent. For how could anyone make a choice at all without having any tastes or preferences upon which to ground that choice? So, if this assumption is indeed a presupposition of the ideal of an ultimately responsible agent, then the moral is: not that this ideal, as thanks to Freud and others we now know, cannot in fact be realised in the actual world; but that it is a will-of-the-wisp which, as a little philosophical analysis will show, could not conceivably be realised in any world at all.

Third, allowing that "unconscious forces drive him into wanting or not wanting to do the thing in question", it still does not follow that his desire to do it or not to do it is an external and irresistible force. Nor does the same premise warrant the earlier conclusions, that the conscious life of the human being is as "merely a mouthpiece for the unconscious" (*Ibid.*, p. 76), and that "our very acts of volition" are nothing "but facades for the expression of unconscious wishes" (*Ibid.*, p. 77).

The objections are two. First, to explain why I have such and such desires, whether that explanation be in terms of unconscious mental ongoings or of solid physiological structure, is not at all to show that I do not authentically, sincerely, and wholeheartedly want whatever these desires happen to be desires for. The desire the origin of which is explained does not by that token become a mere facade. On the contrary: to explain the source of my desire presupposes that I do genuinely want whatever it may be. Where could you find purchase for inquiring why I have a desire if I do not actually have it all? (It is, by the way, extraordinarily common – and one of the intellectual faults which a first course in philosophy should help to correct – to offer or accept an explanation why something is the case as if it were a demonstration that really it is not.)

Second, and more fundamentally, it is totally wrong to construe desires as external and irresistible forces. If I want to go West, then I want to go West; and it is precisely not the case that someone else, or some thing, is pushing me in that direction. Granted that I want Cynthia, then it is no more inevitable that I will set about trying to get her than that it is inevitable that, if I do, I shall succeed. Thus to interpret desires either as alien or as irresistible forces is a gross philosophical error; albeit an error perennially tempting to all who hanker after some kind of psychological mechanics, a new para-physical science of the mind. The truth is that we are not, and we cannot be, puppets on the strings of our desires.

CHAPTER VII

Philosophy and politics

Much of what has been and perhaps still is taught as political philosophy appears to be awkwardly different from what goes on elsewhere. Whereas in philosophical ethics, for instance, the central concern evidently is analysis of the meaning of different sorts of moral utterance, and investigation of their several logical presuppositions and logical implications, here the emphasis seems to be much more on producing very general justification: it has been characterised not too unfairly as impractical and theoretical politics, politics done quarterly and in quarterlies – away from the urgent Westminster world in which a week is, notoriously, a long time.

1. *The Famous Three.* The staple of such traditional courses has been the political writing of Hobbes, Locke, and Rousseau; a factitious collective known to some mischievous tutors as The Famous Three. Sometimes the *Politics* of Aristotle, Edmund Burke's *Reflections on the Revolution in France*, and J. S. Mill's classic essays *On Liberty* and *On Representative Government* have been thrown in for very good measure. Certainly these are all of them splendid things to read and to think about. Yet they do not contain a great deal which is philosophical in our present more technical sense of that term.

(i) Hobbes himself boasted that in *Leviathan* and elsewhere he was producing a new science, a science of the centralised sovereign state, strictly on all fours with the work in physiology and physics of his friends Harvey and Galileo. The contrast for Hobbes was with political science as that is now understood in our own institutions of tertiary education – a discipline started by Aristotle when he organised a team study of the constitutions of contemporary Greek city states. The Hobbist political true science reveals the mechanical function of the sovereign – any sovereign; which is to spare everyone the ultimate catastrophe of squalid insecurity. Where his predeces-

163

AN INTRODUCTION TO PHILOSOPHY

sors had thought of a state of nature as a pre-social condition from which our ancestors had emerged long since, Hobbes saw it as a total war of all against all, into which we may at any time collapse if the essential powers of sovereignty are ever either separated or diminished. This putative natural condition of the unsocial atoms of political society he describes in some of the finest eloquence of an eloquent century. Chapter XIII of *Leviathan*, in a truly philosophical moment, notices that "the nature of war consisteth not in actual fighting, but in the known disposition thereto, during all the time there is no assurance to the contrary". Hobbes then proceeds:

"Whatsover therefore is consequent to a time of war, where every man is enemy to every man, the same is consequent to the time, wherein men live without other security than what their own strength, and their own invention, shall furnish them withall. In such condition, there is no place for industry, because the fruit thereof is uncertain; and consequently no culture of the earth; no navigation, nor use of the commodities that may be imported by sea; no commodious building, no instruments of moving and removing such things as require much force; no knowledge of the face of the earth; no account of time; no arts; no letters; no society; and, which is worst of all, continual fear and danger of violent death; and the life of man solitary, poor, nasty, brutish, and short."

In the shadow of this nightmare we find a curious, uneasy mating between detached science and agitated justification. Since the main force of the Hobbist psychological mechanics is an irresistible drive for self-preservation, a supposed descriptive law of self-preservation is at the same time construed as the fundamental prescriptive rule of prudence, and even morality. This in politics says to obey whatever effective sovereign powers there may be; hopefully a hereditary despot but, failing that, an equally despotic collective leadership. As Hobbes put it in *De Cive*:

"Among so many dangers therefore, as the natural lusts of men do daily threaten each other withal, to have a care of one's self is not a matter so scornfully to be looked upon [in] that one has neither the power nor the wish to have done otherwise. For every man is desirous of what is good for him, and shuns what is evil, but chiefly the chiefest of natural evils, which is death; and this he doth, by a certain impulsion of nature, no less than that whereby a stone moves downward" (I 7).

(ii)　Drafts for what was later to appear in Locke's *Two Treatises of Government* were originally written during the struggle to exclude the Roman

164

Catholic Duke of York from succeeding to Charles II. At that time the author was serving as a one-man brains trust for Anthony Ashley Cooper, First Earl of Shaftesbury and founder of the Whig Party. The *Two Treatises* eventually appeared only after the Glorious Revolution of 1688. They were then intended to justify and to confirm the consequent constitutional settlement; after the final defeat of the long-feared attempt of James II to establish a French-style and French-supported Roman Catholic despotism. Locke's enterprise is entirely justificatory, and without scientific pretensions.

It starts from the traditional idea of a pre-political state of nature, traditionally conceived as the actual and universal past condition of all mankind. In that state our ancestors were subject, as we all are always, to the universal prescriptive law of nature. Although Locke had no nightmare Hobbist vision of a war of all against all, he did insist that this state of nature must have had its "inconveniences". The unwritten law of nature could be no substitute for a written code; while any code needs an impartial judiciary, and an organised power for detection and enforcement. So our pre-political ancestors would, and did, make, even if they could not sign, a social contract:

"And thus that, which begins and actually constitutes any political society, is nothing but the consent of any number of freemen capable of a majority to unite and incorporate into such a society. And this is that, and that only, which did, or could give beginning to any lawful government in the world" (II (viii) 99).

Such an idea is very old, and has taken many forms. It was, for instance, part of the stock in trade of some of the Sophists of Plato's youth; while in Britain in the middle seventies the old label 'social contract' was applied to a new deal between the bosses of the main labour unions and the leaders of one particular party, which happens to be in large part financed by their political levies and controlled by their conference block votes. Typically, and most naturally, the notion of an original or continuing contract is employed as a weapon to promote limited government or government by consent; although Hobbes did contrive to slew it round to defend an individual or collective despotism. For a contract, normally understood, essentially involves give and take by both parties; which is outright incompatible with any unlimited and unconditional subordination.

So, from his fundamental notions of a social contract and of the rights of the contracting parties in a state of nature, Locke proceeds to derive all the guiding principles of the Glorious Revolution – limited and constitutional government, the rule of law as opposed to arbitrary power, no taxation without consent through representatives, and so on. Reinforced by the thought of the Frenchman Montesquieu (1689–1755) and the Scot Hume these were to become in the following century the principles of the Founding Fathers of the American Republic. When in Britain today people speak of any tax cuts, as too many do, as the Chancellor of the Exchequer giving money away, they unwittingly prefer Hobbes to Locke. For in Hobbes all property is the creature of the state, whereas for Locke my income and my property is mine.

(iii) *The Social Contract* of the French-Swiss Jean-Jacques Rousseau (1712–1778) would better have been entitled 'The General Will'. Certainly he does refer to a social contract, albeit as theoretical fiction not historical fact. But his own novel and characteristic notion of the general will is rooted in the omnipotence of the collective rather than any give and take between independent individuals. Rousseau starts from a statement of a problem which should be seen as guaranteed insoluble: "to find a form of association which will defend and protect with the whole common force the person and goods of each associate, and in which each, while uniting himself with all, may still obey himself alone, and remain as free as before" (I (vi)).

The practically wise person, pondering that revealing statement, and taking the measure of the tremendous force and verve of epigram and paradox in Rousseau's writing, will not be surprised to see the sleight of hand which follows. The clauses of the strictly fictitious contract:

". . . may be reduced to one – the total alienation of each associate, together with all his rights, to the whole community; for, in the first place, as each gives himself absolutely, the conditions are the same for all; and, this being so, no one has any interest in making them burdensome to others. . . . Each of us puts his person and all his power in common under the supreme direction of the general will, and, in our corporate capacity, we receive each member as an indivisible part of the whole. At once, in place of the individual personality of each contracting party, this act of association creates a moral and collective body, composed of as many members as the assembly contains voters, and receiving from this act its unity, its common identity, its life, and its will" (I (vi)).

Thus from the admitted fiction of a contract Rousseau generates his brilliant rationale for the total, unlimited power of the collective. It must, it seems, be in the interests of any recalcitrant and dissenting individuals – it is indeed their real wish – to be coerced by the general will: "In order then that the social compact may not be an empty formula, it tacitly includes the undertaking, which alone can give force to the rest, that whoever refuses to obey . . . shall be compelled to do so . . . This means nothing less than that he will be forced to be free . . ." (I (vi)).

Clearly the general will, so defined, must in theory accord with the interests of all. Yet how in practice is it to be discovered? Rousseau felt the force of this objection; even though, it seems to me, he never found any satisfactory answer. About representative democracy – seen as the English system – he had no good to say at all. Plebiscites perhaps might serve, so long as the questions set were suitably general: "Does it please the Sovereign to preserve the present form of government?"; and "Does it please the people to leave its administration in the hands of those who are presently in charge of it?" (III (xviii)). (Here readers of an older generation cannot but be reminded of General de Gaulle.)

But it is to those who see themselves as members of an elite "party of the vanguard" that Rousseau's ideas have had, and continue to have, the greatest appeal. Precisely as members of such a party they can have no doubts but that theirs are the policies best expressing the interests, and hence the true general will, of whatever it is of which they claim to be the vanguard – a rising class perhaps or a chosen people. What matter if most of its actual members want nothing of the kind? The experts know what they truly need. Dissidents must "be forced to be free". Again: those craving revolutionary change must resonate to the essentially dynamic stress on will, and its suggestion of unlimited, all-transforming state action. So in the great French Revolution of 1789 the ultras Robespierre and Saint-Just echo the words of Rousseau, while Lenin later shapes his Bolsheviks as new Jacobins for a Russian October. (See Talmon, passim; and compare Szamuely.)

2. *Democracy and liberty*.   The classical political philosophers of Section 1 presented their often conflicting but always relevant ideas either as science or justification or both. In this and the following sections we return to the more typically philosophical business of making distinctions, and detecting logical presuppositions and logical implications. In *Sense and Sensibilia* that "implacable Professor" J. L. Austin picked 'democracy' as his example of "a notoriously useless word" (p. 127). He was wrong. Certainly it is nowadays employed in many places as a universally acceptable term of commendation, virtually empty of descriptive meaning. Certainly too it is often, and often in

167

bad faith, abused. Yet it remains the best available word for saying various very important things. We need to discover what these things are by distinguishing, if not three precise senses, at any rate three areas of meaning. We can find mnemonic labels for these in the concluding resolution of Abraham Lincoln's Gettysburg Address: "that government of the people, by the people, for the people, shall not perish from the earth."

(i) (a)   First in that order is the understanding in which the word has no essential reference to anything political. The big *Oxford English Dictionary* glosses this, with little enthusiasm: "In modern use often more vaguely, denoting a social state in which all have equal rights, without hereditary, or arbitrary, differences of rank or privilege." It is with this sort of concern, usually, that people speak of democratising an educational institution or a department of state. Democratising the Foreign Office or the Diplomatic Service is thus a matter of ensuring that these are recruited from every sort of school and from families at every social level; while such very widely circulating books as John Dewey's *Democracy and Education* or the Stoneman and Rubinstein collection *Education for Democracy* contain almost nothing on political arrangements or political training. So democracy here is, in one sense, "of the people". But it has no necessary connections with the government of anything.

(b)   Second in the present ordering, although in every other way primary, there comes the application to methods of making state or, more generally, group decisions. If some group as a whole takes decisions by majority vote, then that is democratic. So, too, are institutions under which decisions are made by delegates, representatives, or other officers who can in due course be voted out.

Two points require immediate further attention. First, notice the heavy non-paternalist emphasis upon what the voters themselves decide: as opposed to what they might, by others, be supposed to need; or what it may or may not be in their interests to have. Second, notice the emphasis upon voting out, not voting in. It is sometimes urged as a paradox of democracy that an electorate may give a majority to a party intending to make that the final free election. It is perhaps somewhat less often remarked that there must be parallel possibilities with every other form of government: an oligarchy might decide to hand over the sovereignty either to a dictator or the populace; and so on. But if, as I suggest, we adopt as part of the criterion of democratic legitimacy the possiblity, of – in a good old phrase – 'voting the scoundrels out'; then we shall not be committing ourselves to accepting, as democrats, the verdict of that last election. In this more sophisticated understanding the guarantee of future free elections, and hence the permanent possibility of reversals, are elements of the essence of democracy. It is, therefore, an affront to democracy for any party to threaten irreversible changes; as in the seventies one of Britain's two majors has taken to doing. The democratic alternative is to promise measures which, once implemented, almost no one will in fact want to undo. In an earlier and happier period it was a Labour prime minister who insisted: "Democracy is not a one way street".

(c) The importance of the first of the two emphases in the previous paragraph emerges more fully as we enter the third area of meaning: not "by the people"; but, rather, "for the people". Consider such increasingly common political labels as 'German Democratic Republic' or 'People's Democratic Republic of the Yemen'. Those devoted to democracy in our second understanding may too quickly put down these employments of the term as just so much flagrantly mendacious propaganda. But that is not the whole story, and for us here the other part is the more important.

Consider two revealing and authoritative statements. The first was made by Janos Kadar, addressing the Hungarian National Assembly on 11 May 1957, one year after the friendly neighbourhood tanks of imperial normalisation had installed him in office. The second comes from Abdul Kharume, First Vice President of Tanzania, and it was made on July 7 1967 at the anniversary celebrations of the ruling and only legal party on the Tanzanian mainland. Mr Kharume, who has since been assassinated, was, as his Afro-Shirazi party in Zanzibar still is, strongly influenced by advisers from the German Democratic Republic. The Tanzanian government had recently rounded up everyone in Dar-es-Salaam without visible means of support, and driven them out into the countryside. The statements ran:

"The task of the leaders is not to put into effect the wishes and will of the masses. . . . The task of the leaders is to accomplish the interests of the masses. Why do I differentiate between the will and the interests of the masses? In the recent past we have encountered the phenomenon of certain categories of workers acting against their interests."

"Our government is democratic because it makes its decisions in the interests of, and for the benefit of, the people. I wonder why men who are unemployed are surprised and resentful at the Government . . . sending them back to the land for their own advantage" (Flew 1977, pp. 78–9 and p. 97).

It is evident that Mr Kadar and Mr Kharume are not pretending to be democrats in any sense of our second sort. On the contrary: for them, as for Rousseau, the crux is, not what anyone actually wants or decides, but what satisifies the needs or serves the interests of the people; while for them, though not for him, what those needs and interests are, and who is to count as a person truly of the people, is for the party to decide.

(ii)   Most of us associate democracy very closely with liberty or, better, liberties; we are even inclined to employ expressions like 'a free society' or 'a democratic society' almost interchangably. The philosopher is bound to be curious, both about the nature and the extent of any such connection. Clearly the problem concerns democracy in some sense of our second sort. Almost equally clearly the two ideas are not the same. The one, which we have just been explicating, refers to a way of making and maybe later unmaking, group decisions. The other, as was suggested in an earlier chapter and in another connection, is a matter of the absence of external constraints on individuals.

(a)   The first less obvious point is that there must surely be a logically necessary connection between such democracy and certain minimum general liberties. These are those which are the conditions of its being truly said that citizens made and implemented their voting decisions freely. They include, obviously, guarantees against intimidation. Again, it must be possible to get and to spread relevant information, to discuss issues with other people, and to organise opposition. Exactly what and how much should be included under this head it is here neither necessary nor possible to decide. But that quite a lot is essential can be appreciated by reflecting on how in many countries, which do regularly conduct what they call elections, these proceedings are rendered altogether empty by the lack of such guarantees and such possibilities. What sort of electoral decision can a voter be making when, for instance, every channel of information is controlled by the monopoly governing party; and when there can be – as under full socialism – no unofficial and privately owned presses, or even duplicators?

(b)   Second, there is a very strong case for thinking that a generally pluralist economic foundation, and the various economic liberties which this requires, is, while certainly not sufficient, a contingently necessary condition for democratic politics. The theoretical case, first broached by such classical writers on political economy as Hume and Adam Smith, has recently been pressed with fresh urgency and vigour in books by F. A. Hayek and Milton Friedman, and in speeches in his mission to the universities by Sir Keith Joseph: how can independence and dissent survive and flourish where everything is owned and operated, and everyone is employed, by the state?

170

This theoretical argument appears to be abundantly confirmed by practical experience. For in none of the now numerous more or less fully socialist countries do we find an opposition party contesting elections, or any publication of any fundamental questioning of any of the institutions of a socialist order. 'Where is there a socialist democracy?', students have been heard to ask in Warsaw; and the answer comes back wryly, 'On the moon'.

This is no place, of course, either to develop or to examine such a case. But in order to underline the need for all friends of individual liberties or of "by the people" democracy to take it very seriously indeed, notice two sentences from a document on 'The Falsifiers of Scientific Communism' issued in 1971 by the Institute of Marxism-Leninism in Moscow. It is discussing the tactics of a party of the vanguard: "Having once acquired political power, the working class implements the liquidation of the private ownership of the means of production. . . . As a result, under socialism, there remains no ground for the existence of any opposition parties. . . ."

(c)   In the present subsection we first observed that some basic liberties must be logically necessary to such democracy, and then suggested that economic pluralism with various economic liberties may also be contingently necessary to it. It remains to point out that decisions made even by impeccably democratic procedures, and permanently reversible through those same procedures, may nevertheless be grossly illiberal. There is nothing whatever in the nature of a majority which guarantees that it will respect, or try to cater for, minorities. There certainly have been occasions, for instance, when referenda held after the fullest debate would have supported laws penalising all minority — and hence 'unnatural' — sexual activities; even between consenting adults in the strictest privacy.

So a libertarian, who wants everyone to enjoy the maximum of freedom consistent with the equal liberties of all others, will support democratic institutions only with some reserves. He will want democratic, but always limited government. Where there have to be collective decisions, enforced on all, he will want these to be democratic. But where there is no such need for collectivism, there he will want all the deciding done by each one of us for ourselves. For, in the words of that great essay *On Liberty*: "The 'people' who exercise the power are not always the same people over whom it is exercised; and the self-government spoken of is not the government of each by himself, but of each by all the rest" (Mill, p. 67).

3.   *Kinds of equality*.   In our time 'democracy' appears to have become for

everyone a good word, no matter how various or minute the descriptive meanings which we severally attach to it. Even today this is rather less universally true of 'equality'. But in this case too the prime need is to distinguish three areas of meaning.

(i) (a) The first and the hardest to define seems to have, perhaps for the those reasons, no accepted label. Until and unless someone has a better idea let us call this, baldly, personal equality. Its best yet still cryptic epitome is found in Kant's Formula of the End in Itself: "Act in such a way that you always treat humanity, whether in your own person or in the person of any other, never simply as a means, but always at the same time as an end." This, as we saw in Chapter II (5) (ii), is a matter of treating all others as, like ourselves, persons with their own aims and purposes. It is an ideal, therefore, which entails a political libertarianism. It also supports, surely, the institutions of "by the people" democracy; albeit with the limitations determined by that libertarianism. The argument was superbly put in the Putney Debates of 1647 by the 'russet-coated Captain' Rainborough of the New Model Army. (Here, as so often, he should embrace she!):

> "Really I think that the poorest he that is in England hath a life to live as the greatest he; and therefore truly, Sir, I think it is clear, that every man that is to live under a government ought first by his own consent to put himself under that government; and I do believe that the poorest man in England is not at all bound to that government that he hath not had a voice to put himself under" (Smith, Vol. I p. 301).

The particular emphasis upon initial subjection to government was apt in what was thinking of itself as a constitutional convention. The general point remains. An egalitarian of this first kind will base his support for democracy: not on the false and silly doctrine that majorities are always, or even most often, right; but on the true and vital facts that it is everyone's lives which the collective decisions are governing, and that every individual has their own life to live.

(b) The second sort of ideal is always called equality of opportunity, though a more faithful description might be 'open competition for scarce opportunities'. This is what leaders of the French Revolution of 1789 proclaimed as 'the career open to the talents'. As an ideal it is theoretically consistent with any amount of inequality of achievement or reward; provided only that the rewards do not either include or encourage unequal opportunities for the children and other protégés of the successful.

Two notes need to be made at once. First, we have to ask at what stage in the human life-cycle it is proposed that the desired equality of opportunity should begin. For there is a world of difference: between, at one extreme, applying this notion to adult job applicants or to candidates for tertiary education; and, at the other extreme, applying it to newborn babies or even the freshly fertilized ovum. It is obvious that this ideal poses a bigger threat to individual liberties, and above all to the family, the earlier the proposed stage of application.

The second note applies to other kinds of equality too. The point is that we need to get and keep clear whether the aim really is equality, or only some sort of floor or safety net below which no one is to fall. It was, for instance, this latter conception of the proper health, education, and welfare functions of the state which constituted a main theme of Sir Winston Churchill's domestic speeches in the years after the second World War. That is an entirely different matter, since it is consistent with some being very much better off than others. If, however, it really is equality that you are after, whether of opportunity or of anything else, then you have to insist on monopolies: everyone must attend the same presumably state schools, with no possibilities of opting for different maybe better private provision; and so on.

(c) The third sort of ideal is that of equality of outcome; equality of life-chances, that is, or perhaps equality of lives. Most of the many today for whom this is a value would reject a proposal for complete equality even of wealth and income; although, typically, they always insist that any actual distribution however equal is still scandalously unequal. Hence their position is that this third sort of equality is a value, but one which may, at least in theory and to some extent, be traded off against others: if equalisation produces, for instance, a too severe general impoverishment, then some incentive inequalities may be tolerable.

Most of the drive towards equality of lives is at present directed, as that last illustration suggests, at inequalities of wealth and income. But there is some inclination to condemn differences in other dimensions as inequalities; and it is certainly hard to excogitate any principle of discrimination permitting some and not others. Any teacher is bound to think here of the cries of 'divisive' and 'elitist' raised against the qualitive classification of academic performances. Or ponder another basic and relevant distinction, and a comment thereon by an outstanding Harvard sociologist. The distinction is made in Rousseau's Dissertation *On the Origin and Foundation of the Inequality of Mankind*. On the one hand there is the inequality "which I call natural or physical, because it is established by nature, and consists in a difference of

age, health, bodily strength, and the qualities of the mind or of the soul".
On the other there is what nowadays would be called social inequality, which
"depends of a kind of convention, and is established, or at least authorised by
the consent of men" (Rousseau, p. 160). The comment, and it clearly comes
from the heart, reads: "For a thoroughgoing egalitarian . . . inequality that
derives from biology ought to be as repulsive as inequality that derives from
early socialisation" (Jencks, p. 73).

(ii)   So we have three kinds of ideal of equality. There would not, I think,
be any sort of incompatibility between them if they were presented and
promoted as private moral ideals; which their adherents strove first to
achieve themselves, and afterwards recommended to others by example and
by argument. There would, that is to say, be no problem if it were a matter of
some people wishing to join, and to persuade others to follow them in
joining, such purely voluntary institutions as the kibbutzim of Israel: it is
indeed the main glory of a free and open society that it should provide for its
members possibilities of choice between a variety of life-styles.

In fact, however, contemporary protagonists of the fashionable third ideal
of equality labour to promote this primarily if not exclusively through
measures of legal and administrative compulsion, rather than by personal
conversion and self-sacrificing self-discipline. It is indeed often remarked –
yet never too often – that few if any of our most prominent engineers of
equality volunteer to equalise their own usually well above average resources;
a jarring fact which may, and surely should, suggest that this third kind of
egalitarianism is here, in at least one aspect, part of the justifying ideology of
a new and rising class of political and bureaucratic intellectuals; rather than
an authentically disinterested and self-sacrificing moral ideal. No doubt to
present and prospective members of such a class the price of imposing and
still more of maintaining equality of condition appears not as costs but as a
promise; the promise of more power and more positions for the – shall we
say? – Procrustes people. (Procrustes was a figure of Greek mythology. It is
time that he became recognised as the patron saint of all those striving to
enforce equality of outcome. For it was he who, keeping an inn with only one
bed, used to rack out guests too short to fill it, while also lopping off
protruberant parts from the offensively tall!)

So, in the actual context of enforcement by a Procrustean political bureau-
cracy we have to recognise tensions between ideals of the third sort and those
of the first and second. Because of the intransigent diversity of talents,
temperaments and inclinations in human individuals, the liberties
demanded by the first are surely bound to produce differences repugnant to

the third. In so far as people are free to choose their own objectives, and to do their own things, the outcome is immeasurably unlikely to be a universal equality of condition. The crucial point is well taken by Hume in the section 'Of Justice' in the second *Inquiry*; though he went on there, with too complacent an optimism, to suggest that a wholeheartedly Procrustean state must collapse under the weight of an internal contradiction:

"But historians, and even common sense, may inform us that, however specious these ideas of *perfect* equality may seem, they are really at bottom *impracticable*. . . . Render possessions ever so equal, men's different degrees of art, care, and industry will immediately break that equality. Or, if you check these virtues, you reduce society to extreme indigence and, instead of preventing want and beggary in a few, render it unavoidable to the whole community. The most rigorous inquisition, too, is requisite to watch every inequality on its first appearance; and the most severe jurisdiction to punish and redress it" (Italics original).

The case is similar with the second and third ideals of equality. It seems to be the fact, however deplorable, that for most of us the intrinsic rewards of developing and employing any useful talents we may have are as nothing to the extrinsic rewards we may expect thereby to win. So suppose that some person of power first offers us equality of opportunity; and then explains that, whatever opportunities are or are not taken, everyone is in any case going to be ground down and kept down, or raised up and kept up, in order to fulfil someone else's Procrustean ideal of equality of lives. There will not, I think be much applause for the first offer, once the second intention is understood. For, as Confucius (551–479 BC) really did say, without cynical exaggeration and with traditional Chinese realism: "It is not easy to find a man who was studied for three years without aiming at pay" (VIII 2).

4. *Crime and punishment*.   Another important and ever-topical theme of political philosophy is punishment. The traditional question to ask was, 'What is the justification of punishment?'; while the three recognised rival answers were, retribution, deterrence, or reform. In the small space which remains I cannot hope to develop a satisfactory answer to that traditional and, by the criteria of the present book, not especially philosophical question. But perhaps I can make a modestly useful yet, by those same criteria, characteristically philosophical contribution to the more fruitful discussion of such justificatory issues.

175

(i)   That contribution begins with a question about the question: 'What is the justification of punishment?' This meta-question is: 'What is the context supposed to be, and just what are we being challenged to justify?' (A meta-question, by the way, precisely is a question about a question. When in Chapter IV of *Leviathan* Hobbes said that "'general', 'universal', 'special', 'equivocal' are names of names. And 'affirmation', 'interrogation', 'commandment', 'narration', 'syllogism', 'sermon', 'oration' and many other such are names of speeches.", what he was saying was, in our terms, that they are elements in a meta-vocabulary.)

The points behind the meta-question are that there are quite different things for which justification might be asked, and that the answers ought to be correspondingly different. If we ask about the punishment of one particular person on one particular occasion, then, whatever further supporting reasons there may also happen to be, the first and only essential must be that that person broke a law, and that the punishment being inflicted is the punishment prescribed for that offence. This alone is essential. Anything else is a bonus.

But that first answer given and accepted, the further questions may be raised: 'What is the justification for having that particular law, or for prescribing that particular punishment for those who break it?' Unless one or both of these established arrangements is egregiously outrageous, it will scarcely be possible to give a satisfactory answer to either of these two questions without asserting, or at least presupposing, some solution to the much more general and fundamental problems: 'Why have any systems of law?'; and 'Why prescribe any punishments for those who break these laws?'

Once these questions have been clearly put it becomes almost impossible to return any but the now obvious first answer: 'In order as far as may be to prevent anyone from acting in these ways.' In fact, of course, there always will be offenders. So we may want to go on to add something about retribution or reform. Yet deterrence must always remain the prior and prime object of the whole exercise. For under a perfectly efficient penal system no crimes would be committed; in which case no question could arise either about retribution for crime or about the reform of the criminal.

(ii)   One important corollary is that the chief object of deterrence is not the convicted criminal but all the other potential criminals who might commit offences if they did not believe that offenders are in fact subject to penalties. This should be obvious. It is, nevertheless, something very much worth emphasising. For it is in fact lamentably common for people — including too many people paid to know better — to argue that the facts of recidivism show that 'the system has failed' or that 'deterrence does not work'. (I have actually heard a colleague in a Department of Sociology draw the second conclusion, vividly brandishing a Hogarth cartoon showing pickpockets at work in the shadow of the gallows at a public execution!)

Certainly the recidivist has not been deterred. Nor, for that matter, has the first offender. Certainly too it is a bad business that there is crime, and punishment, and recidivism; and the less of all three the better — always providing, however, that this reduction is consistent with the effective protection of everyone's rights and liberties. As for the ridiculous suggestion that — sociologists know — no one is ever deterred, it should be sufficient simply to ask whether Chancellors of the Exchequer could achieve their prodigious extortions if there were no penalties for tax evasion. The temptation, and it is perhaps for criminologists an occupational temptation, is to concentrate on the prisoner in the dock, being sentenced, or the convicted criminals in jail, being punished. But the enormous majority of those whom the penal system as a whole aims to deter are not present in either place. In this too, as in the Napoleonic wars, what is not seen is crucial. "Those far-distant, storm-beaten ships, upon which the Grand Army never looked", as Admiral Mahan said, "alone stood between it and the dominion of the world."

Now read on

Anyone who has progressed this far is likely to want to go further. If so, then you may already have decided that there is some particular classical or perhaps Classical philosopher whose work you would like to explore for yourself, or that there is some particular philosophical topic which you want to see discussed from more than one point of view. Certainly these are the right next steps.

For the first you will probably need to begin by studying an introductory essay. One excellent single volume collection of such essays, on both major individual thinkers and major movements, is *A Critical History of Western Philosophy*, edited by D. J. O'Connor (New York, and London: The Free Press of Glencoe, and Allen and Unwin, 1964). The decision on which work of your chosen author to tackle first is perhaps best made under the guidance of the appropriate essay in the O'Connor volume; a volume which will be in many public libraries, and should be in all. I will however simply say, without supporting argument, what I should myself recommend.

For Plato it would be at this stage *Theaetetus*, and for Aristotle the *Nicomachean Ethics*. The Scholastics are far less accessible to the modern and secular reader. But the best way of getting acquainted with St Thomas might be to dip into the *Summa Theologica* at a point where he is treating some issue of special present interest; only after that beginning to read more systematically. With Descartes it has to be the *Discourse*, the shattering first publication in which that 'French cavalier stepped forth with so bold a stride'; and then on to the *Meditations*. At Locke I hesitate. For the *Essay* is indeed excessively long; while in any case today's beginning reader may too easily fail to appreciate the stature of Locke's sane and sober greatness. Perhaps the abridgement made and introduced by A. D. Woozley (London: Collins Fontana, 1964) might serve. Berkeley presents no problem: the *Principles* and the *Three Dialogues* should be taken in succession; for both are both brief and brilliant. Anyone with an interest either in physics or in the history of science in general should approach Leibniz through *The Leibniz-Clarke Correspondence*. This is in effect the lucid record of a battle of the giants between Leibniz and Newton. (The best edition is by H. G. Alexander for the Manchester University Press in 1964.) From there go on to the *Monadology*, the *Discourse on Metaphysics*, or even the *Theodicy*. Hume I should start with Book I of the *Treatise*; then on to Book III, the first *Inquiry*, and the *Dialogues concerning Natural Religion*. To Kant the least difficult approach is by way of his own two short handbooks, *The Foundations of the Metaphysic of Morals* and the *Prolegomena to any Future Metaphysics*.

For the second purpose distinguished in the first paragraph above your best bet, I think, would be a strongly edited volume of readings in the area of your choice. Here I can recommend three series, all at the time of writing available in paperback. The first in date of initiation is the Problems of Philosophy Series, the General Editor is Paul Edwards, and the publishers are the Macmillan company of New York and Collier-Macmillan in London. It includes volumes on *The Existence of God* (J. Hick), *Problems of Space and Time* (J. J. C. Smart), *Body, Mind and Death* (A. G. N. Flew), *Perception and the External World* (R. J. Hirst), and *Determinism and Human Freedom* (P. Edwards). The second is the Controversies in Philosophy Series, the General Editor is Antony Flew, and the publishers are in London the original British Macmillan company and in New York the St Martin's Press. This includes *The Private Language Argument* (O. R. Jones), *Philosophy and Linguistics* (C. Lyas), *The Is/Ought Question* (W. D. Hudson), *Weakness of Will* (G. Mortimore), *The Philosophy of Punishment* (H. B. Acton), and *The Mind/Brain Identity Theory* (C. V. Borst). The third is called Issues in Contemporary Ethics, the General Editor is Peter French, and the publishers are Schenkman Publishing of Cambridge, Massachussetts. The quality in this latest case is patchier. But there are challenging volumes on *Punishment and Human Rights* (M. Goldinger), *Assassination* (H. Zellner), and *Abortion* (R. L. Perkins). Another topic which is getting and deserves to get increasing attention is not treated in this series: see *Animal Rights and Human Obligations*, edited by T. Regan and P. Singer, and listed in the Bibliography, below.

Finally, there are two books of quite other kinds. To further the wider aim indicated in the third prefatory motto, the one from Wittgenstein, study Flew (1975). And, as a companion to all future philosophical reading, buy the *Dictionary of Philosophy* which when you read this will have been published in paperback by Pan Books and in hardcover by the Macmillan company of London.

Bibliography

Aquinas, St Thomas, *Summa Theologica*, translated by the Fathers of the
   English Dominican Province (London: Burns Oates and Washbourne,
   1926).
Aristotle, *The Basic Works of Aristotle*, ed. R. McKeon (New York: Ran-
   dom House, 1941).
Austin, J. L. (1961), *Philosophical Papers* (Oxford: Clarendon, 1961).
Austin, J. L. (1962), *Sense and Sensibilia* (Oxford: Clarendon, 1962).
Ayer, A. J., *Language, Truth and Logic* (London: Gollancz, Second Edition,
   1947).

Bayle, P., *Historical and Critical Dictionary*, selections tr. and ed. R. H.
   Popkin (Indianapolis: Bobbs-Merrill, 1965).
Benedict, R., *Patterns of Culture* (New York: New American Library,
   1946).
Bentham, J., *A Fragment on Government and An Introduction to the Principles
   of Morals and Legislation*, ed. W. Harrison (Oxford: Blackwell, 1948).
Berkeley, G., *Works*, ed. T. Jessup and A. Luce (London and Edinburgh:
   Nelson, 1948 onwards).
Black, M., *Problems of Analysis* (London: Routledge and Kegan Paul,
   1954).
Boethius, *The Consolation of Philosophy*, tr. V. E. Watts (Harmondsworth
   and Baltimore: Penguin, 1969).
Bohr, N., 'On the Notions of Causality and Complementarity', in *Dialec-
   tica* for 1948.
Boswell, J., *Boswell's Life of Johnson*, ed. G. B. Hall and L. F. Powell
   (Oxford: Clarendon, 1934).
Brown, R. and Rollins, C. D. (eds.), *Contemporary Philosophy in Australia*
   (London: Allen and Unwin, 1969).

180

Burke, E., *Reflections on the Revolution in France*, ed. A. J. Grieve (London, and New York: J. M. Dent, and E. P. Dutton, 1910).

Burtt, E. A., *The Metaphysical Foundations of Modern Physical Science* (London: Kegan Paul, 1932).

Butterfield, H., *The Origins of Modern Science: 1300–1800* (London: Bell, 1951).

Calvin, J., *Institutes of the Christian Religion*, tr. F. J. Battles, ed. J. T. McNeill (Philadelphia, and London: Westminster, and SCM, 1961).

Carroll, L. (1865), *Alice's Adventures in Wonderland* (London, and New York: Penguin, 1946).

Carroll, L. (1872), *Through the Looking Glass* (Harmondsworth: Penguin, 1948).

Confucius (K'UNG FU-TZU), *The Analects of Confucius*, tr. and ed. W. T. Soothill (Yokohama: Fukuin, 1910).

Cook, C. and Ramsden, J., *By-Elections in British Politics* (London: Macmillan, 1973).

Descartes, R., *Philosophical Works*, tr. and ed. E. S. Haldane and G. R. T. Ross (Cambridge: CUP, 1931).

Dewey, J., *Democracy and Education* (New York: Macmillan, 1916).

Eccles, J. C., 'The Neurophysiological Basis of Experience', in M. M. Bunge (Ed.) *The Critical Approach to Science and Philosophy* (New York, and London: Free Press, and Collier-Macmillan, 1964).

Einstein, A. (1935), *The World as I See it* (London: Lane, 1935).

Einstein, A. (1950), *Out of my later years* (London: Thames and Hudson, 1950).

Engels, F., *The Dialectics of Nature*, tr. C. Dutt (New York: International, 1940).

Flew, A. G. N. (1959), 'Broad on Supernormal Precognition' in P. A. Schilpp (Ed.) *The Philosophy of C. D. Broad* (New York: Tudor, 1959).

Flew, A. G. N. (Ed.) (1964), *Body, Mind and Death* (New York, and London: Macmillan, and Collier-Macmillan, 1964).

Flew, A. G. N. (1973), *Crime or Disease?* (London, and New York: Macmillan, and Barnes and Noble, 1973).

Flew, A. G. N. (1975), *Thinking about Thinking* (London: Collins Fontana, 1975). Also as *Thinking Straight* (Buffalo: Prometheus Unbound, 1977).

181

Flew, A. G. N. (1976a), *Sociology, Equality and Education* (London, and New York: Macmillan, and Barnes and Noble, 1976).

Flew, A. G. N. (1976b), *The Presumption of Atheism* (New York, and London: Barnes and Noble, and Elek/Pemberton, 1976).

Flew, A. G. N. (1977), 'Democracy and Education', in R. S. Peters (Ed.) *John Dewey Reconsidered* (London: Routledge and Kegan Paul, 1977).

Flew, A. G. N. (1978), *A Rational Animal* (Oxford: Clarendon, 1978).

Freud, S., *The Psychopathology of Everyday Life*, tr. A. Tyson (London: Hogarth, 1960).

Gibbon, E., *The Decline and Fall of the Roman Empire*, ed. J. B. Bury (London: Methuen, 1905).

Ginsberg, M., *The Diversity of Morals* (London: Heinemann, 1956).

Hare, R. M. (1952), *The Language of Morals* (Oxford: Clarendon, 1952).

Hare, R. M. (1963), *Freedom and Reason* (Oxford: Clarendon, 1963).

Hobbes, T., *Works*, ed. W. Molesworth (London: Bohn, 1839–40).

Hospers, J., 'Freewill and Psychoanalysis', in J. Hospers and W. Sellars (Eds.) *Readings in Ethical Theory* (New York: Appleton-Century-Crofts, Second Edition 1970).

Hume, D. (1739–40), *A Treatise of Human Nature*, ed. L. A. Selby-Bigge (Oxford: Clarendon, 1896).

Hume, D. (1748 and 1751), *Enquiries concerning Human Understanding and concerning the Principles of Morals*, ed. L. A. Selby-Bigge, and P. Nidditch (Oxford: Clarendon, Third Edition 1975).

Hume, D. (1779), *Dialogues concerning Natural Religion*, ed. N. Kemp Smith (Edinburgh: Nelson, Second Edition 1947).

Huxley, A., *The Devils of Loudon* (London: Chatto and Windus, 1952).

James, W. (1890), *The Principles of Psychology* (New York, and London: H. Holt, and Macmillan, 1890).

James, W. (1896), *The Will to Believe, etc.* (New York: Dover, 1970).

Jencks, C. and others, *Inequality* (London: Allen Lane, 1973).

Jones, E. (1953–7), *The Life and Work of Sigmund Freud* (New York: Basic, 1953–7).

Kant, I. (1781), *A Critique of Pure Reason*, tr. N. Kemp Smith (London: Macmillan, 1929).

Kawnt, I. (1783), *Prolegomena to any Future Metaphysics*, tr. and ed. P. G. Lucas (Manchester: Manchester UP, 1953).

Kant, I. (1785), *The Foundations of the Metaphysics of Morals*, tr. H. J. Paton, in his *The Moral Law* (London: Hutchinson, 1948).

Kant, I. (1788), *A Critique of Practical Reason*, tr. L. W. Beck (New York, and Indianapolis: Bobbs Merrill, 1956).

Kant, I. (1790), *A Critique of Judgement*, tr. J. C. Meredith (Oxford: OUP, 1952).

Kant, I. (1924), *Lectures on Ethics*, tr. L. Infield (New York: Harper and Row, 1963).

Kenny, A., *The Five Ways* (London: Routledge and Kegan Paul, 1969).

Kirk, G. S. and Raven, J. E., *The Pre-Socratic Philosophers* (Cambridge: CUP, 1957).

Leibniz, G. W. and Clarke, S., *The Leibniz-Clarke Correspondence*, ed. H. G. Alexander (Manchester: Manchester UP, 1956).

Leibniz, G. W., *Leibniz Selections*, ed P. P. Wiener (New York: Scribner, 1951).

Leibniz, G. W., *Theodicy*, tr. E. M. Huggard and ed. A. Farrer (London: Routledge and Kegan Paul, 1951).

Lenin, V. I. (1908), *Materialism and Empirio-Criticism*, no editor or translator named (Moscow: Foreign Languages Publishing House, 1952).

Lenin, V. I. (1914–5), *Philosophical Notebooks*, tr. C. Dutt and ed. S. Smith (Moscow: Foreign Languages Publishing House, 1961). This is Vol. XXXVIII of the *Collected Works*.

Locke, John (1690a), *An Essay concerning Human Understanding*, ed. P. H. Nidditch (Oxford: Clarendon, 1975)

Locke, J. (1690b), *Two Treatises of Government*, ed. P. Laslett (Cambridge: CUP, 1960).

Locke, J. (1706), *An Examination of Father Malebranche's Opinion*, in Locke's *Works* (London: Seventh edition 1768).

Lovejoy, A. D., *The Great Chain of Being* (New York: Harper, 1960).

MacNeice, L., *Autumn Journal* (London: Faber and Faber, 1939).

Malcolm, N., *Ludwig Wittgenstein* (London, and New York: OUP, 1958).

Marx, K., *Theses on Feuerbach* in K. Marx and F. Engels *The German Ideology* (Moscow: Progress, 1964).

Mead, M. (1943), *Coming of Age in Samoa* (Harmondsworth: Penguin, 1943).

Mead, M. (1950), *Sex and Temperament in three Primitive Societies* (New York: New American Library, 1950).

Mead, M. (1953), *Growing up in New Guinea* (New York: New American Library, 1953).

Mill, J. S. (1843), *A System of Logic* (London: Longmans, Green, Sixth Edition 1865).

Mill, J. S. (1861 and 1859), *Utilitarianism, Liberty and Representative Government* (London, and New York: J. M. Dent, and Dutton, 1910).

Mill, J. S. (1874), *Three Essays on Religion* (London: Longmans Green, Third Edition 1874).

Montaigne, M. de, *The Essays of Montaigne*, tr. E. J. Trechmann (Oxford: OUP, undated).

Moore, G. E. (1903), *Principia Ethica* (Cambridge: CUP, 1903).

Newman, J. H., *A Grammar of Assent* (London, and New York: Longmans Green, 1891).

Newton, I., *Opticks*, ed. E. Whittaker (New York: Dover, 1952).

Orwell, G., *1984* (London: Secker and Warburg, 1949).

Pascal, B., *Pensées*, tr. J. Warrington (London, and New York: Dent, and Dutton, 1960).

Pearson, K., *The Grammar of Science* (London: A. and C. Black, Second Edition 1900).

Plato, *Dialogues*, tr. B. Jowett (New York: Random, 1937).

Pope, A., *Collected Poems* (London, and New York: J. M. Dent, and Dutton, 1924).

Popper, K. R. (1945), *The Open Society* (London: Routledge and Kegan Paul, 1945).

Popper, K. R. (1957), *The Poverty of Historicism* (London: Routledge and Kegan Paul, 1957).

Popper, K. R. (1963), *Conjectures and Refutations* (London: Routledge and Kegan Paul, 1963).

Price, H. H., 'The Permanent Significance of Hume's Philosophy', in *Philosophy* 1940 (Vol. XV, pp. 1–37).

Radhakrishnan, S. and Moore, C. A., *A Source Book in Indian Philosophy* (Princeton, N. J.: PUP, 1957).

Regan, T. and Singer, P. (eds.), *Animal Rights and Human Obligations* (Englewood Cliffs, N. J.: Prentice Hall, 1976).

Reid, T., *Essays on the Intellectual Powers of Man*, ed. A. D. Woozley (London: Macmillan, 1941).

Rousseau, J.-J., *The Social Contract*, tr. and ed. G. D. H. Cole (London, and New York: J. M. Dent, and E. P. Dutton, 1913).

Rubinstein, D. and Stoneman, C. (eds.), *Education for Democracy* (Harmondsworth, and Baltimore: Penguin Education, Second Edition 1972).

Runyon, D., *Runyon on Broadway* (London: Constable, 1950).

Russell, B. A. W. (1910), *Mysticism and Logic* (London: Allen and Unwin, 1910. The first edition was entitled *Philosophical Essays*.).

Russell, B. A. W. (1912), *The Problems of Philosophy* (London: Williams and Norgate, 1912).

Russell, B. A. W. (1914), *Our Knowledge of the External World* (London: Allen and Unwin, 1914).

Russell, B. A. W. (1918), 'The Philosophy of Logical Atomism', in his *Logic and Knowledge*, ed. R. C. Marsh (London: Allen and Unwin, 1956).

Russell, B. A. W. (1948), *Human Knowledge* (London: Allen and Unwin, 1948).

Russell, B. A. W. and Whitehead, A. N., *Principia Mathematica* (Cambridge: CUP, 1910–13).

Ryle, G. (1948), *The Concept of Mind* (London: Hutchinson, 1948).

Ryle, G. (1954), *Dilemmas* (Cambridge: CUP, 1954).

Schilpp, P. A. (ed.), *Albert Einstein: Philosopher-Scientist* (New York: Harper, 1959).

Schopenhauer, A. (1813), *The Fourfold Root of the Principle of Sufficient Reason*, tr. K. Hillebrand (London: Bohn, 1889).

Schopenhauer, A. (1819), *The World as will and Idea*, tr. R. B. Haldane and J. Kemp (London: Kegan Paul, Trench, Trubner and, Third Edition 1896).

Schopenhauer, A. (1840), *On the Basis of Morality*, tr. E. F. J. Payne and ed. R. Taylor (Indianapolis: Bobbs-Merrill, 1965).

Schopenhauer, A. (1841), *Essay on the Freedom of the Will*, tr. and ed. K. Kolenda (Indianapolis: Bobbs-Merrill, 1960).

Sextus Empiricus, *Outlines of Pyrrhonism*, in his *Works*, tr. R. G. Bury (London, and Cambridge, Mass.: Heinemann, and Harvard UP, 1938).

Sidgwick, H., *The Methods of Ethics* (London: Macmillan, Sixth Edition 1901).

Smith, C. (ed.), *The Clarke Papers* (London: Clarendon for the Camden Society, 1891).

Solzenitsyn, A., *The Gulag Archipelago*, tr. T. P. Whitney (London: Collins/ Fontana, 1974).

Sophocles, *The Theban Plays*, tr. E. F. Watling (Harmondsworth: Penguin, 1974).

Szamuely, T., *The Russian Tradition* (London: Secker and Warburg, 1974).

Thurber, J., *Men, Women and Dogs* (London: Hamilton, 1944).

Talmon, J. L., *The Origins of Totalitarian Democracy* (London: Secker and Warburg, 1952).

Valla, L., 'On Freewill', tr. C. E. Trinkaus, in E. Cassirer, P. O. Kristeller, and J. H. Randall (eds.) *The Renaissance Philosophy of Man* (Chicago: Chicago UP, 1956).

Veblen, T., *The Theory of the Leisure Class* (London, and New York: Macmillan, 1899).

Voltaire, F. M. A., *Candide*, tr. J. Butt (West Drayton, Mssx.: Penguin, 1947).

Waley, A., *Life and Times of Po Chu-i: 722–846 AD* (London: Allen and Unwin, 1949).

Westermarck, E. A., *Origin and Development of Moral Ideas* (London: Macmillan, 1912).

William of Ockham, *Predestination, God's Foreknowledge, and Future Contingents*, tr. M. M. Adams and N. Kretzmann (New York: Appleton-Century-Crofts, 1969).

Wing-tsit Chan (ed.), *A Source Book in Chinese Philosophy* (Princeton, N.J.: PUP, 1963).

Wittgenstein, L. (1922), *Tractatus Logico-Philosophicus*, tr. C. K. Ogden (London: Kegan Paul, 1922).

Wittgenstein, L. (1953), *Philosophical Investigations*, tr. G. E. M. Anscome (Oxford: Blackwell, 1953).

Wittgenstein, L. (1958), *The Blue and Brown Books* (Oxford: Blackwell, 1958).

Young, M. F. D. (ed.), *Knowledge and Control* (London: Collier-Macmillan, 1971).

Zinner, P. E., *Communist Strategy and Tactics in Czechoslovakia 1918–48* (London: Pall Mall, 1963).

Index of notions

187

Index of names

This is intended to include all and only the personal names occurring between pp. 1 and 177. But it ignores the names of the certainly or most probably fictitious, while including those of real people presented or misrepresented in works of the imagination.

PSYCHOLOGY TODAY

W. E. C. GILHAM

This book is a joint enterprise, having been written by members of a large and diverse university department of psychology. Each section covers a defined area of modern psychology, contributed by a specialist in that particular field, and presents a comprehensive survey in language no more technical than the subject-matter warrants. The areas themselves have been defined on arguable but conventional grounds which for a work of this introductory nature may constitute an advantage for the student. Designed as a basis for further study, the text incorporates lists of further reading throughout.

In this multi-level text, the material is presented so as to make it accessible to the general reader, to the student in secondary education whose course includes a psychology component, and to the student commencing a degree course in psychology. Above all, this book demonstrates that psychology today is a relevant and critical discipline, characterised by the broadening of its base as a science and by a radical extension of its practical applications in contemporary society.

TEACH YOURSELF BOOKS

WHO'S WHO IN CLASSICAL MYTHOLOGY

M. GRANT AND J. HAZEL

The Greek and Roman myths and legends are an essential part of our cultural heritage — drawn upon by painters and writers through the centuries, told and retold all over the world.

This scholarly and comprehensive book presents, in alphabetical order, clear and concise accounts of all the characters around whom the myths of Greece and Rome were woven. It describes the principal incidents in the mythological careers of gods such as Zeus and Athena, and mortals such as Achilles and Jason. It is an indispensable reference book to be read and enjoyed in its own right.

TEACH YOURSELF BOOKS

HOW YOUR MIND WORKS

DAVID COX

Jung found that a 'sense of meaning in life' was essential to human health, happiness and even security. In the first half of life, meaning is concerned with the establishment of the ego, the fulfilment of biological needs and duties and the achievement of a place in the world. In the second half of life the sphere of meaning shifts to the goal of inner understanding.

The aim of this book is to introduce Jung's ideas and his analysis of the structural aspects of the psyche. These views are given perspective by an initial consideration of other contemporary theories but the central theme is the same as that which ran through Jung's life and work, a concern for the spiritual nature of man and his need for self-knowledge.

David Cox has on two occasions been Chairman of the Guild of Pastoral Psychology and is at present Vicar of St Thomas' Southborough.

TEACH YOURSELF BOOKS

ETHICS

A. C. EWING

In very simple terms Ethics is the systematic study of what the words 'good' and 'bad', 'right' and 'wrong' mean. As a branch of philosophy it is therefore most immediately concerned with the human character and conduct and this becomes particularly true when one regards the problems imposed upon society by the development of modern science.

Dr. Ewing, an Honorary Fellow of Jesus College, Cambridge, and a Fellow of the British Academy, has made a study of this 'moral science' in which he discusses not only its history and development, but also its importance to the individual in modern society. Through examining and commenting on the work of the great moral philosophers in the past and relating this to the study of Ethics today, Dr. Ewing has written a book which is both humane, learned and a clear and readable introduction to this, the most relevant of philosophical studies.

TEACH YOURSELF BOOKS